MURRAY

Butte Cr.

Prichard Cr.

Beaver Cr.

IDAHO

MONTANA

o Mile Cr.

Hercules ⚒
Union ⚒
Tiger-Poorman   **BURKE**   *Canyon Cr.*
⚒
Standard
Mammoth ⚒   ⚒ **Marsh-Russell**
GEM   **Hecla**
Gem ⚒   Helena-
            ⚒ Frisco   **Tunnel between Hecla
■ Hecla Mill   and Star mines.**

Nine Mile Cr.

Star Morning ⚒

Mill Cr.

MULLAN

South Fork Coeur d'Alene River

WALLACE

Drawn by K. Dalton

HECLA

A Century of Western Mining

HECLA

A Century of Western Mining

John Fahey

UNIVERSITY OF WASHINGTON PRESS

Seattle and London

Library of Congress Cataloging-in-Publication Data

Fahey, John.
  Hecla : a century of western mining / John Fahey.
    p. cm.
  Includes bibliographical references.
  ISBN 0-295-97014-6 (alk. paper)
    1. Hecla Mining Company—History.   2. Nonferrous metal industries–
–United States—History.   I. Title.
HD9539.A3U444   1990
338.7′62234′09796—dc20   90-35872

End-paper maps of Shoshone County area circa 1905 (*front*) and circa 1980 (*back*). Cartography by Katha Dalton, Seattle.

Contents

Illustrations

vii

Preface

FOR MORE THAN FOUR SCORE YEARS, UNTIL IT CLOSED THE EX-
hausted Star mine and moved its corporate headquarters to
Coeur d'Alene, Idaho, the Hecla Mining Company was one of
the sustaining forces of mining in northern Idaho. To the
townspeople of Wallace, it was "Mother Hecla." Now the company is poised for its second century, and the time is right to
look back at the people whose hard work has enabled Hecla
to survive and thrive in a tenuous industry.

This is a book about people. Its narration is topical within a
roughly chronological framework. To maintain pace in the narrative, I focus on presidents and managers and use Hecla as a
metonym for its people. Nevertheless, even when they are not
mentioned by name, the people drive the company. Over the
years, Hecla's people have built a reputation for competent
management, technical excellence, and fair dealing. In earlier
books, I sketched the careers of individualistic mining men:
Charles Sweeny, the promoter, and Harry L. Day, who managed the Hercules partnership largely according to his own design. Hecla has also benefited from singular managers, but it
has all along been a corporate enterprise, the least secretive
about its business of the larger Coeur d'Alene district companies. To the hundreds of Hecla people whose contributions to
company and community are not recorded here, I can only say
that the story had to be brought to manageable length. I simply
could not squeeze in everyone.

In writing Hecla's history, I have worked with a number of
Hecla people. The Hecla company underwrote the writing and
publication, and its staff reviewed a rough draft for accuracy.
All interpretations and conclusions are, of course, mine. Several persons who helped me are credited in the section on
sources. Three accorded me extraordinary help: Elmer L. Bierly,

former vice president for investor and public affairs; Sandra Pope, who guided me through the files; and William H. Love, former president, whose candid observations in long tape-recorded interviews gave me a perspective on Hecla essential to understanding the company's history. I thank them. Without them, there would be no book.

Of course, there would be no book by me—this or any other—without the encouragement of my wife Peggy. For her, saying thanks seems hardly enough.

JOHN FAHEY

HECLA

A Century of Western Mining

I

The Milwaukee Connection

WHEN CHARLES M. KIPP CAME WEST FROM MILWAUKEE IN 1887 to see the Idaho mine his family had invested in, he was too corpulent, at two hundred fifty pounds, to struggle up a hill to peek into the dark portal, so he settled by a shady tree where, with field glasses, he watched a friend climb to the Gem. A local newspaper editor noted that neither Kipp nor his companion from Chicago, Albert L. Gross, was "a practical mining man." And the rough mountain country around Wallace, Idaho, was far removed from brick paving, singing societies, theaters, and prosperous German cousins. "I came out here for nothing," murmured Kipp, a traveling salesman. "I can attend to my part of the business better in Milwaukee or Chicago. My part of the work is to 'put up'."

Kipp and Gross were two of the men who would organize the Hecla Mining Company. Their function would be, as Kipp realized, to put up. Hecla would bring together men from Wisconsin, Illinois, Ohio, and Montana, and how they came together goes back to the discovery of gold in 1883. Kipp visited the mining country four years after its gold rush. He found little to savor.

A pipsqueak railway rattled through the village of Gem, going downhill by gravity from the Tiger mine to Wallace. Gem had a puny mill and a few whitewashed frame buildings. The principal town, Wallace, wooden stores and houses, huddled in a crease between steep hills astride the south fork of the Coeur d'Alene River. The weather, miners quipped, was nine months of winter; the rest, late fall. Barely five years earlier this had been mountain forest, and Shoshone County had embraced all of northern Idaho from its seat at Pierce City. It was Nez Perce Indian country to the Canadian border, with about fifty white

3

residents and three hundred Chinese, whose poll, road, and hospital taxes supplied the county's revenue.

Then pharisaic Andrew J. Prichard, gaunt and belligerent, had descended from the north fork of the Coeur d'Alene River, boasting extravagantly of gold. And the frenzy began. Men defied winter snows, rushing in to stake claims, swapping, stealing, and fighting for gold, and living in mobile tent towns. By spring 1884 hundreds of men had scoured the ground and a thousand claims had been filed. A Montana stampeder wrote home: "The ground was all taken up in 20-acre lots: creeks, gulches, everything. . . . Every claim holder here wants to sell out at big figures, and they have nothing but snow to show for the money." A few prospectors and merchants profited. Most did not. Some dispirited gold hunters stayed long enough to hack roads through the trees for the county, collecting five dollars in discounted scrip for each two dollars' worth of work.

Within months the rush spilled onto the south fork where partners claimed the Tiger, and William R. Wallace (for whom the town of Wallace was named) and his son staked the Ore-or-no-go, both on Canyon Creek, which emptied into the south fork. Unlike the placer gold claims of the north fork, these were lode prospects staked to comply with federal law. The law specified that a prospector must actually find mineral on his ground and lay his claim no more than 600 by 1,500 feet lengthwise along the vein with parallel end lines. In placer mining, the miner washes gold from the earth. In lode mining, he digs tunnels and shafts to remove mineral-bearing rock that is crushed, milled, and smelted. Lode mines and white-pine timber would be the foundations of commerce in northern Idaho.

The Gem, which Kipp and Gross came to see, lay beside Canyon Creek downstream from the Tiger. So did the Poorman, the Sheridan, and dozens of other prospects. So did the Hecla, claimed on May 5, 1885, by James Toner, who staked a hillside tilted like the deck of a storm-tossed schooner just beyond the canvas tents billowing near the Tiger alongside a few shacks and one store. Nobody knows now why Toner called his 19.714-acre claim "Hecla," but probably he named it for the famed Hecla mine discovered in 1873 west of Melrose in southwestern Montana. Five weeks after Toner's discovery, the thirty residents of the shacks voted to name the place "Burke," for John M. Burke, erstwhile manager of the Tiger, who (as they had anticipated) bought several rounds of whiskey in appreciation.

Although the Tiger produced commercial ore, packed over a mountain trail to Montana, the gold claims overshadowed the lead and silver of the south fork until September 1885, when Noah B. Kellogg and his partner Phil O'Rourke located the Bunker Hill on Milo Creek, downriver and west of Canyon Creek. The Bunker Hill's rich ore samples set off a new rush to the south fork. On the hills and along the creeks cascading into the river, miners hastily nailed claim notices to shaved stumps, marking the corners of claims. Here the mining camps congealed into two clusters, one centered on the Bunker Hill, and its companion Sullivan, near the town of Wardner, and the other, to the east, strung along Canyon Creek from Burke to the creek's mouth at Wallace.

The Bunker Hill's samples also magnetized investors (who sent agents) and speculators scheming to pounce on rich prospects at bargain prices. Mining claims changed hands rapidly. Sometimes a claim bought in the morning sold in the afternoon. The governor of Montana, Samuel T. Hauser—banker, railroad builder, capitalist, and part owner of a starving smelter at Wickes, Montana—dispatched associates to the Coeur d'Alene country. One, Anton M. Esler, erected a mill to concentrate Bunker Hill ores for consignment to Wickes. Another, Daniel C. Corbin, relying on Hauser's favor with the Northern Pacific Railroad, built railroads and a connecting steamboat line to the Northern Pacific which by spring 1887 opened the mining district to a substantial ore traffic, and convinced Simeon Gannett Reed, vice president of the Oregon Railway & Navigation Company, to buy the Bunker Hill.

Sometime late in 1887, Amasa B. (Mace) Campbell and John A. Finch reached the Coeur d'Alene mining district as agents of investors in Youngstown, Ohio. Syndicates of businessmen who pooled funds to speculate in mines and timber were not unusual. The men backing Finch and Campbell were the spine of Youngstown's economy: Henry Wick, descended from one of the first families in the Western Reserve, banker, steel-mill founder, and a coal executive, whose home stood on Wick Avenue, and of whom a biographer remarked, "It is difficult to turn anywhere in Youngstown without being confronted with some monument to Mr. Wick's business genius"; his brother,

John Wick; George and David Tod, whose family settled in Youngstown in 1801. George built railroads, including sections of the Union Pacific in Oregon, and David founded a building and supply firm, served on the city council, and then in the state senate. Another investor, H. H. Stambaugh, who married a Tod, had started his own steel company, was a director of others, owned large real estate interests in eastern Ohio, and with another of the syndicate, Henry M. Garlick, was a founder of the Youngstown Foundation.

Finch and Campbell had prospected together near Bingham, Utah, for the Youngstown speculators with indifferent success and had retired to Ohio until something better turned up. Opposites in temperament, both were ambitious to succeed in business. Finch was the son of British parents who had emigrated to Ohio when he was three. He had grubbed in Colorado's mines for a year or so, then traveled Ohio and Pennsylvania as a salesman for a Youngstown manufacturer of bar, hoop, band, and horseshoe iron until the company went bankrupt. At thirty-three he was reserved, not very robust, and out of work.

Campbell at forty-two was chunky, outspoken, and hearty. A native of Salem, Ohio, he was his parents' tenth and youngest child. A blind brother, Walter, distinguished himself as a newspaper editor and as mayor of Youngstown. Another brother, John, rose to brigadier general in the Civil War and served six years as governor of Wyoming Territory. Young Amasa had not matched his brothers; he started working on the railroad at sixteen, prospected in Utah, and settled after that into the routine of chief freight clerk in a Youngstown terminal. He was bored, his ambition stifled. He and Finch were bachelors, reliable, experienced in mining and business—precisely the kind of men that bankers and merchants would choose to reconnoiter a new mining district. And so Finch and Campbell came to Idaho.

They discovered that mining in the Coeur d'Alenes proceeded with only rudimentary notions of the area's geology—hunches, actually. The prevailing strategy was to seize likely prospects next to the few producing mines. Simeon Reed's syndicate of Oregon, Illinois, and California cronies had put the Bunker Hill out of reach. On Canyon Creek, however, the Tiger shipped concentrates, and a handful of other claims looked as if they would make mines. The miners there tunneled directly into the steep hillsides without the initial expense of shafts. There were trees everywhere for cabins and mine timbers, and a miner could slide his sacked ore downhill to the railroad that connected the Tiger to Corbin's narrow-gauge line at Wallace. The terrain of Canyon Creek made mining comparatively cheap, if arduous.

Consequently, Finch and Campbell looked for purchases or partners on Canyon Creek. Throughout their mining careers, their tactic would be to seek bargains in promising claims. As Campbell later explained to a Youngstown backer: "We have made our success out of cheap prospects and the risk is small and the chance to make money very large." Although Campbell located several claims—including the Spokane, Chicago, and Youngstown—he did not waste money to develop them. Their caution in this speculative business would enrich Finch and Campbell and pay handsome dividends to those who bought stock in their companies.

Now, in the fading days of 1887, they uncovered three possibilities: two veteran prospectors, Oliver Durant and Alex Tarbet, had bonded the Union (on the Tiger vein) and needed money to keep it going; two Spokane promoters, Charles Sweeny and Frank Rockwood Moore, held stock in the Union and in other claims near the Tiger and needed money to explore their ground; and Patrick (Patsy) Clark had come over from Butte to bond the Poorman, across the creek from the Tiger, and was grabbing other claims believed to be extensions of the Tiger vein. As agent for Montana investors, Clark had formed the Coeur d'Alene Silver-Lead Mining Company to finance his claims. He welcomed anyone who might put money into it. He had bonded the Poorman for $136,000, was peddling $5 million worth of stock at pennies a share, and driving three tunnels on the vein. He brought Simon Healey from Butte as superintendent and imported Montana miners, paying the Butte wage of $3.50 a day. The Bunker Hill paid $3.00.

In the few months he had been there, Patsy Clark had become the darling of Canyon Creek. With Healey, he ranged up and down the creek bargaining for claims. Now thirty-seven, he had emigrated from Ireland as a lad, mined in Pennsylvania, where a sister lived, and moved on to California and Nevada. In Nevada (as he told his story) he caught the fancy of another Irishman, Marcus Daly, because he sent most of his paycheck to his mother in Ireland. Daly took Clark to Butte as mine foreman, where he rose to superintend mines both for Daly and for William A. Clark, the rival copper kings. (He claimed to have served ten days as a volunteer infantryman against the Nez Perce during Chief Joseph's famous retreat of 1877.) Warmhearted, with a generous blush of the blarney, courtly in manner, Patsy Clark was immensely popular both with managers and common miners. In "east Burke" he built a house, said an editor, that "would be a credit to a town of much greater pretensions."

Finch and Campbell, whom an editor identified as agents "for eastern capitalists," moved with less flourish than Clark while they, too, invested (modestly) in Canyon Creek claims, among them the Union, and hired Durant to advise them on likely prospects. With Sweeny, Moore, and other Spokane men, they organized the Coeur d'Alene Mining & Concentrating Company to raise funds through stock sales and assigned several properties to it, including the Union. Their partnership with Sweeny and Moore would prove inconsequential, however, for Moore, deeply in debt, was forming one company after another in the hope of recouping, and "as far as Sweeny is concerned," Campbell later observed, "we have not much confidence in his honesty, but there is no question about his ability." In any event, Sweeny was less interested in Canyon Creek than in his Last Chance mine near Wardner, where he intended to invade the Bunker Hill's vein.

Campbell and Finch wintered in Ohio. Apparently their impressions of Idaho encouraged the Youngstown syndicate, for in the spring of 1888 both men were back in Wallace, dealing with assurance. They found new competitors in the canyon: Chicago and Milwaukee men, led by Albert Gross and Bernard Kipp, had bonded the Gem and sent out a manager from Chicago. With investors now from Butte, Chicago, Milwaukee, and Youngstown vying for crowded Canyon Creek properties, their agents inevitably bought into one another's claims. Moreover, legal conflicts threatened. One could visualize the lawyers rubbing their hands in anticipation of rich litigants. The Tiger's owners protested that the Poorman stole their ore. The Poorman owners, claiming their surface encroached, dynamited the Tiger dam. The Gem and the adjacent Helena & Frisco (Frisco) squabbled over ores in a fractional claim between them. To the investors and their agents, compromise made more sense than suing.

As a result, Finch and Campbell joined the Milwaukee and Chicago crowd in forming the Milwaukee Mining Company on August 22, 1888, to hold the Gem and other properties. The major stockholders were Charles Kipp, his brother Bernard, Gross, Finch, and Campbell. The company put Campbell in charge and employed R. K. Neill, who had come from Montana with Esler, to build a concentrating mill. (The Gem miners had been using hand jigs to concentrate the ores.) By the next June, the Gem struck high-grade ore four hundred feet into the hillside, began shipping soon after to the Omaha & Grant smelter in Nebraska, and paying dividends. The Gem, "a fine little producing mine" at twenty tons a day, would be the base from which the Milwaukee speculators expanded, although it would be shortlived, with a truncated orebody.

The Kipps belonged to that prosperous German community in Milwaukee which included Charles Pfister, publisher of the *Milwaukee Sentinel* and aspirant to high political office, and Fred Vogel, Jr., a banker, sons of the Vogel and Pfister from Wurtemberg whose tannery had helped elevate Milwaukee as a leather-making center. The Kipps were also Wurtembergers— the father, a tailor; the sons, organizers of a flourishing mattress factory, which grew into the Milwaukee House Furnishing Company. In the eighties, Milwaukee's paved streets, sewers, water system, theaters, restaurants, professional men, and bankers set it far above rural Wisconsin. Its affluent German society relished their singing societies, exclusive clubs, fine homes—their good life.

Apparently Bernard (Ben) and Charles Kipp piloted their brothers into Idaho mining with Gross as their mentor. The Kipps had money to spend and perhaps thought Idaho an adventure. Bernard was a major shareholder in a soda-water plant and the mattress factory. Portly Charles was a founder of Milwaukee's professional baseball team, a league officer, director of an insurance company, and a Republican appointee to the Milwaukee Fire and Police Commission. A younger brother, Frank, normally a circumspect banker, once allowed Charlie Pfister to draw him into spending $20,000 for a whale to exhibit. The Kipps put some money into iron mines. So did Carl Landsee, executor of the estate of Guido Pfister, Charles's father. Charles invested in the Morning mine in the Coeur d'Alenes which had been purchased from its discoverers by Charles Hussey, the young son of a Salt Lake banker who fol-

9

lowed the gold rush to open banks at Murray and Wallace. The Kipps and their business and social congeries personified new wealth with the brashness to speculate.

While the Milwaukee and Youngstown syndicates joined in the Gem, the lightly regarded Hecla fell into the grasp of Patsy Clark, one of many as he assembled ground around the Poorman like pieces of a jigsaw puzzle. Toner had passed Hecla to a Burke miner, A. P. Horton, who did nothing with it. The story goes that George W. Hardesty, a Burke merchant and sometime partner of Simon Healey, set out to buy right of way for a projected rail line, and Horton demanded $100 to cross Hecla. Hardesty asked the price for the entire claim. Shrugging, Horton sold it for $150. Not long after, Hardesty and Healey sold Clark one-third of Hecla, no doubt for funds to drive an exploratory tunnel high on the hill.

"The Hecla . . . is a full-fledged lead prospect," the *Wallace Press* declared in a few months. "The vein is reported to be so well defined that hopes are entertained a mine will be developed." When Hecla showed mineral—very little, and the vein seemed to tail out of Hecla—Clark bought the remaining two-thirds on July 11, 1891. Three days earlier he and Healey had purchased the bordering Katie May, and Healey had passed his share to Clark on the same day. Now that Hecla looked like a mine, Albert Gross and Charles Kipp bought interests in it, and on September 29, 1891, Clark, Kipp, and Gross conveyed their shares to a new corporation, the Hecla Mining Company.

Capitalized for $500,000, Hecla was incorporated in Idaho on October 14, 1891, by Clark, Charles Kipp, Finch, Campbell, John Dorsey of Wallace, Healey, and Hardesty (whose name was substituted at the last moment for Ben Kingsbury, a Clark associate). Of 500,000 shares, Clark took 335,334 and Kipp 151,666—shares to sell rather than hold. Campbell, with 5,000 shares, was designated a director and manager. Finch, with 5,000, was also a director. Some of the men who bought Hecla stock immediately would stay with it: Frank Upman, son of a German immigrant to Wisconsin and now proprietor of the Briggs House apartment in downtown Chicago, and James R. Smith, one of his tenants who worked for the city water department, took 20,000 shares apiece, probably from Kipp on Gross's recommendation, and probably for three or four cents a share—$600 each.

Hecla was only one of dozens of infant companies peddling penny stocks that sped, borne by rumors and hunches, from one buyer to another. A Burke railroad man who took several thousand shares of Hecla at three cents concluded he had been stuck—until someone offered him five cents. Clark advised him to sell quick. For a time Hecla fell to two cents. James Smith bought several thousand more shares, enough to persuade him to move to Burke from Chicago. One buyer, M. L. Humes (neé Martin), would stir newspaper comment briefly in 1917 when she turned in one of these original certificates (number 41, dated May 30, 1892, for 5,000 shares bought at ten cents) to collect $26,500 in accumulated dividends, from which the company subtracted $400 in unpaid assessments dating to the nineties.

The old register of stock certificates shows that Gross and Kipp sold shares mainly to business and social acquaintances in Chicago and Milwaukee. One of the Kipp brothers, Frank, took 10,000 shares, as did Carl Landsee (misspelled "Landersee" in the register). A Milwaukee contractor, George J. Lonstorf, bought 5,000 shares. No Youngstown men appear among the 1891 and 1892 buyers of Hecla stock, although they bought increasingly into the Milwaukee Mining Company, perhaps because Finch and Campbell used Youngstown money to bond the Standard and Banner adjoining the sensational Mammoth, which had struck "two feet of solid ore," according to a newspaper account late in the summer of 1890.

Once organized, Hecla was neglected by its incorporators. They saw too many immediate opportunities at hand to attend to their prospect on the slopes above Burke. They alternately let Hecla to lessees or raised a little money by assessments to drive two short tunnels, the longer 110 feet. By one estimate, Hecla produced ores worth no more than $14,000 in seven years. For the most part, it waited in the wings while other mines (and calamity) occupied center stage.

The last decade of the nineteenth century was a time of transition in American life and of wrenching change in the lead and silver mining industry. In the nation, new constituencies pitted the populous, moneyed East against the emerging West and South. The decade resounded with debate over the gold standard. Western mining states stood solidly behind the free and unlimited coinage of silver. Federal and state governments sought to regulate railroads; the federal government sought to limit the power of industrial combinations. The financial panic of 1893 suffocated westward migration and showered disaster on the Pacific Northwest. America's continuous territorial wrangling culminated in war with Spain.

These commotions upset a mining industry in the throes of its own transformation: power drills and improved explosives made underground mining both cheaper and more dangerous. Electrical energy gradually supplanted water, steam, and mule power and encouraged deeper mining. Near the end of the century, the lead-smelting business congealed into a monopoly—the smelter trust, the American Smelting & Refining Company, dominated by the Guggenheim family. And railroad competition for routes, territories, and markets reached its capshed in the Pacific Northwest. It is hardly surprising that in the Coeur d'Alenes, the last decade of the century was also a time of turmoil.

Finch indulged in politics; he was elected to a two-year term as state senator in 1890 while he was absent in Ohio for his mother's funeral. He was one of ten vice presidents of a Wallace republican club, of which Patsy Clark was president and Campbell, treasurer. Campbell returned to Ohio briefly in 1890 to marry Grace Fox and brought his bride to "the finest residence" in Wallace. No longer itinerant agents, Finch and Campbell had settled near their mines.

In the meantime, the Husseys' Bank of Wallace and the Spokane National Bank failed on December 16, 1890. Creditors seized the Morning mine as a principal bank asset, and Charles Kipp offered to buy the property. With some Milwaukee shareholders in Hecla and others, including Charles and William Allis of the noted Edward P. Allis Company (later, Allis-Chalmers), Kipp organized the Morning Mining Company on November 28, 1891, and sent Gross out to manage the mine. A creditors' committee, which included John Finch, endeavored to release judgments against the Husseys to pay bank depositors. After two years of controversy over the mine's title, Charles Pfister obtained a Milwaukee court order for the sale of Morning, Evening, Silver King, Silver Queen, and Park—the Morning group— and these passed to Kipp's company. Shortly after, Kipp and the same shareholders reorganized as the Morning Mining & Milling Company.

The new owners built a short railway to connect mine to mill on Canyon Creek near Wallace. With the primitive methods of the time, they "gouged" the upper reaches of the mine, leaving the deep ore untouched; and in the mill lost as much as 45 percent of the mineral, dumping it with residue into the creek. (This mill burned in April 1898.)

In the four years since Finch and Campbell had come to Idaho, building and population had snowballed. Burke was now a town of 800 with a water system, volunteer fire department, school, stores, abundant saloons, and a reputation for rowdyism. "You fight your enemies for profit and your friends for pleasure," Burke's residents liked to say, and they quoted the justice of the peace who advised an attorney laden with law books: "If you want law, go to Wallace. If you want justice, come to Burke." When it discovered that a widow's house extended onto its property, a mining company sawed off the offending room and boarded it up. On paydays, the railroads ran a "drunk train" at 11:00 P.M., dumping the comatose and belligerent into a baggage car. Gem, "a solid row of one- and two-story buildings," lay on either side of the tracks, and two miles above Gem stood a hamlet, the Standard's shipping point, named "Mace" for Mace Campbell.

Wallace blossomed as a mercantile, financial, and residential center with two railroads: the Northern Pacific (which took Corbin's road) entered Wallace from the east by a standard-gauge link to its mainline near Missoula, while the Washington & Idaho, a Union Pacific subsidiary, came to Wallace around the southern end of Lake Coeur d'Alene and up the river valley. An electric light company was forming, of which Finch and Campbell were directors, and the pioneer grocery firm of White & Bender, with branches at Burke and Gem, erected a fine brick building in Wallace. Finch was president of the grocery firm, and Patsy Clark, vice president. Soon Finch and Campbell would join in incorporating a new hardware company, the Coeur d'Alene Hardware, to absorb the district stores of an established Spokane firm, Holley, Mason, Marks & Company.

When the Northern Pacific rebuilt the Canyon Creek railroad with standard-gauge rail, the Union Pacific built a parallel line that extended to the Poorman mill, over the objections of Burke merchants that the right of way crowded out their woodpiles. Burke would pop up for years in newspaper oddity columns as the town where merchants cranked shut their storefront awnings for trains to pass.

By now there were more than two dozen producing mines

in the district and thirteen concentrating mills consigning output to smelters in western states. Finch and Campbell had a mill at the mouth of Canyon Creek for the Union. In 1887, the first year of reasonably reliable railroad service, the Coeur d'Alenes had produced lead ores valued at $538,200 and silver, at $337,520. By 1891, lead soared past $2.8 million; silver, past $1.8 million. More than 3,000 men worked in mines and mills and most of the larger mines were directed by resident managers. Gone was the easy camaraderie of five or six years earlier, when men rushed to stake claims on nearly equal terms.

Many of those in the 1884–85 rush had come to Idaho from Colorado and Nevada where they secretly belonged to the Knights of Labor, or from Butte where they openly joined the powerful miners' unions. They formed unions in the Coeur d'Alenes, the first at Wardner in November 1887 to oppose a cut in wages by the Bunker Hill. In Canyon Creek, where Patsy Clark set an example by maintaining the Butte scale, unions were slower to organize, but after the Tiger's crews struck to protest poor food in the company boardinghouse, unions sprang up at Burke, Gem, and Mullan. The Burke union celebrated its formation with a grand ball; the Gem, in October 1891, staged a ball on its first anniversary, declaring that the local begun with 14 members now numbered 580. When the Canyon Creek unions solicited funds to build a hospital, John Finch was among 130 donors.

The mine managers had also organized in 1889 as the Mine Owners Association (MOA) to unite against increased smelting and railroad rates and smelter rebates to railroads. They shut down their mines for three months early in 1892 to compel the railroads to reduce rates. As contention flared between managers and workers, the owners turned their association against the unions, too, using their considerable influence with the government and the courts.

There followed eight years of violence and terror. Management spies infiltrated unions (at least one spy reported by mail to John Finch), armed guards patrolled mines and mills, and managers imported strikebreakers. They shut the mines at will, throwing hundreds out of work, to protest railroad rates or low metals prices, or to coerce miners into accepting their wage scale. Campbell was accused of hiring nonunion men knowing that the unions would drive them away, thereby deliberately constraining the courts to enjoin unions from interfering with mine operations. Finch and Campbell's Union mine received the first trainload of Michigan strikebreakers. Even so, the unions appealed to Finch and Campbell to mediate for them with other mine owners.

Unions harrassed, expelled, beat, and sometimes murdered men who opposed or witnessed against them. During an 1892 gun battle with Gem guards, union men blew up the Frisco mill to compel nonunion miners to surrender, and forthwith marched their captives out of the district. Union leaders saw themselves as liberators of workingmen in the mold of Homestead steelworkers and Pullman strikers. In April 1899, masked union men dynamited the Bunker Hill mill.

Twice the Coeur d'Alenes fell under martial law: from July 13, after the Gem battle, to November 12, 1892, and again from May 3, 1899, after the Bunker Hill destruction, to April 11, 1901. National Guardsmen and army regulars imprisoned union men wholesale and protected the mines and mills.

"The fact is, in that canyon in the last five years, no man, whether he was merchant, saloon keeper, miner, or in any other employment, has tried to criticize even mildly any act of the union," Finch would tell congressional investigators. "We, of course, felt powerless to do anything to protect our men, and have borne whatever they [unions] have seen fit to inflict on us or our men and have said nothing."

The unions were at last repressed when the mining companies, with military support, established a central hiring agency and required each applicant to show a permit indicating he had not belonged to a union. A congressional inquiry found that, of 7,000 permits issued in 1899–1900, only 130 appeared to have gone to men previously affiliated with a union.

One of the effects of labor wars had been to cut off eastern investments in the mines. Finch, who circulated in eastern cities to promote stock sales, discerned "a feeling by outside capitalists that there is likely to be a repetition of labor troubles . . . and they prefer to invest in districts where this danger is not likely."

Another effect had been to drive out those who could afford to get away: Patsy Clark moved his family from Burke in 1892 and, five years later, into a new $80,000 Spokane home, a showplace. Finch and Campbell would build opulent homes in Spokane in 1898. Union troubles were not their sole reason for moving, for, as moneyed men, they were branching out.

Gold and copper mines recently discovered in British Columbia, in West Kootenay and at Rossland and Trail Creek, diverted Patsy Clark and John Finch from the Coeur d'Alenes. Finch and Campbell also put money into orchards, securing the well-known Blalock Fruit Company of Walla Walla, and into timber lands and the Cameron Lumber Company of Harrison on Lake Coeur d'Alene.

With the prospect of union violence and continuing low lead prices, the Milwaukee owners of the Morning sold the mine to its lessees, Thomas L. Greenough and Peter Larson, Montana railroad contractors. The death of Albert Gross had left the Milwaukee company rudderless, their interests largely in the hands of the Milwaukee banker, Frank Kipp, who turned to Amasa Campbell for advice in mining affairs.

Disruptions and erratic markets notwithstanding, Coeur d'Alene mines continued to produce ores, if irregularly and at reduced levels. By one estimate, annual production of 50,000 tons leaped to more than 81,000 as soon as labor troubles ended. Finch and Campbell's Standard, with a vein fifteen feet wide, sent ores to the Union mill. The Standard paid dividends in August 1895 of $70,000; in September, $78,000; in October, $93,000; and in November, $95,000—in any one month, more than twice the $30,840 Finch and Campbell had paid for it. During its life it would yield more than $1 million.

The Standard's first tunnel was highest on the hill above Burke; its lowest, on the valley floor, was named the Campbell tunnel. It went in 3,300 feet. As the Standard's orebodies were depleted, its tunnels were leased to the Mammoth for haulage. The Union (now half owned by a Denver and Omaha smeltermans' syndicate) showed signs of exhaustion, and the Gem was playing out. With the Gem's mill idle, it was time to look again at Hecla.

In 1897 the surviving directors of the Hecla Mining Company—Finch, Campbell, and Clark—bought out lessees and levied two assessments to tunnel and to pay the Milwaukee Mining Company for use of the Gem mill. (Total assessments between 1891 and 1898 would amount to eight cents a share.) Under Campbell's management, Hecla started a third tunnel near the valley floor. The small crew encountered a vein within a few feet of the portal and followed it into the hill. They were near Hecla's boundaries when, at about 350 feet, the tunnel revealed a narrow seam of galena (lead) but it was not commercial. Campbell leased the mine again to men from Burke, who sank a winze (an inclined tunnel) about 150 feet. Without finding ore that would pay, they ran out of money and gave up their lease.

If the lessees had drifted along the seam rather than sinking, they would have run into the original Hecla orebody—but following the seam would have carried them into ground that did not belong to Hecla. To buy these adjacent properties, Campbell, Finch, and Clark reorganized the company. Of the original incorporators in 1891, John Dorsey had sold his interest; Simon Healey had moved to San Diego; George Hardesty had died of heart failure in his bed, vainly firing his revolver into the ceiling to summon help; and on January 28, 1898, almost on the eve of Hecla's flowering, Charles Kipp died at age fifty.

Capitalized for one million shares (double the old company's), the new Hecla Mining Company, incorporated in Washington on July 12, 1898, traded 500,000 shares to the 1891 Idaho company for its assets. Shareholders in the old company received share-for-share in the new and were entitled to buy proportionate additional shares for ten cents. Campbell told Henry Wick, "Stockholders without exception have taken the additional stock they're entitled to." Valued at twenty-five cents par, the new Hecla's stock sold at the outset at twenty cents and within three months rose to forty and forty-five cents a share.

As president, Campbell traded some of the new company's stock for claims around the Hecla. Two owners of these properties, John Frank and James R. Smith, the latter a substantial shareholder in the old Hecla, were among seven trustees named to manage the new Hecla. Frank had been a partner with Edward Ehrenberg and John Van Dorn in claims near the Hecla, but he had abandoned mining for the time being; he was now vice president and treasurer of Frank Culbertson's Wonder Department Store in Spokane. (Culbertson, son-in-law of the Tiger's owner, had once managed the Tiger.) The five other Hecla trustees were Campbell; Finch; Clark; Finch and Campbell's accountant, Harry R. Allen; and the secretary of one of Finch's gold mines, Fred E. Lucas.

From Van Dorn and Frank, Hecla acquired the Burlington, Climax, Denver, Leadville, Muscatine, Orphan Boy, Orphan Girl, and Silvante claims for $36,000 payable in installments over fifteen months. From Ehrenberg, it acquired the Hecla Fraction. Campbell bought the Ore-or-no-go Fraction from three owners for $3,000 and would later buy the Ore-or-no-go itself from the estates of William R. Wallace and Richard Lockey. Hecla's main ore shoot would prove to lie in the Orphan Girl, Orphan Boy, and Ore-or-no-go Fraction. "The Hecla," Campbell jubilantly wrote to Henry Wick, who sulked that he had been left out of Hecla, "is developing into a wonderful mine. We purchased all the surrounding ground."

With the surrounding ground in hand, Hecla's crew could drive ahead without fear of trespassing into someone else's claim. Campbell turned the daily management of his and Finch's mines over to Edward F. Moffitt, who, like so many in the Coeur d'Alenes, had migrated westward after Civil War service looking for a place to put down roots. In an intervening tunnel between the upper and lower, Hecla dug paying ore and sent it to the Standard mill. Campbell soon exulted to Henry Wick that Hecla was shipping enough ore "just out of driving the level" to pay the costs of tunneling.

At last Hecla had come on stage, but even though Campbell believed it would make a mine, he did not guess Hecla's benefic future. He would, he wrote Ben Kipp in the spring of 1899, willingly sell his Hecla stock for sixty cents a share. Neither Campbell nor anyone else dreamed that, of the pioneer companies of the Coeur d'Alenes, Hecla would survive longest of all.

2

Getting Started: McCarthy in Charge

WITH THE BEGINNING OF PRODUCTION, THE THREE OR FOUR
dozen men and women who bought stock in the Hecla Mining
Company clamored for dividends. Mace Campbell held them
off. "Everyone is more or less excited over the property . . .
and they expect dividends at once," Campbell grumbled to
Henry Wick. To Frank Kipp, Campbell suggested that "it would
be a good idea to buy out all the small holders as they are not
familiar with mining and expect too much."

The Youngstown investors generally felt that they had been
left out of Hecla. As the price rose, Campbell found some stock
for Henry Wick—10,000 shares, "a small holding in the mine"—
but warned, "I wish you would not mention in Youngstown
that you have secured some stock in the Hecla." Campbell could
not find enough stock for sale to satisfy his Youngstown or
Milwaukee buyers. And as a major shareholder, Kipp demanded a place on the board. Campbell put him off, too, writing that Kipp "was certainly entitled to representation," but
when trustees lived too far away, "it is hard . . . to get a quo-
rum to do business."

The business of Hecla in 1900 was to enlarge its workings so
that the company could pay dividends. The old tunnel near
the canyon floor, too small for a horse or mule, its timbers rot-
ting, would have to be rebuilt. Campbell accumulated about
$40,000 for renovation and mill rental and warned his friends
that Hecla "will cost considerable before it pays dividends."
Impatient midwestern investors turned in their stock. Campbell rode East to promote the mine, finding new buyers—"The
effect I hoped," he wrote a stockholder. "A great deal of activity in the stock and quite a demand." A block of 20,000 went
at one dollar a share. In January 1900 a small crew of about ten

men started to rebuild the Hecla tunnel, and Campbell predicted the mine would pay a dividend by July.

Campbell now divided his time between the company's office in Wallace and his ornate Spokane home on a south bluff overlooking the Spokane River. In a paneled basement game room, he presided at boisterous poker games. Finch lived two doors away, and Patsy Clark's house, vaguely Mediterranean in style, stood a few blocks south, facing the park. For his ostentation, Clark paid the city's highest residential property tax on an assessed valuation (at roughly 10 percent of market value) of $9,900; Campbell, the second, on a valuation of $8,470.

The Campbells, Finch, the Clarks, and others like them formed a newly rich gentry in Spokane, among whom money surmounted background and breeding. Their wives exchanged formal visits on calling days listed in a blue book. They sponsored elaborate parties, balls, and theatrical performances, and they sent their children to eastern or European schools. Clark enrolled a son at Georgetown. Campbell's daughter Helen studied in Paris. And Campbell ordered shirts tailored in New York. Finch sunned in Santa Barbara, keeping in touch by letter.

In these early days of a new century, troops still guarded the Coeur d'Alene mines. Edward Moffitt, busy with the Standard and his own business, left Hecla largely to its assayer, James Smith, who had come out from Chicago after buying his stock, and who still put whatever he could spare into more shares. Smith was a familiar figure in Burke, carrying his lunch pail to the mine office and, although it did not specify his actions, a newspaper said he had been "a bulwark of strength in the restoration of order" after the Bunker Hill explosion.

While the companies curbed their men by permit and military surveillance, they could not easily influence the smelting industry, dominated by the American Smelting & Refining Company (Asarco)—the trust—reorganized in 1899 by the sons of Meyer Guggenheim to combine eleven companies that now controlled 90 percent of the nation's lead processing. Only ten substantial smelters remained independent of Asarco, but their rates and policies followed the market pattern set by the trust. Moffitt consigned Hecla ores to American's smelters and to the independent Puget Sound Reduction Company at Everett, Washington, a waterfront plant erected in 1892 with money supplied by John D. Rockefeller. In keeping with mining practice of the time, Hecla stationed its own observer, W. Horace Clagett, son of a pioneer judge, at Everett to check the assaying and weighing of its shipments. Even with their own men watching, managers constantly accused smelters of short weights and rigged returns.

As Campbell had forecast, Hecla paid its first dividend, two cents a share, on July 25, 1900. "We could easily pay this dividend every month," Campbell told John Wick, "if we were not making extensive improvements and putting in a large plant." Now that the main tunnel had been enlarged and re-timbered, allowing mule haulage, the Gem mill was proving too small for the mine's output. Nonetheless, by the end of 1900, Hecla had sold $229,550 worth of ore and paid $100,000 in dividends.

At the annual meeting of shareholders, when the mine's unofficial assistant manager, Smith, emerged as the largest individual shareholder with 82,000, the trustees elected him vice president. Now his friends called him "Hecla" Smith, and now that he was making money from dividends and was an officer of the company, he moved back to the Briggs House in Chicago, where he had lived before coming to the Coeur d'Alenes.

With Hecla stock in demand, selling at $1.25 a share and higher, Patsy Clark sold out, taking his profits to invest in a Canadian prospect. Campbell bought 54,300 shares at $1.50 from Clark and distributed them among friends who had badgered him to get them some Hecla stock, telling one, "You are aware that Patsy is a great fellow to sell when the stock gets up pretty well."

While Hecla prospered, the lead market worsened, glutted by too much lead. To hold its customers, American Smelting & Refining promised them a fixed price for pig lead for one year, and to reduce the oversupply, imposed quotas on mines under contract to its smelters, offering bonuses to the mines to cut back production. To Hecla, the trust gave a bonus based on sales for the past six months. The mine closed for the last six months of 1901, throwing its men out of work shortly after the governor of Idaho lifted martial law in the district. The company had earned $58,885 from ore sales and $63,347 in bonuses for not producing that year. The cost of extending its main tunnel and driving two new ones above it, with a three-compartment shaft, had exceeded its income, and Hecla closed its books with a deficit. The trustees reluctantly passed up dividends.

On the other side of Canyon Creek from Hecla, in the hills overlooking Burke, Harry L. Day and his partners in Hercules struck rich silver-lead ore on June 2, 1901, almost at the moment when mines were cutting back production. Both Hercules and Hecla, which were to be the major mines of Burke for the next twenty-five years, looked for independent smelters to buy their ores. Somewhat cocky as vice president of Hecla, Smith negotiated a contract for part of the mine's production with the new Ohio & Colorado Smelting & Refining Company at Salida, Colorado, a subsidiary of the German-controlled American Metals Company. Clagett moved to Denver to represent Hecla at Salida.

With the lead industry under sway of a trust, Mace Campbell proposed that mining companies merge for strength. Shortly after reorganization of Hecla in 1898, he had begun sounding out his Youngstown friends on combining mines (perhaps the Union, Tiger-Poorman, and Hecla) for a stronger company and to save operating costs, writing to Henry Wick, "If I could secure the proper influential man to take hold," he would consolidate the mines of Canyon Creek. Campbell also tried out his notion on David Hyman of New York, absentee owner of the Frisco and soon buyer of the Gem and Galena, who seemed politely in accord. Throughout 1899 and 1900, Campbell had continued to talk merger.

Merging the mines was not Campbell's singular idea, for a good many mining men could see the advantages in combining. Charles Sweeny, keeping his own counsel for once, also thought of merger and started quietly to seek an investor with enough money.

Campbell recommended to Hecla's trustees that they combine with the Standard, as a start, but Hecla's board voted down a merger on Smith's advice. Speaking for himself and Upman, Smith said the proposed division of assets would be unfair—two-thirds to Standard and one-third to Hecla. Frank Kipp sided with Smith and, with their votes, they elected Kipp and Henry Wick to Hecla's board. In a way, Campbell's scheme for merger had backfired, rallying shareholders to Smith and Kipp and setting in motion the events that would emancipate Hecla from Finch and Campbell.

Finch and Campbell had already been approached to sell Hecla, Standard, and other mines to a syndicate represented by former Senator George Turner, who talked in millions of dollars. Behind Turner hid Sweeny, and behind him, the resources of Rockefeller. Few of the mine owners in Canyon Creek would have dealt directly with Sweeny. For one, Harry Day, who regarded Sweeny as a pirate, flatly refused even to talk of selling him Hercules. Bunker Hill and Sullivan would sell, but asked $3 million. Sweeny hesitated, and his hesitation cost him Bunker Hill, for its directors cut off negotiations. Campbell advised Turner that Hecla would sell only for cash at one dollar a share, and Sweeny passed it by.

Consequently, when Rockefeller minions organized the Federal Mining & Smelting Company in Delaware on June 24, 1903, Sweeny proceeded to buy for Federal: the Standard for $2,250,000; the Mammoth for $1,500,000; and his own Empire State-Idaho (at Wardner) for $3 million in preferred stock. Campbell had counseled his stockholders to sell the Standard, "at every level . . . getting poorer," but he delayed closing the sale, piqued because the payment would not be all in cash. The larger shareholders had wanted to sell, anyway, and Henry Wick met Sweeny in New York to sign the sale documents which, to a large degree, closed out Finch and Campbell in the Coeur d'Alenes.

Finch was named second vice president of Federal; Richard Wilson (of the Mammoth), a director; and Sweeny's men, Edward J. Roberts and W. Clayton Miller, manager and assistant manager.

After the sale, Moffitt took the larger Mammoth office quarters for Hecla, but he was busy running his own business in Wallace. He turned over Hecla's daily operations to James F. McCarthy, a mannerly, hard-working engineer who had moved from Mammoth to Hecla late in 1902. McCarthy had been running Hecla for nearly a year when, at their meeting in November 1903, the trustees considered a resolution to appoint him manager. It did not pass but, according to the minutes, "the trustees seemed satisfied with his appointment." In this offhand way, McCarthy came into the post that would make him the soul of Hecla for the next thirty-eight years. At the same meeting, the trustees elected Smith president (on Upman's motion), and Finch, vice president and treasurer. Former president Campbell, his wife and daughter, and Patrick Clark, his wife and three daughters, were in France on a leisurely tour of the Continent.

McCarthy came from clannish Irish in the coal fields of Pennsylvania. He would keep close ties to his cousins all his life. After public schooling, he had sold knitted goods, clerked in a prothonotary's office, and then had gone to New York to sell for a metallurgist while he studied mining engineering at night at the Cooper Union. His first mining job was assaying in Honduras (later, he would sing lullabies in Spanish to his grandchildren), and he moved to the Coeur d'Alenes in January 1898 as engineer and assayer for Mammoth. Shortly after he arrived in Burke, runs family legend, he telegraphed Anastasia Langton in Pennsylvania a proposal of marriage which she accepted.

Republican and Catholic, McCarthy would be one of three men who steered the mining district for the next four decades. The others: Stanly A. Easton of the Bunker Hill and Harry Day of the Hercules. These three would speak for the district, represent it at expositions and government inquiries, serve on national mining committees and on the board of the state university, and contend with smelters, railroads, unions, the government, corporate predators, and the vagaries of mineral veins. Sometimes they fought each other. McCarthy was thirty-six when Hecla's trustees rather casually put him in charge, not realizing how wholly they had delivered Hecla into his hands.

By necessity, McCarthy would pioneer mining technology. Power drills had been used for perhaps a decade. Drill design and explosives continued to improve. Shortly before McCarthy took over Hecla, the Washington Water Power Company of Spokane had begun to deliver high-voltage, year-round current to the mines. Operations need no longer be seasonal. Managers gradually shelved their water wheels and steam plants to convert to electricity for hoists, haulage, ventilation, lighting, mills, and so on. Hecla's last dozen mules would be retired in 1916. Two of them, Toby and Bee, aged nineteen, had not been outside the mine since they started pulling ore cars. McCarthy would also devise Hecla's unique timbering and stoping methods and would drive the mine deep, establishing its reputation for innovation which has lasted into the present day.

In addition to ingenuity, McCarthy needed adroitness to deal with the smelter trust. When the new Federal company bluffed that it would build smelters, Asarco expanded its holdings: it bought the independent Tacoma and Selby (San Francisco) plants, and in March 1905, Daniel Guggenheim acquired control of Federal itself. As the preeminent supplier of lead to manufacturers, Asarco manipulated prices, smelter charges, and railroad schedules and rates. Harry Day complained to other mine managers that "independent smelters are perforce following their lead, and the miner is being mulct." A manager who dealt with Asarco either accepted its dictates or risked not selling his ores. To assure themselves of a market, the directors of Bunker Hill & Sullivan signed a twenty-five-year contract with Asarco.

Under McCarthy, Hecla dealt not only with trust smelters but also with independents, now one and then another, relying on their gasping need for concentrates in a monopolistic market to negotiate favorable rates. Hecla played the smelting game cautiously, as if steering a canoe through rapids, for, as F. W. Bradley of Bunker Hill observed, "All . . . smelting companies had what I call their 'personal equations.' That is, some of them were more honest in the weighing, sampling, assaying, settling, etc., than others were. They had different ways . . . all calculated to be in favor of the smelterer against the shipper."

In this risky business climate, Theodore Sternfeld, president of American Metals, finding Smith "rather offish," appealed to Harry Day to intercede with Hecla for its business, and then asked if Day might join him in buying Hecla. Day held 32,000 shares of Hecla stock, but he would never have entered a partnership with the skittish Sternfeld, and the pipe dream of buying Hecla evaporated.

For most of McCarthy's first ten years as manager, Hecla ores went to Salida. Smith, Upman, and the Wallace attorney, C. W. Beale, had made a formal visit to the plant. For a brief period in 1906, to nudge Salida into line on returns, McCarthy diverted ores to the Pennsylvania Smelting Company at Carnegie, the nation's smallest independent. In 1913, when International Smelting & Refining completed a modern mechanized smelter at Tooele, Utah, and offered reduced rates to attract customers, Hecla became its first patron and, thus, a preferred one. Throughout these years, Clagett watched over assays, weights, segregated car lots, and moisture in concentrates, often

25

calling an umpire to settle disputes. Since smelter reports could be as much as four months late, every mining company showed "ore in transit" as a line item in financial statements.

Easton and McCarthy occasionally traded information about their smelting contracts, suspicious that Federal, as an Asarco subsidiary, and Hercules, with ores desirable as flux, might secretly be getting better rates. In emergencies, Clagett and McCarthy exchanged coded telegrams—frequently garbled, McCarthy sighed, by telegraph operators' poor spelling.

Mine managers also contended with railroads. Both the Northern Pacific and the Oregon-Washington Railroad & Navigation Company (Union Pacific) ran from Wallace to Burke on parallel tracks on the narrow canyon floor. They competed for the mines' traffic and fought over routes, largely owing to the Union Pacific's failure to live up to an 1890 understanding that it would obtain right of way for both lines.

The Northern Pacific, with the only trackage to the Tiger-Poorman, demanded use of the Union Pacific's way to Hecla on a hillside route known as the highline. The Union Pacific also served Hecla at a lower level, where Hecla, with high cribbing to hold back earth and waste, hoisted supplies and ores by crane—"hand to mouth," McCarthy grumbled, urging a better loading arrangement. McCarthy was stuck with the Union Pacific, for it owned the spur to the Gem mill. At Hercules, Day's men resorted to stealing the Tiger's ore cars, and Day finally wangled a spur to his loading area only by agreeing to a smelting contract with the trust.

Not until 1908 would the railroads compromise on joint use of spurs, and they would not share a single track in the canyon until 1927, when the county commissioners demanded space for a highway. Until the railroads settled their differences, McCarthy, Day, and other managers played one line against the other for better schedules, more cars, and even for favored rates. Jim Smith promised the Northern Pacific "not less than 50 percent of his ore shipments" for improved service and even offered to build a spur at Hecla's expense, but the railroad declined to maintain it. To honor Smith's compact, for some years McCarthy gave all Hecla's business to one railroad for six months, and then to the other for the next six months.

Railroads often provided open cars unsuited to hauling concentrates, or leaky cars, or too few cars, and sometimes after loading them, lost the cars en route to a smelter. "What a slow mover the railroad is," McCarthy fussed, tracing ores foresaken in transit on a siding somewhere.

The mine managers also watched their men carefully for signs that unions were coming back, using detectives in the towns, spies among the shifts, and the employment bureau. For years, Hecla and other companies regularly imported Missouri miners through a Joplin agent, and company patrols checked the payrolls for former union members, discharging any they discovered. The managers saw themselves as assuring their companies of reliable workmen at predictable costs. Beginning in August 1906, they voluntarily established an eight-hour work day, cutting pay accordingly from the customary ten-hour day. And faced with gathering political support for workman's insurance in Idaho, the Hecla, Federal, and Morning in February 1905 set up company-endowed liability associations, to which each miner paid one dollar and each company paid fifty cents a month per man. Hecla's Provident & Accident Insurance Association, which started, McCarthy acknowledged, despite workers' antagonism to self-insuring, would pay an injured miner ten dollars a week for up to ten weeks, a lump $1,500 to a man permanently disabled, or the same amount to the family of one killed on the job.

The specter of violent unionism hovered over the district, nevertheless, with the arrest of Harry Orchard, a onetime Burke wagon driver, who confessed to the bomb murder of former governor Frank Steunenberg. In June 1907 three Western Federation of Miners officers were kidnapped by the state, to be tried—and acquitted—on charges of conspiring with Orchard.

Now that Smith was president, visiting Burke annually and writing often from Chicago, and now that James McCarthy was managing the mine, Hecla transferred its records from the offices of Finch and Campbell in Spokane to Wallace on October 14, 1904. The Hecla office would stay in Wallace for more than eighty years.

Fortunately for the Coeur d'Alenes, the nation's consumption of lead was rising with heavy demands for sheeting from the chemical industry, sheathing for cable, and paint manufacture. The oversupply turned to a shortage and the price rose steadily; it would hit six cents a pound on the New York market early in 1907, its highest in thirty years. Hecla prospered in the rising market with a net income in 1903 of $152,263, and the directors happily declared a $60,000 dividend and voted to

27

buy the Milwaukee mill at Gem for $50,000. In 1904 Hecla re-
alized a net of $224,779 and more than doubled dividends to
$150,000; the next year it paid $240,000; the next, $450,000; and
in 1907, $520,000 in dividends. Incidentally, when Hecla bought
the Gem Mill, Campbell, Frank Kipp, and Adolph Speigel
bought the 85,167 shares belonging to Julia, Charles Kipp's
widow, for three cents a share and also took her dividend of
ten cents a share. On the back of stock certificate 103, someone
wrote: "rather a rough way to treat the widow."

Even though prices were good, McCarthy spent as little money
as practical on the mine. He reduced costs to $1.93 a ton during
1905–06 and reported a net profit of $4.32 a ton. While the costs
of lumber and timber doubled in three years, he held costs at
$2.22 and pushed profits per ton up to $5.25. The grateful trustees raised McCarthy's salary to $500 a month and elected him
secretary and treasurer of the company.

McCarthy's careful management piled up surplus earnings—
idle money—amounting to more than $320,000 at the end of
the 1906 fiscal year. The directors had talked for some time about
reincorporating Hecla in another state or increasing its one million shares to take advantage of demand for its stock, but each
time they put off a decision. Now with some surplus funds,
they voted to lend Frank Kipp's First National Bank of Milwaukee $100,000, and to lend to selected large firms, perhaps
Swift or Armour packing companies. At Kipp's urging, Hecla
also deposited $271,628 in the Wisconsin Trust Company and
the First National of Milwaukee, as well as in the First National
Bank of Wallace, on which it drew for operating expenses and
dividends.

At the shareholders' meeting in 1907, Smith's and Kipp's
proxies elected as a trustee the sixty-year-old Milwaukee bachelor Carl Landsee in place of Charles Bender, a Wallace merchant associated with Finch and Campbell. Finch and Campbell rarely attended Hecla meetings now, sending in their stead
Spokane attorney W. J. C. Wakefield, who was often invited
to sit in on trustees' meetings. With Landsee's election, Milwaukee and Chicago men constituted four of Hecla's seven
trustees—Upman, Smith, Kipp, and Landsee.

The board, now often called directors rather than trustees,
had authorized Smith to declare dividends from surplus. He
took for himself the privilege of soliciting borrowers, a role that

flattered him in Chicago where the *Daily News* called him "a wealthy mining man . . . said to be worth about $1,000,000." On his own, Smith negotiated a loan of $27,000 by Hecla to Swift & Company and, after first turning down Armour because the packer offered too low an interest rate, lent Armour $51,000. Kipp was astounded at Smith's call for a special meeting to ratify his loans. "The idea of Smith making a loan . . . without the consent of the Directors is awful," he told Mc-Carthy. He and Landsee wired Smith, protesting the Swift loan because, Kipp declared, "my opinion of Swift and Company is not very good." And to McCarthy, Kipp went on, "I think Smith's actions ought to be curbed; he is taking too much responsibility. . . . I think he is acting very peculiar."

The huffy directors could do nothing but approve the loans, but Kipp and Landsee shifted their confidence from Smith to McCarthy, whom they now regarded as the steady man in the company.

Smith's conduct was not Hecla's greatest worry, for in the last months of 1907 the price of lead collapsed in a general business depression. The stock market had softened in March, businesses failed, and on October 22, the Knickerbocker Trust of New York closed, toppling eastern finance in a panic—a "Wall Street depression," western businessmen sneered. All across the country, banks stopped lending. Spokane banks issued clearing-house certificates to be used as currency. "No bank here is lending any money," Charles Hussey wrote Campbell from Spokane. Campbell was trying to raise funds in Youngstown for a Hoquiam lumber company in which he, Finch, and Henry Wick had invested. A recently started Wallace stock exchange disbanded. The Spokane exchange halted trading until times improved.

Mining companies closed or cut back, throwing men out of work—effectively ending mine workers' muttering about a strike for four dollars a day. To add to the misery, the Idaho legislature had enacted a Sunday rest law which, although it excluded mine workers, covered bartenders, forcing saloons to close on the sabbath. Easton estimated the district's production at 13.6 percent lower in 1907 than in 1906. Smelters cut off some mines, and when Upman hurried to Salida, he was able to arrange a contract only for 1,300 tons of Hecla ore a month, compared with a monthly average of 8,430 in 1906. The smelter's directors urged Hecla to cut back to 900. Upman and Campbell both wrote McCarthy to close the mine "for the best interest of the Hecla Mining Company."

At the directors' meeting in December 1907, McCarthy told them that "in the past 90 days, the demand for ore has practically disappeared." He had already advised Landsee, and now he advised the board that Hecla should shut down rather than exhaust its reserves at low prices, estimating that maintenance of the idle mine would cost $60,000 for a year, "an amount we can make in one month with favorable conditions." With a surplus of $438,914, Hecla was in no peril, but McCarthy pointed out that Federal had closed, concluding that "if the situation warrants them making such a drastic cut, . . it seems a safe sign for us to follow."

The somber board agreed to shut down on January 1, but, at the insistence of Kipp and Upman, to pay dividends of at least one cent each month through April. Before adjourning, the directors lent Grace Campbell $50,000 at 8 percent on the collateral of 499 shares of Washington Water Power and 200 of Traders National Bank of Spokane. Perhaps she handed the money to her husband for the Hoquiam lumber venture.

Closing the mines fell heavily on Burke and Wallace. Smith seemed unaware of the distress. The president of the Wallace bank, Frank Johnson, asked that Hecla withdraw only $20,000 a month to pay dividends, "which would enable us to go along with our liquidation without forcing things." But Smith warned Johnson he would need $100,000 and took $110,000. Johnson sadly wrote his old friend Mace Campbell, "It would have been better for the community if they had let the balance stand after paying the dividend, and allowed us to carry some of the people who were entitled to credit."

Hecla would be closed for five months before lead prices revived halfheartedly, and the company's dividends fell from $520,000 in 1907 to $190,000 in 1908. McCarthy used the down time to renovate the mine workings, but a new electric hoist consistently burned out pulleys and started with such a surge that it sometimes disrupted service throughout the system. When he braced D. L. Huntington, president of Washington Water Power, about the hoist, McCarthy learned that the utility intended to raise rates for all of the mining companies—for Hecla, from $22 to $100 per horsepower.

Smith instructed McCarthy to resist the rate increase, of

course, and McCarthy appealed directly to Campbell, recently
retired as first vice president but still a director of the power
company. As he led Campbell through the rate structure, however, McCarthy saw Campbell's eyelids flutter. "You know you
can never hold Mace's attention in matters of detail," he wrote
Smith, and he tried a new strategy. Convinced that the power
company could not accurately measure power use, McCarthy
went into a lengthy exchange with Huntington on the accuracy
of meters.

Other managers, meanwhile, determined to break the district monopoly of Washington Water Power by underwriting a
hydroelectric plant at Thompson Falls on the Clark Fork River
in Montana. They intended their new contracts with Washington Water Power to be their last, and in 1915 Federal, Bunker
Hill, and Hercules took their first current from the Idaho Transmission Company, a new utility in which they held stock.
McCarthy had joined the other managers in their planning for
the Montana project but decided—perhaps because Campbell
was connected with the Washington company—to stay with
Spokane.

At the same time, promoters of a revived Panhandle smelter
at Ponderay (on Lake Pend Oreille near Sandpoint) solicited
Coeur d'Alene mine owners to buy stock and patronize their
plant. At one time or another, every manager of a major mine
had considered the advantages of a captive smelter. Spokane
and Portland hungered for smelters—one would become a
Chicago of the West, they often said—and both cities built them.
Spokane's smelter never operated, and Portland's was a fiasco
from its start.

In 1907 the former Panhandle Smelting Company at Ponderay had failed, changed its name to the Idaho Refining &
Smelting Company, and reorganized under control of J. Herbert Anderson of Chicago. About three million shares of its
stock had been sold to farmers and other small investors in
midwestern states. Anderson pressed Easton, Day, McCarthy
and other mine managers to buy shares. Mostly they put him
off. In June 1907 the 200-ton smelter blew in—as the mines
were closing—but shut down soon. With "moral support," if
not financing, from Montana mine owners, it started up again
in November 1908.

James McCarthy pondered the usefulness of the Ponderay
smelter to Hecla. Privately, he told Campbell, he felt the plant

could not survive without Hecla's patronage but its management impressed him as unreliable and its finances shaky, and he could not hang this millstone on Hecla. He turned aside Anderson's importuning. By March 1909 the smelter again went into receivership, its president accused of overissuing stock. Rumors that it would reopen circulated from time to time but, aside from fitful puffs, it never did. Its assets would be auctioned by the sheriff in 1922.

For eight years after the depression, Hecla's income would not equal that of 1907, for mining, farming, and lumbering recovered slowly from panic. McCarthy, like others, experimented with cheaper milling methods and, although he reduced his costs to $1.88 a ton, income fell. Hecla merely held its own.

Not all the news was bad: Late in 1908 the Ninth Circuit Court of Appeals denied damages to farmers along the Coeur d'Alene River who had sued the major mines alleging that wastes polluted and choked the stream. During seven years of litigation, the Mine Owners Association hired detectives to check farm income and agents to adjust the claims of willing farmers, and built dams near Osburn and Pine Creek to collect mill tailings.

As Hecla gingerly resumed operations after its closure, James Smith created one last surprise: On September 8, 1908, giving his age as forty-four, he obtained a license to marry thirty-four-year-old Sarah E. Peterson, a Chicago public stenographer. Sixteen days later, Smith was hospitalized with pneumonia complicated by Bright's disease. As he worsened, he and Sarah were married hastily on September 25 by a hospital chaplain. At 6:30 that evening, Smith expired. He left no will. To Sarah passed his 92,000 shares of Hecla stock. His death certificate gave Smith's age as fifty-six. Obituary notices in Spokane and Chicago newspapers, based on his friends' recollections, did not mention Sarah. Nonetheless, Hecla's largest shareholder was now a woman nobody in the company knew.

3

The East Orebody

WITH THE NEWS OF JAMES SMITH'S PASSING, ONLY FOUR MEN— Mace Campbell, John Finch, Charles Hussey, and James McCarthy—showed up for the scheduled annual meeting in October 1908 and, as a gesture of respect for their late president, they adjourned until November. In November, the shareholders elected Smith's widow, Sarah, a director, and his friend, Frank Upman, president of the company. Upman would be an absentee president; he was caught up in his investments in municipal and utility bonds, building his dividends for retirement. He left the business largely to Frank Kipp and McCarthy.

Sarah Smith, about whom they were curious, turned out to be a well-spoken, intelligent, not unattractive, plump woman in expensive clothes. At first she listened to the men and did not say much, but the clubby maleness of board meetings evaporated. At the time, Hecla employed no women, and females rarely attended stockholders' meetings. No matter. Sarah seemed unruffled, even though they shut her out of the cigars and whiskey. When they knew her better, they discovered in her a streak of arbitrary stubbornness. When the directors met in Wallace, Sarah was handed over to Anna McCarthy to be entertained—she always arrived a few days early and stayed a week or two—and Anna often took her to moving pictures, silent then. Because her deafness encouraged her to read lips, Anna sometimes whispered to others what the actors really said. That seemed to irritate Sarah. She preferred to be the center of attention.

If Sarah's election changed the board, the company itself seemed to be in transition. The two founding fathers stood apart: Finch, who had suffered a nervous breakdown several years earlier, conserved his strength in California or at Hayden Lake, where he built a fine villa; Campbell traveled often and was wrapped up in other businesses. They sent Charles Hussey or

W. J. C. Wakefield to meetings. The shareholders chose Wake-field as a director in 1908, not only as Finch's and Campbell's representative but also for his good sense. A partner with Archibald W. Witherspoon in one of Spokane's prestigious legal firms, Wakefield moved familiarly among the city's leading men.

Wakefield's Spanish stucco home sat between those of Campbell and Finch, and their yards ran together like a park. Henry Wick felt himself outnumbered, and sometimes ignored, by the Spokane-Chicago-Milwaukee crowd; he had once written Smith, asking that Smith and Kipp, who were talking about selling the mine, do nothing "without our being considered."

The directors had authorized an audit of the years 1903 to 1907; it showed that, of Hecla's $250,000 capitalization, only $175,000 had been paid. At each meeting the directors considered reorganizing Hecla in another state, but they held off. After McCarthy, in a printed letter to stockholders, pointed out that Hecla's low capitalization and par value had a "tendency to lower the selling price of the stock," and that many shareholders complained about it, the directors met to consider raising the capitalization to $5 million. But at this special meeting, Landsee offered, and the majority approved—over Youngstown opposition—a motion authorizing the board to sell Hecla for $3 million, or to place its stock for trading on the New York or Boston curb exchange, where it would attract a wider sphere of investors.

The company's net had tripled in 1909 to $329,888, and it had paid $200,000 in dividends. Although income rose and fell with the market for lead, dividends flowed steadily: $200,000 in 1910; $240,000 in 1911, $300,000 the next year, $320,000 the year after, and so on. Charles Sweeny, who had resigned from Federal, offered to buy Hecla. Vogelstein & Company, a German-owned New York metals trader, also wanted to buy, but as McCarthy told Clagett, "the directors would not even let these people inspect the mine."

And when shareholders responded with "fierce criticism" to a letter outlining prospects for a sale, the directors rescinded their vote to sell the mine or list its stock for trading. The past decade had been occupied with improving and expanding the company's workings and mills, ensuring its markets and bringing it to a position to pay regular dividends. Frank Kipp would snap that the "Hecla treasury is run in the interest of the First

National Bank of Wallace" and push through a resolution that, when the Wallace account exceeded $50,000, funds must be placed in Milwaukee and Chicago banks, but that was incidental. Their objective now, the directors agreed, must be to secure the company's future.

Perhaps they should do their own smelting. Even though Asarco cast a lowering shadow across the marketplace, and though Hecla's contract with International saved it $54,000 a year compared with Salida, the board reviewed again the possibility of building a smelter. Cyaniding ores at the concentrator had substantially reduced the concentrates that warranted high treatment charges, but instead of lowering rates, smelters had raised them. When its contract with International expired, Hecla might have little chance for another as favorable. "It is generally believed that whatever competition there was amongst large smelters several years ago has disappeared," McCarthy advised his board. "There is a pretty good understanding among them as to the prices they will pay."

McCarthy conferred with George Faunce and John Williams of the Pennsylvania Smelting Company, who guessed that Hecla could save $4,000 a month by smelting its own concentrates. The Coeur d'Alenes were alive with rumors that Bunker Hill or the Day brothers—Harry, Eugene, and Jerome—would build a plant in the district. The Days bought riverside flatlands that might serve as a site. But the trust's grip, as well as vicissitudes of the lead market, invested smelting with high risks. Frank Upman, brooding on Hecla during four months in Europe, fairly well summarized the directors' consensus. He wrote McCarthy that he did "not think it advisable for us to engage in the smelting business . . . [owing to] too many elements . . . we are not familiar with." Hecla renewed its International contract for five years.

The board had been pleased with McCarthy's work. At their 1910 meeting they voted him and Upman their appreciation "for able management" and in October 1911 they offered a more tangible expression of how wholly they relied on McCarthy. They awarded him a $1,000 bonus and elected him president as well as general manager, Upman vice president, and Lewis E. Hanley, secretary. To Hanley, who had come over from Mammoth about the same time as McCarthy and had been his right hand since, they gave $500 as a wedding gift.

McCarthy's installation as president marked a change in

management philosophy, for it was the first time one of the large shareholders had not held the post. Despite falling lead prices (again), the costs of sinking a deeper shaft, and heavy depreciation charges for a federal corporation tax (imposed to replace revenues lost by lowered tariffs under the Payne-Aldrich Act of 1909), the directors charged their new president with continuing to pay monthly dividends. They agreed to keep a surplus of $200,000 and to disburse any profits beyond that as special quarterly dividends.

And to continue the company in business, the directors decreed that McCarthy "should be on the lookout for a new mine in the Coeur d'Alene district." They acceded to McCarthy's request that he be awarded a 5 percent interest in any mine Hecla acquired because he would be blocked from looking for new properties for himself. Managers commonly bought shares in prospects that their companies, for one reason or another, did not take up—and often, if the prospect proved worthwhile, sold their shares to their own companies. McCarthy, for one, held stock for years in the Argentine claim.

McCarthy felt that he had an attractive prospect almost in the family: the Star, whose largest stockholder was John Finch. Immediately west of the productive Morning mine, the Star consisted of ten patented and seven unpatented claims; it was well equipped, had one and one-half miles of underground workings, and, although exploration in two drifts on a vein had failed to turn commercial ore, samples from drill holes indicated salable mineral. "This seems to me the most desirable partly developed property in the district," McCarthy explained to the directors. He negotiated with Finch for an option on two-thirds of Star's capital stock at sixty cents a share, promising that during the option period Hecla would complete a crosscut at the 5,700-foot level, estimating that the work would require three and one-half years and $125,000. Finch agreed to pursue the offer with other stockholders.

Hanley summoned the board to a special meeting at that massive old pile, the Auditorium Hotel in Chicago, to consider bonding the Star. Sarah Smith, Landsee, Upman, and McCarthy attended, and George Lonstorf, a Milwaukee shareholder and president of his own exploration company, sat in. McCarthy described Star in detail. The directors seemed interested but declined to vote until they talked with Frank Kipp.

The meeting adjourned to Milwaukee where Kipp, Landsee, and McCarthy were joined by Lonstorf, George P. Mayer and Albert Trostel, shareholders. McCarthy told his story again.

But the Milwaukee directors and shareholders dragged their feet; they merely bade McCarthy to continue negotiating with Finch. McCarthy sensed that for some reason the Milwaukee men did not want Star. Some objected that the price was too high (Smith later quoted Lonstorf as saying Star was "not worth the money"), and Landsee cited congressional deliberations for further tariff reductions. "Under present conditions," he soon wrote McCarthy, "I feel we should drop all negotiations for a bond on the Star mine." To which McCarthy replied, "I regret this change of position. . . . [It is] too early to admit defeat in the tariff matter."

While Landsee and McCarthy exchanged letters, another of the founders died—Amasa Campbell, wasted in body from throat cancer. For nearly two years Campbell had been slowly, painfully starving as his throat closed. A Paris physician inserted a tube to ease breathing, but the Mayo brothers refused to operate, saying it would hasten death. For his last two months, Campbell spoke in a faint whisper and swallowed only ice. He died in his sleep the night of February 16, 1912.

When the Hecla directors convened for their regular meeting in April, Wakefield moved, and the directors unanimously agreed that the company should drop negotiations for Star. McCarthy remarked to Henry Wick that the Milwaukee shareholders rejected Star because "some of them would rather have the profits from the Hecla without any further speculation." The Star dismissal had not been an encouraging portent for a president and general manager charged with finding a new mine, but Star was not out of the picture.

In June 1912 Harry Day became president of Federal Mining & Smelting Company. He, too, was charged with finding new mines. Day employed a New York mining engineer, E. Percy Smith, to evaluate Star for Federal, encouraged (and a little surprised) by learning that Federal crews in the Morning had overshot their boundaries and were digging commercial ore from Star ground. Day reached a compact with Finch for an option on the Star nine months after the Hecla had abandoned it. But Smith, on closer inspection, recommended dropping the option, opining that the ore was too low grade to pay. And Federal, too, called off bargaining. Thus the Star stood anathematized, optioned and discarded by two of the district's able companies.

Campbell had not lived to hear about a new discovery in the Hecla—the east orebody. Late in 1910 McCarthy had offered a bonus of fifty cents a day to his tunnelmen if they speeded up driving a crosscut from number 3, the oldest and lowest of three Hecla tunnels opening on the hillside above Burke. Although no mineral appeared as months passed, McCarthy insisted that the crew go on, and in February 1912 they struck good ore east of the original Hecla shoot.

The "east orebody," this find would be called, and McCarthy, in his report to the directors in April 1913, informed them that crews had drifted five hundred feet in mineral one- to four-feet wide, not quite as clean as the original shoot, carrying more zinc and iron, but commercial ore that would "materially add to the value" of the Hecla.

Then, when the men drifted on the 900-foot level to undercut the east orebody, they "unexpectedly encountered ore within 350 feet of the old shoot," McCarthy reported. They followed this 325 feet in mineral one- to ten-feet wide with slightly higher silver content than the original shoot. If this ore persisted, it could be reached on five other levels "as fast as we can spare funds for drifting and crosscutting." Thus assured that their mine would endure for some years, the directors voted to expand the concentrating plant, build cottages at Burke for six shift bosses, and buy a company automobile.

The exhilaration of finding new orebodies was dampened only slightly by fluttering lead prices and pockets of business depression, compounded in the Northwest by layoffs of thousands of workmen as transcontinental railroads completed their mainline construction. Men put out of work by farm machines, or ill-housed and ill-fed in logging camps, or dropped from a mine crew for missing the first shift after payday could feel themselves oppressed. A number joined the radical Industrial Workers of the World—the IWW or Wobblies. In 1909 the Wobblies fought Spokane's government for the right to speak at street meetings; then they opened an office in Spokane for organizing men and distributing union literature. Organizers signing on as experienced hands in mines found a ready-made forum in boardinghouses for single men—places like the Tiger Hotel at Burke—and the union grew. To the dismay of mine managers, unionism was filtering back into the Coeur d'Alenes.

McCarthy stayed close to his men and, as a consequence, the IWW was perhaps weaker in Hecla than in other major mines at Burke and Mullan. He spent at least half a day each week at Burke, talking with miners and shift bosses, looking over workings and mill, listening and counseling. The men's word for him was "gentleman." McCarthy treated each with respect. At Wallace, he lingered in his office each evening until 6:00 or after, giving his foremen time to come in with their day's problems or his men a chance to drop by to talk.

With hard times, the district's towns bulged with men looking for work—and speculators sniffing for a lucky buy. For every man who lost his job, a dozen others leaped to apply. No matter how slow other industry, the mines ran at full speed. Bunker Hill and the combined Federal properties each tallied net profits of more than $1 million in 1912; the Hercules partnership, $715,763; and Hecla, more than $335,600, its highest net since 1907.

But the lead market would not sweeten. Smelters piled up surpluses, Congress reduced tariffs on imported metals for the second time since 1909, and in 1914 war in Europe cut off lead sales to nations that had been taking one-fourth of the Coeur d'Alenes' output. Although Asarco continued to hold the market to an arbitrary price, McCarthy warned the directors that production must be curtailed again. He did not want to shut down, for "there is something due the men and the community . . . and reduced output would permit the men sufficient income to live on."

Obviously, McCarthy had become bolder in advancing the interests of his men. Seven years earlier he had let Jim Smith heedlessly siphon funds from the Wallace bank. Now he spoke up. When a faithful employee's health failed, McCarthy recommended voluntarily retiring the man at $125 a month, remarking, "I don't think he should be turned away because of his advancing age."

Butte and the copper districts had already cut back to half capacity. Slowdown notwithstanding, the Milwaukee directors insisted on dividends. Landsee declared, "We have been paying regular monthly dividends since March 1904 and this should be kept up . . . even if we have to reduce our surplus."

McCarthy reduced Hecla from its normal six days a week to five. Even though lead prices remained low, smelters demanded freight increases of two to three dollars a ton which would cost Hecla $60,000 a year, and that possibility resurrected the campaign for a smelter in the Coeur d'Alenes. Incensed, the directors authorized McCarthy to pledge ores and financial support to one. On the first of January 1915, McCarthy was obliged to restore the six-day week and to stop development work in order to build up funds for a one-cent dividend. The company's net had fallen roughly $100,000 a year for three successive years.

McCarthy urged John Finch to attend the April meeting in 1915 to support his recommendation for a renewed contract with the Washington Water Power, saying that, because Federal, Bunker Hill, and Hercules were going to buy Montana power, the Spokane utility had offered Hecla rates "better than the Montana Power Company." But Finch did not show up; he had come home tired from San Francisco and had worked wanly in his flower garden. On a Sunday morning in June, Finch fell dead in a bathroom of his Hayden Lake villa. He had pushed himself for two years, working with newspaper publisher William H. Cowles to solicit subscriptions for a new Davenport Hotel in Spokane, a building for the city's future. The hotel's architect, Kirtland K. Cutter, and his wife, were visiting the Finches. They heard a thump on the floor and rushed to find their host sprawled lifeless. Finch's followed by thirteen days the death of Patsy Clark, taken by a heart attack in the middle of the night at his Spokane home.

For some years Charles Hussey had managed Finch's mining investments, so at a special meeting in July the Hecla board elected him a director. As they passed the customary resolution eulogizing a lost associate, the directors were feeling bullish. The lead market had spurted suddenly upward. Revolution in Mexico had cut off lead shipments. Demand shot up for American lead as well as zinc for galvanizing and lining cartridge boxes. Silver prices, depressed for more than a decade, also started to rise. The old Success mine and the Interstate-Callahan—lame, zincy prospects in peacetime—reaped spectacular profits from war. Mining companies hurriedly put on extra crews for higher production to ride the tide of rising prices.

A brokerage house in Chicago touted the Success. Envious, Kipp prodded McCarthy, "I presume we will get the limit on output." McCarthy had already extended the underground workings and was expanding the mill to sell as much ore as he could. Now Kipp again asserted the Milwaukee opinion that the company's stock should be listed on a national exchange. He, Landsee, Lonstorf, and other large Milwaukee shareholders (with 340,000 shares among them) agreed this was the "proper" time. They approached Upman in Los Angeles; he was ambivalent and thought to put them off by consenting, if Kipp would "do the organizational work," but he felt it a "task bigger than he [Kipp] now realizes," observing that considerable capital would be tied up for a year or two. Henry Wick came around, although Youngstown had opposed listing in 1911. Perhaps he was gratified to be counted in, and now he favored the plan. Confident of their majority, the Milwaukee crowd called for a special meeting in July to vote on listing.

The company's original 500,000 shares, raised to 1,000,000 in 1898, had sold for pennies a share but, as an earlier audit showed, $75,000 had never been paid in. Perhaps the solution to this deficiency was Wakefield's, for he offered a successful resolution to levy a 7.5 percent assessment on the stock and simultaneously to declare a 7.5 percent dividend. Each shareholder would come out even and, on paper, the $75,000 would be made up. This done, the board designated Lonstorf to arrange for listing Hecla stock on the New York curb exchange. Not only would new investors fatten the company, the Milwaukee group predicted, but present stockholders "could dispose of their stock without causing a disturbing fluctuation in price." Much of the discussion at this meeting concerned increasing the number of shares to two or three million at a par of perhaps one dollar, but the directors could not agree on that. They closed the special meeting by authorizing President McCarthy to pay dividends of two cents a share each month, with five cents extra whenever income allowed, beginning the next month "and continuing as long as possible without impairing the reserve fund of $200,000."

Two months later, Lonstorf reported that he had retained the Security Transfer Company as agent and the Metropolitan Trust as register, and trading in Hecla stock had begun in New York on September 23, 1915. The New York curb—it once actually had been an outdoor market—in those days dealt largely in mining stocks with a few industrials. As a safeguard against chicanery, its listings committee required that a stock be recommended by a specialist and that the company provide a statement of assets, a map, assay reports, and similar data. A specialist who thought he had spotted a likely security would write the company's name on a blackboard, where it stayed for five days. If the listings committee approved and no trader objected, trading in the company's securities would begin on the sixth day. Due to the curb's investigation of complaints, confidence had grown in its listings, and a listing on the curb usually ensured a rise in a stock's quotation.

With listing, Hecla commenced printing its annual report, previously a typewritten statement from McCarthy's handwritten draft. And McCarthy soon would grumble that "the cost of mailing in some cases exceeds the amount of the dividend." As the roster expanded to more than 2,100 shareholders, some with no more than five shares, monthly dividend mailings taxed the office staff—Hanley and a male secretary—until the directors changed in 1918 to quarterly dividends.

For the Coeur d'Alene mines, the year 1916 was the most prosperous in the thirty-three years since discovery, piling up record profits for Bunker Hill, Hercules, Morning, and Hecla, "whose wise policy of advanced development put them in a position to take material advantage of the runaway metal market," said the Idaho inspector of mines. In June, McCarthy leased an idle mill from Federal, increasing output by 300 tons a day, and Hecla produced its largest tonnage to that time—40,832, compared with 19,937 tons shipped three years earlier.

The price of lead reached an average quotation of 6.9 cents a pound, up from 4.8 a year before. McCarthy happily advised the directors late in the year that the company "can pay a ten-cent dividend in December and finish the year with a surplus as large as we had at the beginning. . . . We are distributing all the profits we make, as we make them." Mine and mill ran seven days a week, and McCarthy estimated that, even with accelerated production, Hecla's reserves would last at least another six years.

Hecla's men, poking into a stringer in the Ore-or-no-go, crosscut into commercial ore, too zincy to process with Hecla ores. McCarthy rented the old Marsh mill for this ore until the Marsh took back its mill at the end of 1917. For the first time, Hecla's net income passed $1 million—$1,793,525, virtually triple its 1915 net—and dividends leaped to $1,550,000, almost three times those of the preceding year.

Meanwhile, Harry Day, angered by Asarco's threats to Hercules, bolted Federal early in 1916; he and his brothers bought the idle smelter at Northport, Washington, for conversion from a copper to a lead plant, and with it, the Pennsylvania Smelting Company as refinery and marketing agent. And Bunker Hill, after months of indecision, began construction of a custom lead-silver smelter at Kellogg, proposing to treat not only its own low-grade ores but those of other mines as well. The Kellogg smelter, crowed the weekly *Wallace Miner*, was "the most important event in the history of the Coeur d'Alene district . . . the realization of a hope that has been cherished for a quarter of a century." But the Days' smelter took only their ores, and Asarco sued Bunker Hill, charging breach of contract. Neither plant seemed available to Hecla, although McCarthy, privy to Easton's intentions, planned to divert Hecla's ores to the Bunker Hill smelter. He would wait, renewing the International contract for one year at a time.

With Finch gone, Hussey resigned from the board at the April 1916 meeting. The shareholders elected in his place Hugo C. Lambach, a Spokane dentist associated with Finch in real estate, who voted the 60,000 shares of the Finch and Campbell heirs.

In the midst of these prosperous times, another of the old-timers, Charles Sweeny, died in his favorite city, Portland, on May 31, 1916. Thirteen years earlier he had been, in the words of the *Spokesman-Review*, "the dominant power in the Coeur d'Alenes," but at his passing he was almost forgotten, no longer an avaricious conspirator with Rockefellers and Guggenheims.

By this time, Sarah Smith was a familiar member of Hecla's board, relishing the deference paid her as the largest shareholder. During her two weeks or more in the Coeur d'Alenes each year, she discussed mining with the managers and engineers of other companies who treated her courteously and respected her quick mind. She showed a dismaying willingness to talk freely about Hecla, as she formed her private opinion of its management. McCarthy could not, of course, shut her out of the company's business, but he became guarded with Sarah. She found a ready listener, however, in Eugene R. Day, now manager of the Day properties. Perhaps they drew together as outsiders—he, the youngest brother seeking to prove himself in the office Harry Day had held, and she, the one woman in Hecla's otherwise male constellation.

And Sarah met Ralston Wilbur, two years her junior, a tall,

athletic, dark-haired womanizer and prankster who sold min- ing machinery. He had left Stanford University in the wake of a collegiate caper, played football at Yale, and returned to Cal- ifornia. There he was remembered for staging a bogus funeral, complete with fifty taxicabs, on San Francisco's Market Street and for his tempestuous courtship of Helen Clifford, a drama critic and a friend of actress Maud Adams. Helen soon sent her eccentric spouse packing.

Now, in mid-1916, Wilbur rented rooms in the Davenport Hotel and set about courting the wealthy widow Smith (divi- dends of $11,883 a month). He "rushed" her into marriage, as Sarah later told her story. Shortly after their September wed- ding, she lent him money, then more—in all, about $130,000. They built a native-stone house with flowing arches in the shadow of basalt cliffs at East 2534 Seventeenth Avenue in Spo- kane but had hardly moved in before Sarah sued for divorce. Ralston Wilbur chased women—"vile women," Sarah called them—and although he sweet-talked her once out of separat- ing, she soon sued again and was granted an uncontested di- vorce in September 1918. She again called herself Sarah Smith.

Sarah's rash marriage, like her garrulity, may have tickled some skepticism about her business judgment but, for the present, McCarthy had little time to think of her. Epochal events engulfed Hecla. In April 1917 the United States entered the war in Europe, and the mining industry abruptly conformed. Men enlisted or were drafted. The labor surplus evaporated. Harry Day, apprehensive that the federal government meant to seize the mines, served on a national committee for voluntary allo- cation of lead supplies to meet federal needs. The tariff bill of 1913 had imposed personal income taxes, and now the gov- ernment added, as a war measure, an excess profits tax on cor- porations—a confusing law. For years, as they negotiated their taxes, the Hecla and other mining companies set aside reserves against possible tax liabilities.

When many of the remaining experienced men went to Butte for higher wages, the Coeur d'Alene mine owners adopted a sliding scale of bonuses that increased or lowered pay in tan- dem with the price of lead. By early 1917 underground work- ers, at a base wage of $3.50 a day, earned $5.25 a day. The flow toward Butte ebbed, and Bunker Hill and Hecla, the only re- maining clients, closed the central employment bureau set up nearly two decades earlier to weed out union men. A. W. Muir, vice president of the Idaho Federation of Labor, perceived closing of the bureau as his opportunity to organize the district. Within a few months locals formed at Burke, Gem, Mullan, and Wallace in support of his demand for a wage increase of one dollar a day.

Without higher pay, a number of men refused to work. Butte, brimming with "radicals," struck. Wobbly agents, McCarthy warned, maintained a "constant effort to organize this camp . . . with some success." Mullan had gone over to the IWW. At Burke, managers discharged Wobblies whenever they uncovered them. Turnover was high (170 men in one month), McCarthy sighed. "We are working many men who have never heard of the process of underground work." Boys took jobs hand-sorting ores. Wobblies, demanding better housing and food, closed lumber mills and logging camps. McCarthy sent his men to cut stulls, guarded from Wobbly intrusion by five armed deputy sheriffs. The union halls offered a fraternal alternative to the saloons, closed by Idaho on January 1, 1916.

The mining towns rustled with whispers of German saboteurs, and the mine operators, fearing union or enemy violence, appealed to Democratic Governor Moses Alexander for troops. When the governor declined, Harry Day, a powerful Democrat, quit the state defense council in protest. Alexander came to see for himself, and eventually fifty Montana National Guardsmen arrived, to be succeeded by green Sandpoint state militia outfitted from the university's cadet corps. Hercules erected fencing and revolving searchlights at its Burke property. Citizens' vigilante patrols rooted out men suspected of anti-American sympathies. To ensure uninterrupted lead supplies, the army sent an arbitrator, Captain E. D. Birkholz, who brought about a patriotic truce between management and the unions for the duration of the war.

As the price of lead spiraled upward, the mining companies squandered reserves, producing as fast as manpower and the overburdened railroads allowed. (One-fourth of each mine's output went to the government below market price.) Hecla pushed its net income in 1917 to $1.8 million, third highest in the district, behind Hercules' $3.6 million and Bunker Hill's $2.4 million. The pleased directors voted McCarthy a $4,000 bonus and raised his annual salary to $10,000, but they deferred his suggestion that they suspend dividends to put their funds, instead, into tax-exempt Liberty Bonds. Upman favored suspending dividends to build up the reserve, but not bonds; Frank Kipp proposed that the company pay dividends and buy bonds. Finally, when Hecla was the only company that had not subscribed for bonds, McCarthy fretted that, as the county's bond chairman, he was "chief booster and chief slacker." The directors relented; they bought $50,000 worth and would buy more.

For the Milwaukee shareholders, wartime was melancholy. Most had relatives in Germany; they cherished their memories of their native country. Carl Landsee had emigrated in 1867 from Rottenburg am Neckar; he had remained that town's patron, sending substantial sums to Germany for village causes and institutions. Never was there a doubt of the Milwaukee men's loyalty, but the angry suppression of everything German, including their beloved Deutscher Club, saddened them all.

In July 1917 Hecla began sending its ores to the new Bunker Hill & Sullivan smelter at Kellogg at a large saving in freight costs. Horace Clagett moved to Kellogg, where he would spend the rest of his career. For the Coeur d'Alenes, the smelter, which blew in on July 5, was a signal benefit. It enabled operators of many low-grade mines to profit except in the worst times.

The year 1917 proved to be the wartime peak for production and profits in the district. Near the end of the year, Hecla's potential liability for federal income tax, corporate tax, and excess profits tax induced the board to consider suspending dividends until they could be sure how much they would owe. A national committee of mining men, trying to interpret the tax laws, offered "no word . . . of any assistance," McCarthy boiled. In April, Hecla hired A. Wade Strowger, a Portland accountant expert in tax matters, to negotiate with the revenue bureau— a discourse that went on for years. Although Landsee and Kipp wanted to continue paying dividends, even to cashing certificates of deposit, the other directors reluctantly consented to suspend, "due to the so-called excess profits tax," after a January 1918 dividend. Hecla had distributed $6,955,000 in monthly dividends without interruption since March 1904.

High prices and headlong wartime production piled up a national surplus of lead. Consequently, in 1918, while war still raged, mining slacked off. Morning and Hercules halved their outputs. Hecla cut back after midyear, but continued to deepen its shaft to 2,000 feet. The board voted to pay quarterly rather than monthly dividends—then suspended dividends because of uncertainties about taxes. Saving dividends increased the earned surplus to more than $1.9 million by the end of 1918, a million higher than the year before.

At the armistice, the lead market collapsed and the patriotic truce between management and labor in the Coeur d'Alenes ended. Both the Industrial Workers of the World and the state Federation of Labor resumed recruiting. After a fifty-cent wage cut, the mine operators agreed to continue bonuses even though the price of lead had fallen, partly as a conciliatory gesture to their employees because men were still scarce, and partly because a survey of retail prices for foods, clothing, and fuel showed the cost of living had risen 65 percent in the district. Miners at Kellogg petitioned for higher wages. McCarthy told his board: "The man with a family is having a difficult time to make ends meet on the present $4.75 [a day] for a six-day week."

Yet, without markets, mines closed. The Day mines had not reopened after a Christmas holiday. By March Interstate-Callahan, one of the wartime zinc producers, had shut down. Its manager apologized: "We did not want to close down, particularly on account of the married men," but his stockholders would not "take the loss." A general postwar depression washed over the district. Men left for work on farms or in the woods, if they could get it. McCarthy reported "a vigorous campaign" by the Idaho Federation of Labor to organize the miners, and he thought the men at Burke in Hercules and Hecla, "pretty well organized."

Wooed by two unions, workmen tended to join both. Their locals recognized both membership cards. Consequently, the Mine, Mill, and Smelter workers, the Federation of Labor affiliate, was overrun with "radicals," in the opinion of the mine operators. The operators regarded the Mine, Mill, and Smelter Workers as their adversary of twenty years earlier with a new name, and they refused to treat with either union. McCarthy had complained of men "inefficient and deliberately so," describing the Wobbly tactic of slowing down on the job to force managers to accept their demands. Less than five months after the war ended, the managers cut wages one dollar a day and the unions, outraged, threatened a strike. At the request of the Mine, Mill, and Smelter Workers, the federal government sent in a conciliator, Robert M. McWade, a veteran labor negotiator, an editor and a scholar of ancient history and mythology, decorated by the empress of China. McWade proposed that the companies recognize the AFL union, grant its demand for an eight-hour work day but not for higher wages, and in partnership with it, squash the Wobblies. The managers hotly refused to recognize any union.

Pointing out that he had "consistently and persistently . . . hunted these people [Wobblies] out of our organization," McCarthy stated Hecla's position. A census showed, he explained, that Hecla employed 61 percent native Americans and 51 percent married men, even though "Burke . . . does not lend itself to the employment of married men." Like the other managers, he considered his men to be working eight hours— but they entered and left the mine on their own time. Three men required thirty-four minutes to reach work stations. He felt the conciliator and the unions did not recognize "the depressed condition of the industry." Hecla had lost 35 percent of the "war price of lead," but costs had not come down, and the company continued to face "unsettled income taxes. . . . We will probably owe the Government anywhere from $1,200,000 to $2,000,000." Hecla had not distributed its 1918 operating profits because its taxes were uncertain. And on the question of union recognition, McCarthy said flatly, "It can't be done," alluding to the union strangulation of mining two decades earlier.

The conciliatory McWade, oddly enough, suggested the method that the operators adopted to rid themselves of Wobblies; he recommended hiring gunfighter Jack Foster, known for intimidating Wobblies, and deputizing him—"to avoid the accusation of bringing in gunmen," as Jerome Day observed. Seven men were arrested for trials under Idaho's 1917 criminal syndicalism act. They were held in jail for months, until the IWW feared to send organizers into the district. The United States attorney general's national roundup of Wobblies destroyed the union's vigor.

Denied recognition, the Mine, Mill, and Smelter Workers struck the mines at Burke and Mullan, but the strike lasted less than six weeks. "The time is almost here when someone must back down," McCarthy realized, and the strike broke when the mine operators announced they would reopen if the men would come back to work. The Burke local voted to continue striking, but the others gave up. McCarthy, who had recruited men in Joplin, Missouri, rather proudly wrote his directors that the labor supply was better after the strike than before it. The managers had not changed hours or wages, and now they reopened their central employment agency to scrutinize every man who applied for work in the mines.

During its confrontation with unions, Hecla sustained its worst accident. Four men were killed and three injured when the hoist, signaled to descend, shot instead to the top of the gallows frame and the men were drawn into the sheave wheel. One survivor hung by a foot from the cage; he would never work again.

Now, a legal challenge. Hecla's east orebody (in the old Katie May claim) lay close to the northeast boundary line where the Marsh Mining Company worked the Russell under lease from its owner, Federal Mining & Smelting Company. Four years earlier, Federal had protested that Hecla trespassed, claiming that the vein in the east orebody reached its apex in Russell ground. (Under mining law, the owner of an apex or top, the highest point of a vein—where it rises nearest the surface—has the legal right to follow the vein downward even into ground beneath the surface boundaries of other mines, as long as he stays within parallel end lines.)

Hecla's board retained Myron Folsom, an able attorney, but in the ferment of war and union revival, Federal had not pursued its allegation. Apex suits were expensive, after all, and their outcomes chancy. In the fall of 1919, however, McCarthy heard again—by the district's lively grapevine—that Federal was talking trespass. After conferring with the directors nearby— Sarah Smith, Wakefield, and Lambach—he engaged John P. Gray, a Coeur d'Alene attorney noted for his knowledge of mining law.

Not long after, Fred Burbidge, the mincing manager of Federal, called on McCarthy, asking to inspect the Hecla underground to see if trespass had occurred. Managers did not blithely open their workings to competitors, so McCarthy refused, saying the matter was in Gray's hands. He wrote fully to his board that same day, telling them that Federal's claim "might conceivably have a very important influence on the future of the company." Indeed it might—it might deny Hecla its east orebody, its principal source of mineral.

If James McCarthy perceived the Federal suit more as blackmail than a quest for justice, he did not say so publicly, even when Marsh joined the suit, asking $6 million in damages. He was exasperated, however, by fanciful accounts spread by brokers who favored Federal, and was deluged with letters from stockholders demanding to know if the brokers' stories were true. Sarah Smith frankly regarded the loss of the suit as "fatal" to Hecla. Moreover, McCarthy was in a delicate position with another competitor; he suspected the Day brothers of trying to direct the Marsh suit behind the scenes. During the union troubles, Eugene Day had sat in on several Hecla meetings; he could not have avoided learning something of the company's affairs.

Representing his family's shares, Eugene showed up at Hecla's annual meeting of shareholders in 1919, where Lambach nominated him as a director to succeed Frank Upman, who was too ill to attend. An awkward silence followed the nomination. The shareholders sat flintily mute, and when no one seconded, Day manfully withdrew his name. Soon after, McCarthy petitioned Hecla's directors to bail him out of the Tiger Hotel, "the beanery" at Burke which he owned jointly with Eugene. Single men in Burke had virtually nowhere else to live, so the directors acquiesced, but they reflected that Eugene Day seemed to be mixed into Hecla's business.

Perhaps as Burbidge had intended all along, he and McCarthy settled Federal's claim of trespass, agreeing that Hecla would buy Federal's claims near Hecla—Russell, the idle Tiger-Poorman, Wide West, and others—for $750,000. The directors approved the agreement at their special meeting on October 9, 1920. McCarthy correctly discounted as "gossip . . . entirely unfounded," a rumor that Eugene Day, miffed when Hecla spurned him as a director, would finance a separate Marsh suit. Without Federal, the Marsh case collapsed. Hecla had bought off the threat to its east orebody.

Frank Upman's death in Los Angeles on September 30, 1919, seemed to close an era, to extinguish the circle of founders— sons of German immigrants—and to end twelve years of transition from a company of friends to one of business associates. Nonetheless, friends would pose the next challenge.

4

Hitched to a Star

ONE OF THE PREDICTABLE RESULTS OF LISTING HECLA'S STOCK on the New York curb was a shift in voting power toward James McCarthy. Many new stockholders, knowing little of the company but what their brokers told them, simply mailed their proxies to the president. Beginning with the war years, consequently, McCarthy voted his own 8,050 shares and 247,000 or more by proxy, the largest single block.

Kipp voted his 44,000 and 101,050 by proxy; Landsee, his 30,200 and 121,970 by proxy; and, although she remained the largest individual shareholder with 93,500, Sarah Smith voted only 2,000 by proxy. At annual meetings, McCarthy, Kipp, and Landsee, with more than 525,000 votes among them, usually held 60 percent or more of the shares represented. And so long as these three agreed, they controlled Hecla.

Now in his early fifties, after more than a decade as president and general manager, a grayhaired, stately James McCarthy commanded respect in the Coeur d'Alenes. And through his service on committees of the American Mining Congress, as county bond chairman, as director of the First National Bank of Wallace and the Coeur d'Alene Hardware & Foundry Company, as one of the men (with Stanly Easton) who had framed Idaho's workmen's compensation program, and as regent of the state university, James McCarthy had become a personage in Idaho and in mining in the United States.

He was neither conceited nor lofty; he worked hard—ten or eleven hours a day in the Hecla office and many evenings at a desk in his home. He and Anastasia lived quietly, their social life limited to a few friends, the Elks Club, and St. Alphonsus Church. She was a homebody, frugal and proper; she insisted McCarthy go out on the porch for his evening cigar. The social strata of Wallace segregated owners and managers from workingmen. McCarthy had purchased one of Wallace's largest homes, that of August Paulsen, the former dairyhand grown rich, who had moved to Spokane.

McCarthy could not ignore his conspicuous role in western mining, nor could he set aside the fact that he had conducted Hecla's business well; he knew it and so did his board, who regularly passed resolutions testifying to his salutary performance.

McCarthy was chagrined, therefore, to receive a caustic letter in November 1920 from Sarah Smith, who complained that "since our last directors' meeting . . . you have seen fit to keep me absolutely uniformed as to your location, your movements, your progress, acceptance or rejection" of a settlement with Federal over the Russell property. She demanded "full and accurate information." Well, perhaps he had neglected Sarah; he certainly was circumspect in what he told her, lest she talk too freely. He felt, in fact, that she had "used the information" from the Russell settlement prematurely.

And a few days later, Kipp warned that "the feeling among the large shareholders in Chicago (including Mrs. Smith) is very bitter against the management and they threaten trouble and the only way we can ease this condition is to give them more information." Kipp feared that the Chicago proxies might "be lost to us." Like Smith, Kipp complained that his knowledge of Hecla came from western newspapers

McCarthy faced incipient revolt. He wrote Smith and Kipp jointly a conciliatory letter: "I agree that perhaps I should have written oftener . . . although there has been little of a definite nature to say." Absurd tales of $6 million in damages spread by Marsh and its friendly brokers had left Marsh "in an awkward position to settle for a small sum." He sent a copy of this letter to each director, resolving that he would write more often.

Yet, McCarthy could not bring himself to inform Sarah when Frederick Bradley, president of Bunker Hill & Sullivan, proposed that Hecla join his company in buying and operating the Star mine—the mine that Hecla's directors had turned down nine years earlier. McCarthy relayed Bradley's proposal to Frank Kipp, who was vacationing in California before coming north for the annual meeting. Landsee was also there, and they talked with E. J. Nolan, the Los Angeles attorney who handled Upman's estate. McCarthy encouraged the three men (Nolan had been elected a director in place of Upman) to visit Bradley in San Francisco, to "form their own opinion" of the Bunker Hill man and his offer. But they insisted that McCarthy accompany them, and he took Wakefield. Consequently, during the first week of April, Kipp, Landsee, Nolan, Wakefield, and Mc-Carthy of Hecla, and Bradley, Easton, and Frank Smith of Bunker Hill talked for two hours in Bradley's San Francisco office.

Bradley was betting on expansion of the nation's zinc market. The Star was tangled in a lengthy lawsuit with Federal, alleging trespass into Star ground over a ten-year period ending in 1917, and when Star ran out of money, Bradley lent its owners $125,000 to continue their litigation, taking in return its stock and an option to buy the mine. Before taking the option, however, Bradley instructed Easton to test 100 tons of Star ore.

By the time Star would agree to a compromise with Federal, Bradley held 89.4 percent of its stock. Star ore was admittedly low-grade and zincy, but its lower workings showed a favorable proportion of lead. On the west end of the Star-Morning orebody, Star had yielded little ore; it had been idle for fifteen years. But if the Morning vein continued into Star, and if Federal had taken commercial ore from Star as contended, and if samples from drill holes and that 100 tons could be trusted, Bradley—and McCarthy—believed Star was a sleeping giant.

Everything Bradley said was familiar to Wakefield, the Star's acting president representing the Finch, Wick, and Moffitt estates, principal owners of Star. Now, Bradley disclosed that once Star's lawsuit was settled, Bunker Hill intended to build a zinc reduction plant at Kellogg, using a method it had been testing for four years to process Star's ores. As he studied Star, Bradley had concluded that the easiest and cheapest route to its supposed orebody would be through a long tunnel—7,500 to 8,000 feet—from the lower workings of the Hecla. And if Hecla provided the route to the Star, Bradley went on, Hecla could also operate the Star. It would, of course, have to obtain permission to pass through several intervening claims, or perhaps buy them outright.

As Hecla's men headed north for the annual meeting, McCarthy asked them to keep Bradley's plan secret until they were ready to decide whether to accept it.

Other than the possibility of opening the Star, the directors had little to cheer them. The Coeur d'Alene district was mired in yet another recession. "After the war the decline in prices and market demand, combined with the excess profits tax, high freight rates, cost of commodities, and high wages, had such a demoralizing effect on mining," the state mining inspector asserted, "that the State experienced the greatest depression it has known for over 20 years." Only three large mines continued operations: Hecla, Bunker Hill & Sullivan, and Federal's Morning. Half of the district's men were out of work. In this gloomy atmosphere, with Sarah Smith's coterie perhaps in revolt, the Hecla board met in Spokane in advance of the annual meeting to prepare for any problems that might arise when the shareholders gathered. They agreed that they would recommend reorganizing Hecla in Idaho with a capitalization of $5 million, if tax difficulties allowed.

At the annual meeting, the mood was clearly in favor of change. The uneasy directors had seen scurrilous letters, purporting to reflect the views of Hecla employees, asserting that McCarthy was "dominating the entire company" with directors "who know little of the mining game." For some weeks, rumors had circulated that Eugene Day, with Smith and dissident shareholders, would try to take control and, as shareholders gathered, an attorney for the Day brothers—lanky, dour John Wourms—joined them.

Some shareholders wanted to close the mine until the market brightened; others feared that the Hecla would play out at depth. McCarthy suggested they hire an engineer for a disinterested evaluation, and the shareholders elected Smith, Wakefield, and Lambach as a committee to find a consulting engineer. Wakefield, with Archibald Witherspoon, was also delegated to study reorganization of the company with an increase in capital stock.

When McCarthy called for nominations, Eugene Day was nominated as a director. Sarah Smith seconded. Adroitly, McCarthy named Wourms as one of three inspectors of ballots. Eugene tallied the fewest votes and was declared not elected. Sarah remained a director, the *Wallace Miner* observed, "through sufferance due her sex." A few icy moments after the voting, the shareholders adjourned. No one had whispered a word of the Star.

The next few months would be seminal for Hecla. Not only was the board deliberating the Star, but Wakefield, seeking a consultant, came up with a noted San Francisco engineer, Fred Searls, Jr., who, in the years to come, would play a central role in the company.

McCarthy recited most of Bradley's proposal for Star in a for-

54

mal letter to the directors May 12, 1921, reminding them that they had earlier rejected Star. Now, the mine "represents an opportunity to get into a very promising enterprise under the best of circumstances," he wrote, "where our present plant and equipment can be used and the company's existence prolonged." Bunker Hill had put $871,529 into Star and would vest Star's stock in a new organization, the Sullivan Mining Company, which would control the mine and operate the projected zinc plant. Hecla's anticipated cost amounted to approximately $323,260, which, McCarthy felt, could be paid from royalties on the sale of ore. His letter did not mention the San Francisco meeting, but he entreated the directors again to keep the Star proposal to themselves until they came to a decision.

On May 24, the day before the directors met at the Pfister Hotel in Milwaukee for a special session, the Wallace *Press-Times*, a newspaper controlled by the Days, published a report of the proposed partnership in the Star between Hecla and Bunker Hill. McCarthy's secret was out. Incensed, he blamed Sarah Smith for talking too much (although later under oath she denied it). The Star plan had really not been very secret. Attorney Nolan had asked the opinion of John Gray, who had represented Star against Federal, and Hugo Lambach, who had other mining interests, had talked to one of his managers, Ed Ehrenberg, about Star. Both Gray and Ehrenberg had recommended that Hecla participate in Star.

No matter who spilled the secret, premature publicity widened the rift between the McCarthy and Smith factions. Moreover, the editor of the *Wallace Miner*, Alfred Dunn, persisted in writing that the Days plotted to seize Hecla. McCarthy was convinced that Harry Day had encouraged Federal and Marsh in their suit against Hecla—he would say so later in court, pointing out that Hecla was "surrounded by properties owned or controlled by the Days. I am satisfied that the Days urged the Gertie company to start suit against the Hecla and I know that Harry L. Day urged the Federal not to settle the litigation with us over the Russell claims." (On the other hand, Jerome Day asserted that the Day brothers declined Federal's solicitation to join the Marsh suit.)

Secrets were hard to keep, at any rate. The Coeur d'Alenes teemed with spies, amateur and professional. A district grapevine sped rumor. Mine managers rarely discussed business by telephone, lest someone eavesdrop. Some of them sealed letters with wax to discourage prying. For anyone who knew the mining district, it was not hard to imagine intrigue.

Looking back, Sarah Smith must have realized the limit of her voting strength and hoped, at most, that seating Eugene Day as a director would strengthen her hand against Mc-Carthy. Eugene could not realistically have expected, in that hostile group, to exercise control over Hecla, although he might have thought to build a constituency that would eventually give the Days command of Hecla. Although she had been a guest in his home, Sarah disliked McCarthy, and she opposed the Star. Reputable engineers and geologists disagreed about its worth. Fred Burbidge declared Star "worthless." Eugene Day respected Burbidge's opinion, and so did Sarah Smith.

At their special meeting, Hecla's directors took Wakefield's advice that they postpone reorganizing the company or increasing its capital, and they agreed to hire Searls to inspect the mine. On Nolan's motion they voted to join Bunker Hill in Star—only Smith voted against it.

McCarthy now scheduled a special meeting of shareholders to ratify a Star contract and to hear Searls's report. As usual, Sarah appeared in Wallace a few days early. She came to McCarthy's office to demand that no contract be signed with Bunker Hill. McCarthy looked at her for a long moment and then said, in a low voice, "It's already been done." He had signed, in fact, the previous day, contingent on stockholder approval.

On August 17, the day before the special meeting, Eugene Day and Sarah Smith obtained an order from the Spokane County Superior Court restraining Hecla from proceeding with the Star, and they sued both in Washington and Idaho for a permanent injunction. Their complaint, in flamboyant language smacking of Wourms, charged that Hecla "for a number of years has always been under the immediate control of . . . McCarthy . . . dominated, controlled, and dictated by Mc-Carthy, arbitrarily, and not in the interest" of the shareholders. They accused McCarthy and Wakefield of conniving for the proxies of unwitting shareholders and alleged that the two men really acted in the interest of the estates of late owners of Star. "The said so-called mining properties of the Star Mining Company are absolutely of no value," the complaint went on, "the ores of no commercial value, and cannot be sold, used, or in any manner applied by the Hecla." The Days' newspaper, the

Press-Times, translated the Day-Smith complaint into plain language; Bunker Hill, it said, was "anxious to ditch as much of the lemon as possible" on Hecla.

Although Hecla's shareholders were enjoined from ratifying the Star contract, they heard about taxes and listened to Searls's report. Wade Strowger, the Portland accountant, told them that the company's tax liability remained up in the air after three years of negotiation.

Dissident shareholders may have regarded Searls's review of the mine as an appraisal of McCarthy's stewardship. They found Searls supportive of McCarthy, for despite a difference of twenty years in their ages, he and McCarthy had formed a lasting friendship. Fred Searls, at thirty-three one of America's preeminent mining engineers, was already fashioning the legend: born in a California mining town, Nevada City, he had graduated at twenty from the University of California in engineering. As an engineer, Searls was thoroughly professional. As a man, he was short in stature, with a nose smashed from boxing as a youth. He was decisive in manner and speech, somewhat raffish and rumpled, and he seemed always to wear the same black oilcloth bow tie.

His report, read in full to the shareholders and later printed for distribution among them, avoided judging the company's management or suggesting future objectives. "The [Hecla] mine is neither in as good condition as it ought to be," he commented, "nor in a condition so bad as to be properly a cause for alarm, or even for serious concern." The older sections had been neglected in order to drive new drifts on the east orebody, exposing mineral "far in excess of the requirements of present production." Searls felt the mine, which produced 700 tons a day, could turn out 2,000. Two small cave-ins had blocked old stopes—the engineer's precise mind calculated this at .4 percent of the underground works—but "the rest of the mine is in fairly good shape" except for a "tendency to run drifts . . . larger than necessary." He suggested experimental changes in timbering and haulage.

The *Wallace Miner*, biased for McCarthy, called the report "a complete vindication of management," and so it seemed to most shareholders. Their meeting was adjourned until September 14, and would be put off again, awaiting a decision on the injunction against the Star. The directors, Sarah Smith stonily among them, met briefly after the shareholders to authorize

McCarthy to defend the company against the Day-Smith coalition.

Smith and Day now mailed a printed letter to stockholders
setting out their views, although Sarah complained that
McCarthy refused her a current list of shareholders. They argued that McCarthy showed "poor judgment" in the Marsh
case, that he relied wholly on Bunker Hill's data on Star, that
the costs of reaching the Star from the Hecla were "underes-
timated," and that large water flows would stop the work. They
asked rhetorically: "If the Hecla authorities have accepted the
figures and arguments of the vendors (the Bunker Hill Mining
Company), who then is looking out for the interests of the Hecla?" A second letter, expanding these arguments, concluded
that the Star "bids fair to lead the Hecla Mining Company to
disaster."

Meanwhile, the courts heard arguments over the injunction.
Day and Smith dropped their allegations of fraud against
McCarthy and of negligence against the Hecla's directors for
entering into the Star contract, and they based their case on an
intricate argument that participation in the proposed Sullivan
Mining Company ran against public policy because Hecla would
give up control of its business. On February 3, 1922, the judge
denied Smith and Day a permanent injunction. His order found
the Star contract valid, legal, and not opposed to public policy.
On the next day, the much-adjourned special shareholders'
meeting reconvened in Spokane without Sarah Smith. After the
shareholders present heard five engineers discuss the Star, all
662,492 shares represented voted in favor of the contract with
Bunker Hill.

In the last days of argument in court, Jerome Day had taken
Eugene's usual seat in the courtroom while Sarah sat quietly
among the spectators. Eugene was hospitalized with Bright's
disease. Eight days after he and Smith had been denied, as
their attorneys prepared to appeal to the state supreme court,
Eugene Day died unexpectedly. Smith would carry on alone;
she had paid three-fourths of the $75,000 spent in an attempt
to overturn McCarthy and the Star. The supreme court upheld
the lower court, ending what the *Miner* insisted had been "a
Day-Smith conspiracy to grab control of the Hecla." The newspaper's editor speculated that "if the Star deal had been declared illegal and void . . . the effects on stockholders of the
Hecla might have been such that the Day-Smith combination

might have eventually gained control of the Hecla, the real purpose back of the litigation." Speculation, of course—but that was how the Hecla's directors saw it, too.

At their next meeting, the Hecla's board raised McCarthy's salary and voted him bonuses for 1921 and 1922. They also elected George P. Mayer, a sixty-two-year-old Hecla shareholder from Milwaukee, to replace Sarah Smith on the board. Mayer, one of three brothers who had inherited their father's business, was president of the Mayer Boot & Shoe Company, which owned a controlling interest in the Washington Shoe Manufacturing Company of Seattle. He was a vice president of the National Bank of Commerce, an insurance broker, and a substantial member of Milwaukee's German community.

Freed from the threat of injunction and stockholder insurrection, Hecla embarked with Bunker Hill on an audacious adventure—a new refining process with ores from an unproven mine to produce high quality zinc for a market dominated by two powerful competitors. Nonetheless, one of America's leading authorities on zinc, the mining engineer Walter Renton Ingalls, termed the Sullivan a "reasonable venture . . . not an idea of unjustifiable boldness."

Bunker Hill and Hecla estimated that developing the Star mine and its mill would cost $1.4 million; the zinc refinery, another $1.1 million. The refinery would be modest in size compared with others in the country. In June 1921 McCarthy set crews to digging around the clock, six days a week, at a pace of 300 feet a month, to drive a 8,203-foot crosscut from the bottom of the Hecla shaft to the Star. Bunker Hill had been experimenting with electrolysis for eleven years to recover zinc from low-grade ores. As it neared production, it negotiated for current from Washington Water Power.

The project was daring enough that when Bradley offered Hecla a half interest in Sullivan, the directors voted to wait to see whether there really would be commercial ore from the Star. Searls told them there were enough zinc plants in the country already, and Anaconda proffered a low rate "to prevent erection of a plant at Kellogg."

The refining process adopted was the Tainton-Pring, used commercially for only twelve months in 1920–21 in a 10-ton plant at Martinez, California, but never attempted on a large scale. To adapt electrolysis to the Star ore, Bunker Hill hired a young metallurgist, Wallace G. Woolf, giving him a crew of five or

six in its old north mill, where he experimented with concentrates from the Constitution mine. Woolf could not rid his process of a gelatinous silicate until U. C. Tainton himself came
to work with him. As a student in England, Tainton had leached
(dissolved) zinc ore with sulphuric acid, then removed the zinc
from the resulting zinc sulphate solution by electrolysis. (A party
of engineers copied the Bunker Hill process for a plant in East
St. Louis, which would be the second in the United States to
use the Tainton method).

When Woolf and Tainton finally contrived to coat an elec-
trode with zinc, they melted it in a tiny furnace to form a silvery lump and carried this prize to Stanly Easton, who for years
showed it proudly in his office.

The Sullivan Mining Company, an Idaho corporation with
37,442 issued shares of capital stock split between Bunker Hill
and Hecla, was a holding company. Its charter provided that
Bunker Hill would choose three of its five directors one year,
and Hecla, three of five the next year, and so on, trading control back and forth. Hecla agreed that if it abandoned the Hecla
mine, it would operate the Star and Bunker Hill would manage
the zinc smelter, with most costs and profits to be divided
evenly.

Perhaps the boldest part of the Sullivan scheme was marketing, for Bunker Hill meant to produce nearly pure zinc for
a small but growing clientele, largely in die-casting. During the
war the New Jersey Zinc Company had sold its premium
Horsehead brand (75 percent zinc) to selected users, and early
in the twenties, partly to supply a subsidiary, American Brass,
Anaconda entered the zinc field. Anaconda, Consolidated Mining & Smelting at Trail, British Columbia, and the Judge Mining Company in Utah used electrolytic processes.

As the Sullivan took shape, New Jersey Zinc and Anaconda
dominated high-purity zinc sales. The Sullivan, however, would
revolutionize this business with Bunker Hill brand 99.99 percent pure zinc, a "new" metal. To sell it, Sullivan contracted
with the St. Joseph Lead Company, which maintained New
York offices. As Walter Ingalls would marvel a few years later,
St. Joseph Lead "brilliantly" solved the problem of "introducing a new kind of metal." So brilliantly, in fact, that New Jersey Zinc, Anaconda, and Hudson's Bay Zinc of Canada changed
their processing to compete in the market that the Sullivan had
created, and the use of high-purity zinc spread beyond die-

casting to radios, household appliances, telephone bases, automobile radiator grills and windshield frames, fuel pumps and carburetors, machine valves and bearings, and other products that needed a strong, ductile, malleable metal that resisted corrosion.

McCarthy's tunnelmen had started their crosscut to the Star from a bore already driven 335 feet that way. They carved and timbered an eight-by-nine-foot passage, wide enough for electric trains with spurs for passing, and dumped their waste rock into exhausted stopes of the Hecla. As they dug, they hit two strong water courses. McCarthy had anticipated underground water—all Canyon Creek mines battled water—and had ordered a special pump from Hecla's shop to force grout (thin, coarse mortar) into fissures to seal off the water flow. In November 1924, Hecla's men entered the Star vein, thirty-two months after starting. They stopped to cheer, and the men on the surface picked up their celebration. McCarthy sent the tunnelers forward another 1,235 feet to find any possible mineral paralleling the vein. By then, this longest tunnel in the world at such depth had cost $531,887.

McCarthy also started his men drifting on the vein which, after showing stringers, widened into commercial ore. An editor who went to see this new wonder wrote that, after descending 2,000 feet by cage down the Hecla shaft, "we stepped onto steel floors, from which radiated galleries in a number of directions, with . . . tracks and overhead trolley wires, the whole . . . lit up with electric lights." The caverns echoed with voices, rattling trains and drills, and the clank of rail switches. An air pipe hung overhead in the Star on which a wag had painted a popular advertising slogan, "Picture ahead . . . Kodak as you go." The temperature turned hotter as he neared the Star (rocks there would reach 100°), and the editor left the train to walk along the drift to its face, estimating that he saw seven to eight feet of ore.

Mining the Star would test men's endurance and ingenuity. Although at first crews stoped upward from tunnel level, the heavy ground was treacherous. "At the Star," a Hecla engineer would explain, "the source of all ground weight is straight wall pressure . . . pressure actually squeezing the ore out between the walls, such as squeezing the ice cream out of an ice cream sandwich. Most of our ground support efforts are in holding the walls." Later the men would mine deeper in temperatures so high that cold water had to be pumped continually for air-conditioning.

For managers, the Star demanded efficiency—often experimental methods or special machines—to hold down costs, for the ores would not pay otherwise. The daily struggle against costs, not as dramatic as new discoveries or secrets told in court, was nonetheless exacting and ceaseless. In time to come, Hecla's managers would reflect that the Star taught them lessons they used in other mines.

Beside the Hecla's ore bin at Burke, the company built a massive concrete bin for the Star. Ore went from there by rail to the Bunker Hill concentrator until a Star mill could be built, and was treated in the smelter until a zinc plant could be completed. The Star produced no crude ore or coarse concentrates, like the Hecla, but fine ore carrying a high smelting charge.

For half a century Sullivan would flourish, but these early years were shadowed with doubts and problems. Ingalls had warned of hazards in "a new process in a new works, which will inevitably meet with new obstacles." The Star produced ore in 1925, nearly a year before Bunker Hill commenced building its zinc plant. Until completion of its mill, Sullivan sent zincy ores to Anaconda at Great Falls, and for two years to the Vieille-Montagne, a Belgian company. The Belgians charged seven dollars a ton less than Anaconda, leading McCarthy to reflect that "one cannot avoid having the opinion that the Belgian company is driven to very great extremes for their tonnage, or that the Anaconda company is making a very extraordinary profit from its zinc customers."

As costs outran forecasts, both Bunker Hill and Hecla diverted funds from other operations, and eventually from dividends, to pay for Sullivan. The Star's underground workings in its first seven years soaked up more than $1.4 million in costs. During construction, the outlay for the zinc plant, predicted to be $1.1 million, seemed to rise almost monthly—it mounted $230,000 between March and July 1928—eventually to reach $3.4 million. To satisfy his directors that they were not being bilked, McCarthy hired Ingalls again to analyze the expenditures. Ingalls attributed the expense "mainly to overbuilding . . . in anticipation of doubling capacity," and he recommended putting off further development of the Star until the plant caught up—advice Hecla ignored. Rather than a 50-

ton plant to be enlarged gradually to 150 tons, Bunker Hill insisted on building the entire shell from the start and adding electrolytic units as needed to increase capacity. Consequently, a hillside structure of 70,000 square feet went up at Silver King. On a Sunday morning in April 1928, McCarthy and Easton together would ceremoniously press a button to start current flowing for a test run.

The zinc plant started operations six months behind schedule, after the Belgian contract had expired, forcing the Star to shut down to wait for processing. McCarthy cautioned his chafing shareholders that at least another year must pass "before profits flow back to the Hecla company" from Sullivan—but it would be longer than a year.

The price of lead, which paid most of the costs, fell before the plant opened. "The reduced price, with our obligations on account of the zinc plant," McCarthy wrote his board, "raise a serious question as to what our future dividend policy should be." He pointed out that Hecla either must lower dividends until the plant was ready or spend from accumulated cash surplus.

Just when it appeared that mill, mine, and markets might come together, the Star's ore grade fell off. In 1929 it yielded 119,000 tons of frustratingly low-grade ores, and the zinc-plant managers turned to other mines, chiefly Sidney. Then, to protect Star from potential apex suits, Sullivan spent more money for the Alice No. 2, the Morning Star Fraction, and other claims near the Star. And not surprisingly, once the zinc plant started up, unfinished because its owners were in a hurry for income (it produced its first spelter in October 1928), it required "extensive reconstruction and correction . . . the natural consequences of introducing a new process," explained a Hecla analyst.

Although the 99.99 per cent pure Bunker Hill brand zinc found a ready market, the new plant was wrung to supply customers because performance of mine and plant remained erratic. Hecla's directors spent worried hours weighing their next move to sustain Sullivan. After metals prices began their slide in 1929 toward depression levels of the thirties, they voted in April 1930 to shut down the Star altogether to wait for better times. The zinc plant cut back to one-third capacity and, as a result, lost newly won customers to New Jersey Zinc. By then, eight years after the Day-Smith revolt, the Sullivan Mining Company had cost its stockholders $6.6 million without returning one penny.

If Sarah Smith, reading the newspapers, concluded that her gloomy predictions for Star were coming true, no one at Hecla heard about it. But they heard about her. She sold her Hecla stock and, between 1921 and 1925, profited spectacularly from investments in Chicago real estate. Some accounts bandied a figure of $8 million. In Chicago, said a Spokane newspaper, she was known as the "Hetty Green of LaSalle Street." (Hetty H. R. Green had used her husband's fortune to buy and manage Chicago real estate. She was a popular subject for newspaper writers who called her the "richest woman in America . . . the greatest woman financier in the world.")

In 1925, about the time Star disgorged its first ore, Sarah married an adventurer, George F. Scollard, who had divorced his wife, with her assent, to wed Sarah for her money. The Scollards built a mansion in Bellingham, Washington, and traveled often until, in Buenos Aires, Sarah caught her husband bedded with her maid—his former wife.

Instantly estranged, Sarah and Scollard raced homeward by ship, airplane, and railroad, each seeking to grab community assets before the other, while newspapers enthusiastically chronicled their dash. Sarah angrily sued Scollard, then reconciled, and then sued again; he fled to Canada with $1.6 million in cash to rejoin his first wife. But $800,000 in securities, thought to be hidden in the Bellingham house, were never found, although a sheriff's deputy, summoned to guard Sarah, discovered ninety $1,000 bills in a mattress.

Divorced again, the aging and eccentric Sarah—she was said to carry thousands in her handbag—soon fell in with Reese Brown, a man who seemed to charm women. (A schoolteacher had sued for $175,000 she claimed Brown took from her by a fake marriage.) Brown did not propose marriage to Sarah, but he represented himself as an experienced manager, and she appointed him her confidential agent. He put Sarah's money into a Spokane house, land near Toppenish, a woolen mill near Seattle, a mercantile company in Montana, and his own lavish living. Eventually his fiscal flimflam led to indictment by the Internal Revenue Service, and he hid Sarah from federal agents in Montreal. There she died alone in a hotel in 1932, with $5,000 in travelers checks in her purse and $1,000 wrapped in an old dress. Notified by the hotel, Brown had Sarah's body cremated and carried her ashes back to the United States in a silver jewel case.

Not until Reese Brown died in January 1934 in an automobile accident near Wapato did anyone other than Brown and his wife know what had become of Sarah Smith. Brown's widow produced Sarah's ashes for the court when Sarah's nieces and nephews sued the Brown estate, alleging that $5.2 million had been squandered or unaccounted for. Every newspaper report of Sarah Smith mentioned her days with Hecla.

5

Searching

PARTICIPATING WITH BUNKER HILL IN THE SULLIVAN CHANGED Hecla from a company with a mine to a company bent on extending its operating life indefinitely. For two decades, James McCarthy and the Milwaukee shareholders had steered the Hecla company as they pleased, taking into account only the caprices of the market and their mutuality with the Mine Owners Association. And even though they had charged McCarthy with finding them another mine or two, when he did, the Milwaukee crowd backed away.

The Star changed that. With it, they were deliberately committed to another mine—and by consensus, to more if they could find them. They had given up some independence for the comfort of shared risk; they conceded the obvious—that the Hecla mine could not go on forever—and they tacitly faced the likelihood that the company would outlive them, as they had outlived its founders.

The twenties had started with fending off Sarah Smith, and by the middle of 1922 Hecla was back to business as usual. Jerome Day had promptly sent over a check to pay Eugene Day's share of court costs, but Hecla had had to sue Sarah for hers. For the next two decades, business as usual would mean roller-coaster rises and falls in the lead market, gliding to peaks of prosperity near the middle of the twenties and again near the end of the thirties. The market fell off abruptly after World War I, resulting in closure of marginal mines, a cut in wages "because of the poor condition of the lead market," and a sudden drop in income for mining companies. Hecla's earnings fell from $1.39 a share in 1918 to fifty-six cents in 1919. Earnings would not reach one dollar again until 1923.

A fluctuating market aside, mining in the twenties cost a lot of money: technical advances required new investments, and a race for new mines cost millions. Ravenel Macbeth, secretary of the Idaho Mining Association, estimated that $3 million was gambled in the Coeur d'Alenes alone during 1925 to buy or develop mining properties that paid no immediate returns—most never paid—and during 1926, the ante rose to more than $4.5 million. Two-thirds of this money flowed from outside the district, demonstrating that the Coeur d'Alene mines intrigued a national following of citizens eager for a fling in mining stocks. Hecla now had 906 shareholders, about half of them in eastern states.

One major technical improvement, differential flotation, required converting mills during the twenties from gravity concentration to flotation, or adding a flotation unit to the gravity. The flotation process uses a chemical frothing agent to catch and float finely ground mineral particles on the surface of a liquid pulp in huge vats, while waste material settles to the bottom. It saves more of the metals in ore, yields higher-grade concentrates (and thus higher returns from smelting), and treats complex ores at about the same cost as gravity systems. In the Coeur d'Alenes, the ore from one mine often differs from that of others, so that each company devises its own process. Some like Hecla kept their gravity mills to recover perhaps 85 percent of the mineral, adding flotation for a second treatment of the same ores. Others, like Morning, switched entirely to flotation. For perhaps fifteen years the major companies of the district, including Hecla, had experimented with flotation, but they could not make it work satisfactorily until wartime or shortly after. Then flotation came into general use.

Patents for flotation belonged to a British firm, the Minerals Separation Company. Using miniature mills as exhibits, the company sued in American courts to protect its patents. After conferring with the company's agents in San Francisco, McCarthy paid $50,000 for unlicensed use of their process, agreeing that Hecla would take a license later when a royalty basis had been established for Coeur d'Alene district mines.

Business as usual stopped abruptly for Hecla on the afternoon of Friday, July 13, 1923, when a destructive fire swept Burke, starting at the lower end of town and racing on a brisk wind toward Hecla's buildings and shaft. Hecla's hoist lifted out the men working as far down as the 1600 level, but when flames, toppling posts and burning wires, cut off current, the hoist stopped. The mine fell silent. Its pumps stilled and tunnel lights flickered out. Men still underground, with only their cap lights to guide them, clambered out of the eerily hushed maze by ladders in the manways. They could hear faintly the sounds of water trickling in the tunnels and the distant calls of other men. Some who took a wrong turn in their haste finally found a manway to climb hand over hand 2,000 feet to the surface.

No one was killed or injured in the mine. The fire leveled Burke's business district and perhaps fifty houses. It destroyed the Hecla surface plant as well as timber cribbing that held the mass of waste on which the plant stood. In the upper town, Hercules miners dynamited the old Tiger works and shot arches of water from hydraulic rams to save the Hercules cribbing and buildings and the Tiger Hotel. Early the next morning, Washington Water Power crews strung temporary cable 4,000 feet across the smoldering debris of Burke to restore power for pumps to keep the Hecla from flooding. Even so, levels below 2,000 feet had to be dewatered.

Writing his directors, McCarthy told them that the Hecla mine itself had suffered "no damage on account of the fire . . . for which we should be very thankful." All the other mining companies offered help. Bunker Hill sent a truckload of shop supplies and offered financial aid if Hecla needed it.

Hecla did not need financial rescue, however, because six years earlier, in 1917, the cautious directors had purchased Use and Occupancy Insurance, then relatively novel in mining. As McCarthy remarked, the fire insurance companies sold it at about the same cost as standard fire policies and it had sounded like a good investment to Hecla's board—mindful of their total reliance on one mine, its wooden buildings, extensive timbering, and the cramped Burke canyon, where fire might leap quickly out of control.

The *Engineering & Mining Journal-Press* published an editorial calling Hecla "a brilliant example" of the benefits of insurance, "a lesson for many other companies." Herman J. Rossi, the Wallace insurance man, sold a good deal of Use and Occupancy Insurance in the district after the Burke fire. Hecla's policy had insured it against lost gross income while the mine was shut down. The workings had been appraised as recently as 1920, and fifteen months before the fire, the board had increased coverage from $500,000 to $1,000,000. For the shareholders, the insurance proved golden; it allowed the company to pay two quarterly dividends of $400,000 while the mine was down after the fire. But it did not extend to the men; three-fourths of Hecla's crew would be out of work for nearly six months. One-fourth stayed on to rebuild the plant.

Hecla was actually out of commission only five months and eighteen days. It hoisted its first ore after the fire on Sunday, January 27, 1924. Insurance adjusters, McCarthy told the directors, "say this has been the most difficult loss they ever had to deal with," while Hecla's claims livened the shoptalk in offices and clubs throughout the district. As Hecla resumed production, the adjusters pressed McCarthy to settle, and he recommended to his board that, in addition to $337,000 in fire insurance, "we accept now a settlement on the basis of payment for seven months' loss of operations, plus $25,000, which would be $641,014, based on a daily loss of 1/365 of $1,000,000." The extra $25,000 represented a compromise of claims for metallurgical loss and the lowered capacity of the unfinished sorting and crushing plant. Realizing that they were setting precedent, the adjusters convened in San Francisco to review Hecla's terms, then accepted them.

In the meantime, as thirty carloads of twisted steel and wood ash were hauled away from Burke, McCarthy and his engineers scoured the West for used equipment and building materials. They bought 160 tons of steel buildings from the abandoned Granby smelter at Grand Forks, British Columbia. Consequently, the widths of some new Hecla buildings at Burke were determined by the roof-truss spans of the old Granby smelter. The Ingersoll-Rand Company diverted to Hecla a pump already on its way to a Montana mine, and a Seattle secondhand dealer offered another, once used in the Treadwell in Alaska. As soon as pumps could be installed, Hecla pumpmen worked in relays of twenty-four hours, preferring the long vigils to eight-hour shifts that required ninety minutes of climbing to reach pump stations at the 1200 level and another ninety minutes to come out. The Marsh Mining Company lent one compressor. Another, consigned to a Seattle shipyard during the war, was bought in its original crate, never unpacked. And so it went, Hecla rebuilding with materials and equipment lying unused, secondhand, or hurried to Burke by sympathetic suppliers. When new machinery had to be manufactured, insurance companies supervised the work, paying bonuses for rapid completion to reduce their liability.

With secondhand heaters from the former Day smelter at Northport, Hecla's men built an oven to dry waterlogged equipment. They thus restored all but one electric motor, six of eight transformers, and four locomotives (with batteries) which had been submerged. Cable was harder to dry. Much of it was lost. Due to oxidizing, trolley wire in the Star crosscut had to be sandpapered by hand its entire length.

The new Hecla plant, as fireproof as concrete and steel could make it, rose twice as large as the old one. It would process ore from the Star as well as the Hecla. And as they rebuilt, Hecla corrected old problems; they eliminated the steep railroad grade by excavating 1,600 yards of rock from an area earlier occupied by town stores and houses and by rerouting Canyon Creek by conduit, so that they no longer needed cribbing to hold ground from falling into the stream. The conduit, incidentally, improved sanitation at Burke, where outhouses stood on stilts over the creek. Concrete ore bins, scorched but usable, were enlarged to handle Star and Hecla ores separately. The first carload drawn, however, yielded 500 pounds of burned nails.

In his haste to rebuild, McCarthy persuaded the Northern Pacific to move its tracks to make room for the enlarged ore bins, promising that he would work something out. But he did not. Hecla's bins not only took the railroad's land but encroached on the Galena's surface. Then county commissioners demanded a fifty-foot right of way for a paved highway through Burke, forcing the Union Pacific and the Northern Pacific, at long last, to a single track.

As the upshot of Burke's fire, Hecla gained an enlarged crushing and sorting plant with the newest machinery of the time. This was the modern mill the company would have wished. In the Hecla mine's ore, galena occurred in large lenses and streaks, fine-grained and hard, an ideal ore for gravity concentration or hand-sorting. Hecla did both. In the sorting plant, experienced men, standing beside moving belts carrying ore cleaned by water spray, picked off chunks of galena and waste rock and dropped them into separate bins. The ore thus hand-sorted could be shipped without concentration, a crude that assayed about 50 percent lead and 28 ounces of silver a ton, nearly equal to the proportion of concentrated ores. Ores sent to the crusher passed through a series of machines that broke the ore and dropped it through screens for sizing before it went by rail to the mill at Gem, where Hecla had added pulp vats for flotation.

In the mine, machines gradually took over more of the work underground, where technology is traditionally slow to change. Machines allowed managers to reduce crews and set higher production quotas. Reciprocating pneumatic drills ("widow-makers") took the place of double-jack hand-drilling teams, although teams remained a feature of miners' picnics. Because Hecla ran drifts under ore deposits, as did most district mines, and then stoped (dug upward to extract the ore), ore-breaking required boring overhead, using machine drills that trailed air and water hoses and were equipped with hollow steel cores through which water was forced at 85-pounds pressure to reduce dust and to lubricate the whirling bits. A new class of surface worker appeared: the bit sharpeners, filing dozens of bits a day. In 1939, James F. McCarthy, Jr., with two associates, would found Bitco, Inc., a company to sharpen the tons of bits required daily for drilling in district mines.

Machine drills shook tunnels with ear-splitting chatter. Most miners emerged from a shift deafened for several hours. The companies favored the Leyner drill, standing on a one-leg brace, spurting air and water under pressure, for drifting, and Ingersoll-Rand jackhammers for sinking shafts.

Ventilation of tunnels by natural convection currents and slow vane fans could not keep up with the dust and fumes of machines. The larger mines pumped air down shafts for ventilation. As deeper tunnels grew hotter, chilled water was piped downward for cooling. But tunnels remained shadowy, cluttered, suffocating, and dangerous. Some threatened to collapse. In fact, McCarthy's method of timbering in the Hecla resulted in frequent caveins in unused sections. In the Morning mine, crews continually watched tunnels for threats of caving, and when Hecla drove into the Star, heavy ground there also required heavier timbering and constant watchfulness.

From a drift under an orebody, Hecla miners normally built a raise (a shaft driven upward) approximately nine by eighteen feet with separate compartments for an ore chute, a timber slide, and a manway. By drilling and blasting upward, the crews blew out space for successive floors above the drift. Some stopes rose 135 floors before crews spent too much time climbing. The miners generally blew out sixteen or more feet above a floor, making room to timber a new floor with seven or more feet above for drilling. An average of thirty holes, five- or six-feet deep, would be bored upward into the rock and filled with 300 sticks of dynamite and paper cartridges tamped in with a long wooden pole. The explosion brought down tons of ore to be drilled and blasted a second time and then dumped down an ore chute to a haulage level. Improved packing, higher power, and electrical detonators reduced the hazards of blasting only slightly. Gelatin fumes still induced splitting headaches.

Mucking machines (mechanical shovels) moved the rock to the chutes. Hecla was among the first to adopt the Armstrong "Shuveloder," a machine that flipped muck backward. Hecla's unique ore cars, ten-feet long, low and narrow, were manufactured in its own shop; they carried five-and-one-half tons and ran on a twenty-five-inch track. By removing the wheels, crews could lower a Hecla ore car through a shaft only four by five feet.

For work underground, a Coeur d'Alene miner wore a cap with carbide lamp, hob-nailed boots, woolen shirt, socks, underwear, and bib overalls covered by a "jumper," a rough work coat. A man working in wet drifts donned rubber coat and hip boots.

Hardrock mining was dirty, stifling, sweaty, fatiguing, and perilous. The men who mined did it largely because they knew no other occupation or because they hoped to save a little stake before moving on. Many were poorly educated immigrants from Central Europe, or their sons; they banded together in Irish, Swedish, Finnish, Italian, or other enclaves. A comradely bravado pervaded the miners, a sense of beating dangerous odds together, a loyalty to fellow workers rather than companies.

About half of the miners at Burke were single. As McCarthy often said, few men willingly settled families in the cramped canyon. After the fire, Burke offered 125 to 130 fewer houses. Men boarded in town or at the "beanery," the Tiger Hotel, for $1.25 to $1.50 a day. At Mullan, the Morning also ran a barracks for its single men. Mines remote from a town erected boardinghouses near the portal. Because single men tended to move often, to log or to harvest seasonally or to work in another mining camp, the companies put up recreation halls and donated to local churches and YMCAs to make life a little more tolerable and to keep their men longer.

More than most, Hecla instilled loyalty among its employees, because McCarthy, Hanley (whose office was at Burke), and the other managers knew their men, talked to them, kept office doors open, and went underground to see conditions for themselves. For a time, Hecla conducted a "school," training at the 1600 level for novices willing to learn mining. But no company could make the work safe, clean, or easy, and as more machines appeared, the men felt themselves displaced and newly endangered. Hecla experimented briefly with radio as a warning device, but radio could not transmit clearly underground. Instead, electric buzzers were installed for shaft signals with auxiliary lamps to flash when noise drowned out the buzzers. At least, they were more reliable than rapping on air pipes.

The mine owners had agreed as far back as 1916 to adjust wages with the rise or fall of the lead market, from a basic rate of $3.50 a day. As lead prices fell between 1920 and 1940, the wage bonus would be reduced four times—in 1921, 1926, 1931, and 1933. The work week would be shortened to four and then three days—in 1930, 1931, and 1932; and the bonus would rise five times—in 1922, 1923, 1925, 1929, and 1933—usually to lure back men who had left for higher pay in Montana mines. To justify lowering wages in 1921, the Wallace Board of Trade surveyed grocery, meat, drygoods, and hardware prices in Wallace, reporting they had fallen 31 to 36 percent since the war.

As the third largest employer in the district (behind Bunker Hill and Morning), McCarthy aimed to attract what he called "a better class"—married men who would stay on the job, show up sober after payday, and learn the ways of the Hecla and Star. The slightly more genteel residents of Wallace and Kellogg regarded Burke as a nest of rowdies, but in Burke one could always find someone offering French, piano, or art lessons. Although wages were tied to those of other companies, in 1922 Hecla's directors agreed to set aside $30,000 as a fund to lend to its men, at no interest, to buy houses. Many then commuted to Burke by jitney and even by private automobile. With the backing of the Wallace Board of Trade, Burke's mine owners defeated a Northern Pacific petition to the state public utilities commission to discontinue passenger service between Wallace and Burke.

In addition to maintaining wages and trying to improve housing and transportation for their men, in 1924 Hecla, Bunker Hill, and Sullivan mutually established group life insurance programs offering accident and death benefits, in addition to the state Workmen's Compensation Act of 1917, which permitted companies to self-insure.

Overseeing technical advances at Hecla fell chiefly to Lewis

Hanley, who was promoted to general superintendent in August 1922. The post was new, intended to relieve McCarthy of direct management of operations. Hanley had, the *Wallace Miner* remarked, "practically grown up with the Hecla." As a Wallace high school student, he had won an A. B. Campbell scholarship to study mining and metallurgy at the University of Idaho. After graduating, he worked as an assayer at the Standard and the Helena-Frisco until 1903, when he joined Hecla. There, he and McCarthy constituted the entire office staff. Hanley assayed ore samples in the morning and kept accounts in the afternoon. In nineteen years with the company, he had risen to chief of an enlarged business office, purchasing agent, and secretary. A man of standing in Wallace, a school trustee, he resigned as president of the Board of Trade to move to a company house at Burke when he was named general superintendent. Leo Hoban took over as head of the company's office in Wallace.

With Hanley to carry more of the load, McCarthy could bend his efforts toward finding other mines to extend the company's life. New geological opinion suggested that orebodies in the Burke and Mullan areas might be expected to play out as they reached sea level. F. H. Brownell, president of Federal, in his annual report for 1924, produced a map showing the relative depths of the Hecla, Hercules, Standard-Mammoth, Tiger-Poorman, Gem, Frisco, Morning, and Gold Hunter shafts, pointing out that only the Hecla, Morning, and Gold Hunter were still active.

Deepening the Hecla another hundred feet or so would thrust the mine into what the *Wallace Miner* ominously called "the fatal zone," where mines died. McCarthy had been talking about a larger hoist for the Hecla, both to handle the Star output and to reach deeper into the Hecla. He invited Fred Searls to inspect the Hecla "to advise as to the probability of great depth" before deepening the shaft, and could report to the directors that Searls believed the orebody would persist deeper. Even so, McCarthy would hesitate four years longer, exploring by winze, before sinking the Hecla shaft farther.

A quest for new mines would take Hecla as far as Newfoundland, but the search centered on the familiar fields of Idaho and Montana. Every successful manager, James McCarthy among them, received begging letters from prospectors sure they had found new El Dorados. If a letter sounded plausible and its writer seemed reliable, managers sometimes sent an engineer to look.

One of McCarthy's essays involved a gold property in Alaska in which some Hecla directors owned stock. He, Searls, and William A. Corey, the Spokane accountant who co-managed the Finch estate, visited the place on a tributary of the Yukon River 100 miles out of Fairbanks. McCarthy enjoyed the scenic steamer voyage from Seattle, but he and Searls agreed the claim was too far from transportation to warrant investment by Hecla. In a future day, Hecla would try to conquer a wilderness almost as solitary.

Among dozens of possibilities that McCarthy, his engineers (principally Searls, as consultant), and Rush J. White scrutinized in the next fifteen years was the Olson claim, a forlorn furrow in the hills above Enaville near the confluence of the north and south forks of the Coeur d'Alene River. After tunneling 250 feet, Hecla miners cut the vein. It was barren.

Hecla took an option (800,000 shares at six cents) on the Wall Street near Burke, thinking it might contain an extension of the Hecla if the vein persisted through the intervening Maher-Hearn, owned by the Days. But the Wall Street's owners were difficult to deal with, and when the company's secretary billed McCarthy $25 a month for his services, although Hecla had performed the administrative work, that was the last straw. Exasperated, McCarthy cut off the Wall Street. He and Searls had already convinced themselves that the Hecla vein "fails and loses itself" rather than continuing. And so it would go. Newspapers trumpeted Hecla's interest in this claim or that one, but in a few months, McCarthy would tell his board that a prospect had proven worthless.

In Custer County, however, Henry Ford, the auto maker, leased the old Red Bird from Robert N. Bell, a one-time state mines inspector. The Red Bird had been located in 1878 by A. H. Conover, who also ran a stageline to Montana. In a cut-rate scramble for mail and express contracts, Conover had eventually carried passengers free. Predictably, he went broke. The Red Bird's ore, hauled by wagon sixty miles to the railhead at Mackay, could not bail him out. Ford refused comment on his mine but was rumored to want it as a source of lead for batteries. A good many speculators, thinking that Ford knew something no one else did, snapped up claims near his.

Hecla took an option on the South Butte, marked by a surface outcrop of oxidized iron perhaps 50 by 400 feet, between the Red Bird and the Dryden, owned by New Yorkers. McCarthy negotiated to buy Bell's $120,000 interest in the South Butte but could not come to terms, while a railroad car of Hecla machinery sat on a siding at Mackay. Then Ford abruptly shut the Red Bird, puncturing Custer County's boom. McCarthy backed away, too. He visited the Northern Pacific at St. Paul, learning that the railroad's officers "have no plans for building into central Idaho." Hecla gave up the South Butte for lack of transportation.

Hecla also dickered for the Mountain King, on Sheep Mountain, reachable only by snowshoes much of the year. McCarthy sent in a crew with hand tools, but 633 feet into rock the ore pinched out, "completely disappointing." Next to it, his men rebuilt the caved tunnels of the Hasbrouck mine. It showed too little ore to pay its way.

Not far off lay the Minnie Moore, the preeminent mine of the Wood River boom of the eighties, when Ketchum, Hailey, and Bellevue were robust mining camps. In its boom days, Bellevue had been known for its Cornish miners' band and dances and for a flourishing racetrack built by British capitalists who bought the Minnie Moore for $1.5 million. Repeal of the Sherman Silver Purchase Act and national economic depression put Wood River out of business, and the Minnie Moore's vein was lost, snipped cleanly by a fault, a rock wall created by slippage in the earth's crust. But in 1925 a Philadelphia company claimed to have rediscovered the vein, guided by Oscar Hershey, a noted geologist. If Hershey had not been so cocksure, perhaps no one would have looked at the old mine. When miners blasted into five feet of ore early in 1925, Bellevue's remaining residents staged a Minnie Moore jubilee, certain that their glory days were back.

Then the vein again butted against barren rock. The Philadelphians, who had put half a million into Hershey's hunches, gave up. Federal Mining & Smelting Company tried briefly to find the vein without success. And in the middle of 1926, James McCarthy took an option on the Minnie Moore for Hecla, banking that Fred Searls could locate the severed vein. Searls had only recently joined Newmont Mining Corporation, which collaborated in the Minnie Moore, and Searls himself supervised the exploration. Late in August, McCarthy told the directors that he and Searls would grant the stubborn old girl a few more weeks to divulge her secret. "If . . . no ore by December 1," he wrote them, "we will conclude that the broken end of the vein cannot be recovered." By Christmas, their search in the Minnie Moore had failed, and McCarthy returned the mine to its owner.

The Minnie Moore paid off for Hecla, nonetheless, for it brought Hecla and Newmont together in a marriage of convenience that would endure for half a century. Newmont was the invention of William Boyce Thompson, native Montanan, a rotund, cigar-chewing New York promoter who made millions in mining stocks. Thompson conceived Newmont as a holding company, a portfolio of mining and petroleum stocks, and a vehicle for developing and managing potentially profitable properties anywhere in the world. He held Newmont to a small group of fast-moving managers, Searls among them as exploration geologist.

While Searls had searched for the Minnie's lost vein, he gave McCarthy a diffident letter, suggesting that the two companies share other enterprises too expensive for Hecla alone. "Another thought that occurred to me, if I may venture it without seeming to try to horn in on any other plans you may have," he wrote, "is that possibly this syndicate that we have more or less accidentally got together for the Minnie Moore purpose, might be available for other developments in the general region, if opportunities should arise." For Hecla, as McCarthy pointed out, Newmont's interest "divides a highly speculative venture with people well qualified to judge the value of the properties."

Moreover, Newmont had ample resources: incorporated for $8 million, it was traded (as was Hecla) on the New York curb and held properties, chiefly copper, throughout North America. Hecla's directors welcomed Newmont as a working partner. They authorized McCarthy "to join Mr. Searls in any of his operations" in the Pacific Northwest, "participation . . . to be optional with either party."

Although the central Idaho prospects had fizzled, McCarthy had an eye for the Red Ledge in the Idaho hills above the Snake River, owned by the Idaho Copper Company. In the midst of negotiations for it, however, the chief promoter of Idaho Copper, George Graham Rice, was convicted of fraud for manipulating its stock on the Boston curb and was sent to prison. The Red Ledge had become a hot potato. McCarthy gingerly laid it aside.

If Hecla was not finding new mines, its directors were learning about the vagaries of prospecting. McCarthy looked over the Stampede group in northern British Columbia, gold mines worked from thirty-five open slashes in the ground. Too remote, too risky. The Imperial group showed ore—in streaks "of no length and consequently no commercial value." The names of mining prospects examined and discarded flashed like prairie villages past a speeding train. McCarthy toured Newfoundland with Searls. The outlook was "disappointing." The Loyd, a zinc-lead property near Metaline Falls, Washington, proved too low-grade.

After five years spent examining dozens of prospects, McCarthy wrote the board in the fall of 1927, "The only property we have under consideration now is one in British Columbia . . . a silver and gold property . . . offered for $175,000, to be paid out of profits." This was the Union mine on the Kettle River about twenty miles from the railroad at Grand Forks. Seven months later, McCarthy told his directors, "I am quite satisfied that we have a reasonably good chance to find sufficient ore to make this a commercial operation."

The Union was not to be the long-lived mine wanted by Hecla to ensure the company's future, although it produced what was said to be the richest carload of ore mined in British Columbia, fifty-four tons that returned $43,178 from the smelter. That carload, mused an editor, came from "a little streak of ore [that] gave an awful thrill and inspired hopes that others like it . . . would be found." But none was. Hecla erected a flotation mill, barracks, and sawmill at the Union, mined there for four years, prospected adjoining claims, and then shut down when silver prices fell. The Union, virtually exhausted, had netted $63,000.

In its own backyard, Hecla poked into the Wide West, one of the claims near Burke acquired in settling the Russell apex suit, finding no mineral. Hecla pumped out the pioneer Tiger-Poorman, another legacy from the Russell, shooting water driven by compressed air from the rotted shaft at 1,200 gallons a minute, splashing through flumes to Canyon Creek. The old mine was worn out. It was allowed to fill with water again. McCarthy took options on the Pilot group and the Mountain Goat near Mullan but, after three years of fruitless exploration, let them expire.

One reason for reopening old mines like the Tiger-Poorman was that improved mill technology—fine grinding and especially flotation—allowed profitable treatment of ores once left in place as too low-grade to pay. Dumps of tailings (discarded mill residue) held minerals not extracted by ruder methods that now could be recovered by flotation. Several small contractors, in fact, mined only tailings dumps. Consequently, while Hecla searched for a new mine, in 1925 it also began reworking its dump, building a plant for this purpose beside the Gem mill. The tailings mill used two Hardinge fine-grinding units and flotation to treat 300 tons a day, tailings both from the dump and from the Gem mill, and recovering 85 to 90 percent of the mineral.

The tailings mill was designed by Vern L. Zeigler, a slight, soft-spoken graduate of the University of Idaho with a pencil habitually cocked behind one ear. Zeigler, who had joined Hecla in 1924, had planned flotation mills for several mining companies in British Columbia, Washington, and Idaho before McCarthy captured him for Hecla, bragging thereafter that Hecla employed "the best mill designer" in the district. Zeigler would give the company ingenious, efficient mills in his thirty-two years as its millman. The *Wallace Miner* once remarked that "Hecla milling costs are always lowest in the district." Operating at thirty cents a ton, the tailings mill repaid its construction expense in four months and produced a modest profit—about fifteen cents a ton—for Hecla for twenty-four years until it closed in 1949.

While Hecla's geologists had been looking for new mines, a surprise popped up in the southern part of the Coeur d'Alene district, generally regarded as a region of superficial veins that would fail at depth. Prospects there had been neglected, even though two brothers, True and Dennis Blake, took silver from their Yankee Boy mine in the hills overlooking Big Creek: a two-man mine—that was pretty much the best that experienced miners expected of Big Creek. From 1904 to 1916, this belt produced only a few hundred tons of ore a year. When silver flourished with federal support, it turned out about three thousand a year. When silver prices rose, the Blakes mined, and when silver fell, they farmed on their homestead two and one-half miles up Big Creek from its confluence with the south fork of the Coeur d'Alene River. Over the years they were said to have mined $100,000 worth of silver, but they did not trouble themselves to patent their claim until twenty-five years after discovery. Then they let it to lessees.

In the early twenties, a Spokane stockbroker, Eugene E. Tousley, bought the Yankee Boy and adjoining Yankee Girl for his Sunshine Mining Company. On the promise of silver, he peddled 100,000 shares at six cents to a Yakima businessman, John Sawbridge, whose purchase entitled him to be president of Sunshine, and Sawbridge in turn enlisted more than two hundred modest plungers in the Yakima area, who bought their stock for pennies. With stock sales and bond issues, Sunshine erected a small mill and sank a shaft. When the managers of other mines paid Sunshine any heed, they looked on the company as amateurs pouring money into a sterile siren hole. Indeed, Sunshine produced only a few thousand tons a year and lost money until 1926. Then it struck a rich vein, confounded the old-timers with a carload of the highest grade silver seen in the Coeur d'Alenes, and turned a modest profit.

With that, Sunshine began to change the traditional pattern of the district. In older mines, silver had been extracted as a by-product of lead (although sometimes only silver returned a profit) but after 1926, the silver, or dry belt—the mines around Sunshine—produced silver as their primary metal. In May 1927 Sunshine paid its first dividend of $30,000, two cents a share, and retired its outstanding bonds.

Instead of rushing to gobble properties in the silver belt, the old managers hesitated to see if Sunshine would keep going, while sleepy little companies near Sunshine wakened, strutting like male peacocks, to sell their penny shares in a rising market triggered by Hecla's adoption of a minimum dividend of two dollars a year in 1925. Spokane brokers said they took orders then from buyers who had not been in the market since 1917. The market peaked near the end of 1927 when regional stocks on the Spokane and Vancouver exchanges moved at the fastest pace in memory.

Hecla was drawn into the silver belt by lending money to Harry W. Woodward of Lynn, Massachusetts, principal owner of the Polaris, a mine directly northeast of the burgeoning Sunshine. A few years earlier Woodward and a partner had taken an option on 600,000 shares (of an authorized 1,500,000) of the Polaris and, although they made their payments, they let the mine lie. But after Sunshine paid a dividend, Woodward, who by now held about 900,000 shares of Polaris, hired a mining engineer, intending to sink a shaft.

Unsung, the Polaris was one of the district's oldest claims, staked on August 30, 1884, by the porcine pioneer lawyer, Weldon B. Heyburn, and two partners he soon bought out. The Polaris discovery was twenty-six days earlier than the Sunshine, née Yankee Boy and Yankee Girl. Heyburn had held onto his Polaris and two adjoining claims, Omega and Southern Cross, until his death in 1912, but as Charles Sweeny's outrageous attorney in predatory apex suits, and then as United States Senator, 1903–12, he had had no time to develop them. He would not sell, however, convinced that he would have a mine someday. After 1912, a nephew managed the Polaris briefly, taking some ore from a tunnel near the surface to ship sporadically. The mine was said to have yielded $250,000, the "ugly duckling" of the Coeur d'Alenes, well equipped but going nowhere. The Polaris Development & Mining Company's stock sold slowly at thirty-five to forty cents a share until, under Woodward's direction, it halted operations.

When Woodward failed to repay his loan, Hecla pocketed the 100,000 shares of Polaris given as collateral and, having thus acquired an interest, negotiated for the remainder of Polaris, taking an option on 969,500 shares at twenty-five cents. Early in 1930, whispers went around that Hecla had taken over Polaris and the *Wallace Miner* editorialized that "what is lacking [in the silver belt] is the public confidence that would be supplied by the prestige of a great and successful organization such as the Hecla. . . . Even the most pessimistic are now forced to admit that the Sunshine has made good."

Sunshine, in fact, had paid dividends in 1929 of twenty-two cents a share, built a cash surplus of $134,000, enlarged its mill, and installed a new hoist. Under an agreement ratified (by a split vote) by Hecla's directors on November 8, 1933, Hecla would buy Polaris stock, and the proceeds would be used to develop the mine. The directors limited expenditures there to $90,000 in the next thirteen months. They were still not sure that, in Polaris, they had a mine.

Before the 1923 Burke fire, James McCarthy had been contemplating a deeper Hecla mine. He was not sure what he might find below 2000, the lowest operating level, although Fred Searls had predicted that ore would persist. McCarthy moved cautiously, perhaps hoping that if he had to tell his shareholders their mine was bottoming out, he could accompany the bad news with that of the purchase of a new mine. But he had not found another mine, and he could not postpone indefinitely looking deeper in the Hecla. In 1924, McCarthy's men sank a winze (an inclined tunnel) 400 feet downward. The orebody was still there. The next year, they drove the winze to 2,800 feet, showing "a very substantial amount of ore," McCarthy reported. No doubt now—Hecla's orebody went deeper.

At the same time, crews in the Star found ore. There, McCarthy wrote in his annual report for 1925, "development has been very satisfactory. . . . We have drifted the whole length of this orebody," and there could be no doubt that the Star would pay. This was the news Stanly Easton had been waiting for. Finally, Bunker Hill had started construction of its long-delayed zinc plant.

As they reached the boundary between the Star and the Morning, Hecla's men, by agreement with the Federal company, ran their tunnel into the Morning's 2250 level, creating an escape route from either mine in an emergency and improving ventilation in both.

"We have hesitated a long time in deciding what we should do concerning the deeper development of the Hecla," McCarthy acknowledged to his board in October 1927. "We finally decided that it would be better to sink the main shaft and install hoisting equipment." Taking out deeper ore by winze, he explained, would require double handling and, in the long run, cost more.

Hecla's new hoist would lift about 2,000 tons every nine hours. Built by the Nordberg Manufacturing Company, Milwaukee, with electrical controls from Allis-Chalmers, it could reach down 3,500 feet. Before ordering it, McCarthy went to Butte to inspect three large hoists recently installed by Anaconda. Hecla's new double-drum hoist would be in operation by November 1929.

If a deeper Hecla and commercial ore in the Star sounded like unmitigated good news, McCarthy sounded warnings. In his annual report for 1927, he told the shareholders that, despite a large tonnage in the Star, "It is not to be expected that promptly upon completion of the zinc plant profits will flow back to the Hecla Company. . . . It will take several months, possibly a year, before such results can be secured . . . as earnings will probably be deferred owing to the adjustments and delays incident to the operation of a new plant."

And although the Hecla would be deepened, his company ought to expect lower tonnage, due "partly to a shortening in length of the ore body and partly to a widening of the Hecla dyke, a mass of post-mineral igneous rock that has always followed the ore shoot. . . . This statement concerning the present condition of the bottom of the mine is made so that shareholders may be informed concerning prospects for the future in that part of the Company's property on which we have depended in the past for a large part of our income. It is hoped," he went on, "that shareholders will not undervalue the remaining reserves in the Hecla mine nor its assets represented by its holdings in other properties." They had come at last to the prospect of a Hecla company without the Hecla mine.

6

The Thirties

HEAD BOWED, HANDS THRUST INTO POCKETS, NEWSPAPER rolled under one arm, James McCarthy paced the four blocks between his home and office. As usual in 1932, on a Sunday morning in Wallace, the streets were nearly deserted. Stores were locked, and here and there stood an empty storefront— a business failed in the hard times of the thirties. Now sixty-five, McCarthy regularly toiled at the Hecla office on Sundays, as though single-handed he might bay the dragon of depression that stalked the mining district during the worst metals markets in thirty-five years.

Mining had not been this discouraging since McCarthy joined Hecla three decades earlier. Most of his old companions on that arduous pilgrimage had fallen away. Frank Kipp died in December 1925 after nearly a year's illness. One of his last letters asked McCarthy to recommend his son, Clarence F. Kipp, for his seat as a director, and the sorrowing board had honored his request. They found Clarence well schooled in the family business but, as a newcomer to Hecla, less than the forceful leader his father had been. In his day, Frank Kipp had been sometimes critical, sometimes volatile, occasionally acerbic, but he had held together the Milwaukee shareholders.

The younger Kipp and his wife had first visited Wallace as McCarthy's guests, shortly before Frank's death. After donning miner's garb, they had gone down into the Hecla, dutifully declaring themselves impressed. "It looks like a railroad terminal," ventured Mrs. Kipp after their two-mile trolley ride to the Star.

Hugo Lambach resigned in April 1927, at McCarthy's request, posting a curt letter from Hollywood, California. Ah, that had been a delicate showdown. Lambach's former wife had written Carl Landsee a damaging letter. Neither Landsee nor McCarthy would say what was in it, but they agreed that

Lambach must go, despite his nearly eleven years as a director. Lewis Hanley had succeeded him on the board.

Then, at a tearful directors' meeting in April 1931, Landsee himself resigned, saying that at age eighty-four he was too old to carry on. The last of the Milwaukee originals, a quiet, sentimental bachelor, Landsee had come into money in middle life. Having no family, he had adopted his native village in Germany, Rottenburg am Neckar, which he had last seen as a boy of eleven. At his death in 1934, he would leave $100,000 to the town for charity, and $30,000 to the nearby University of Tübingen. He also left bequests to thirty-six relatives there. William G. Hanson, a Milwaukee attorney, took Landsee's seat on the board.

On the night of July 4, 1931, only three months after Landsee resigned, the sensible, reliable W. J. C. Wakefield, a director and vice president of Hecla since 1908, expired peacefully in his sleep. His estate went to five children, and his law books to his son Channing, also a lawyer. Wakefield was succeeded by Archibald Witherspoon, his law partner.

Thus Hecla's veterans had gone. By 1932, four of the seven directors of 1925—Frank Kipp, Landsee, Wakefield, and Lambach—were no longer on the board. In the spring of 1930 McCarthy himself suffered a mild heart attack. Overwork, ruled his physician, citing such exhausting days as the one in which McCarthy and Vern Zeigler had risen at five, driving by auto to Felts Field (the Spokane airport), flying to Seattle, working there for six hours, flying back, and driving home by eleven. In 1930 air travel to Seattle by Ford tri-motor aircraft was adventuresome, indeed. McCarthy's doctor packed him off to Hawaii, accompanied by his younger son, James, Jr., for two months of rest. McCarthy left Hanley in charge at Wallace.

Now in 1932 McCarthy—the survivor—was hard at work. Some time after reaching his desk on a Sunday morning, McCarthy customarily telephoned the neighbors of his secretary to send the boy up to the Hecla. After a few months, embarrassed by this regular imposition, McCarthy raised his secretary's $88-a-month pay by $2.75, enough for the boy to pay for his own telephone.

As he did nearly every day, McCarthy spent his Sundays devising ways to reduce the costs of mining and milling. Often enough, cutting costs meant fewer working days for his men. With lead at its lowest price since 1914 and silver lower than anyone remembered, the Star had been closed indefinitely in April 1930, "until the metal situation justifies resumption," McCarthy said, and 125 of its 200 men laid off. Seventy-five stayed to maintain the mine and continue development, but even development had been suspended in March 1931. After that, only watchmen and pumpmen prowled the gloomy tunnels. Hecla, which in good times ran every day but the Fourth of July and Christmas, had been limited to 229 days in 1931 and reduced to 167—13 days a month—in 1932. McCarthy had thus halved the company's operating expenses from $1.4 million to $722,000. Nonetheless, in April 1932 Hecla failed to pay a dividend for the first time since 1902.

Ironically, the value of ores produced from the Coeur d'Alene district in 1929 had been the highest since 1918, roughly $35 million, but high output had built surpluses. By the end of 1929 Hecla, and Federal's Page and Morning mines, had shortened work weeks. With the Star down, the zinc plant cut back, too, operating at one-quarter capacity or less with ores from Hecla, Bunker Hill, and small mines—and losing customers it could not supply. Sunshine took out no ore during 1931. Morning ran in the red in 1932. Net operating profits for the district's mines plummeted from $4.2 million in 1930 to $437,013 in 1932, that of the bellwether Bunker Hill from $1.6 million to $52,801, and Hecla from $1.2 million to $85,486. The annual report of the state mines inspector called 1932 "the leanest . . . in 40 years."

In such dismal times, Arthur J. Pellette, a Milwaukee attorney who had succeeded E. J. Nolan on the board, regularly voted to close the Hecla and opposed even modest development funds for the idle Star. But Pellette voted alone in these instances. The other directors left such decisions to McCarthy, as the reasonable voice of long experience. Pellette's situation emphasized a shift in power within the company. Represented by heirs or lawyers, the Milwaukee shareholders no longer breathed that familiar air of proprietorship that had guided Hecla for four decades.

Hecla's directors were unanimous, however, in questioning continued operation of the Sullivan zinc plant. In 1932 the Sullivan plant lost an average of $6,600 a month and, despite its long-range promise, was becoming an abrasive issue between Hecla and Bunker Hill. In Hecla's annual reports, McCarthy simply quoted Easton's review of the zinc plant from Bunker

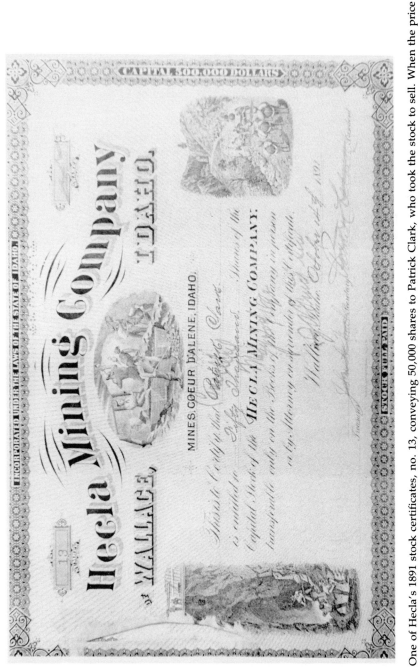

One of Hecla's 1891 stock certificates, no. 13, conveying 50,000 shares to Patrick Clark, who took the stock to sell. When the price of Hecla's stock began to rise, Clark sold his shares to invest in Canadian mining claims.

Amasa B. Campbell, who came to the Coeur d'Alene mining district in 1887 with John A. Finch to represent investors in Youngstown, Ohio. Campbell's strategy was to buy mining properties cheaply and pay for development with stock sales. (*Eastern Washington State Historical Society*)

John A. Finch, Campbell's partner, who became prominent in business and Republican politics before moving to Spokane from the mining district. Finch's estate would be noted for generous gifts to Spokane's park system. (*Eastern Washington State Historical Society*)

The *Spokesman-Review*, Spokane's morning newspaper, showed a natty, vain James R. "Hecla" Smith, president of Hecla from 1904 until his death in 1908. This photograph was published on October 24, 1936, during lawsuits to recover his widow's vanished estate.

The Standard Mine, with a gravity tramway running to the railroad in the Canyon Creek valley below. Promoters of the Hecla mine prospered from this and other mines before turning their attention to Hecla. (*Spokane Public Library*)

Hecla's frame surface buildings before the fire in 1923 which destroyed much of Burke, Idaho, and the Hecla plant. The Hercules buildings, in the background, were saved by using ram jets to play water on the flames.

Lunch break at the Hecla mine in the early 1900s. The squared timbers will be hauled underground to shore up tunnels and stopes. Although the photograph is not dated, it apparently goes back to the days when the Hecla was mined by tunnel directly into the hillside.

Frank Kipp, the Milwaukee banker who served as a forceful director of Hecla until 1925. The Kipp family and associates, largely second-generation German immigrants, dominated Hecla's board for four decades. (*Milwaukee County Historical Society*)

The gentlemanly James F. McCarthy, who managed Hecla for more than thirty years, established the company's reputation for technical innovation and conservative policy. McCarthy was one of Idaho's prominent spokesmen for the mining industry. (*Photograph courtesy of Anne [Hoban] Foreman*)

Hecla's offices in the Gyde-Taylor Building, Wallace, on June 28, 1919. Hecla, expanding into the entire two-story building, purchased it in 1964 and occupied it until moving the corporate headquarters to Coeur d'Alene in 1986.

The Hecla office building, the company's headquarters until it moved to Coeur d'Alene. Hecla rented a few rooms in what was originally the Gyde-Taylor Building and, as the company grew, took over the entire structure.

Marking the Russell claim, September 9, 1920. During a 1919 lawsuit with Federal Mining & Smelting and Marsh Mining, the precise boundaries of the Russell claim were questioned. The corner is indicated here by white tape nailed to a corner stake. (*Photograph by W. Earl Greenough*).

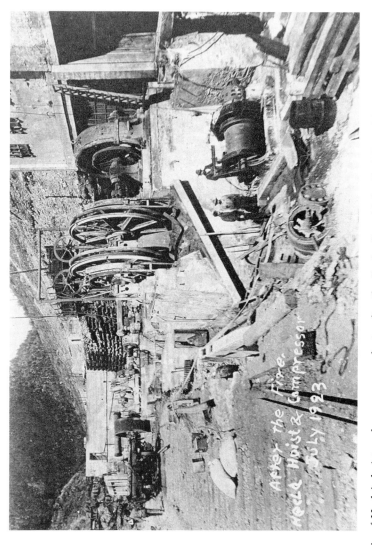

After the Fire.
Hecla Hoist & Compressor
July 1923

The debris of Hecla's hoist and compressor plants after the Burke fire of July 13, 1923. Although the surface buildings burned, the mine was not damaged, and Hecla was covered by insurance. (*Photograph by A. Standow, Mullan, Idaho*)

After its 1923 fire, Hecla rebuilt its surface plant of fire-resistant concrete and steel, using secondhand materials from mills throughout the West. No longer used for mining, these structures look much the same today. (*Photograph by Tolman, Spokane*)

Hecla's old mill at Gem, leased and then purchased in 1903 from the Milwaukee Mining Company. The mill was enlarged piecemeal over the years as ore production increased and mill technology changed.

Governor H. C. Baldridge of Idaho, visiting the Hecla mine on June 11, 1927, toured its underground workings. The numbered persons are: *1*, Baldridge; *2*, James McCarthy; *3*, L. E. Hanley; and *4*, J. M. Plumlee, superintendent.

The globe-trotting Fred Searls, Jr., who formed a close friendship with James McCarthy and brought Newmont Mining into partnership with Hecla in several exploration projects. (*Photograph courtesy of W. H. Love*)

Lewis E. Hanley, who succeeded McCarthy as president of Hecla. Wallace citizens liked to say that Hanley was "destined" to be president of Hecla because he knew every nook and cranny of the company. (*Photograph courtesy of Thomas E. Hanley*)

Leo J. Hoban, the accountant who steered Hecla through its early confrontations with the federal internal revenue bureau and became an effective lobbyist on taxation for the mining industry. Untimely death cut short Hoban's career with Hecla. (*Photograph courtesy of Anne [Hoban] Foreman*)

When Hecla hired women for its office force during World War II, Hanley directed that they tour undergound to "see what our business is all about." In hard hats, *left to right, front:* Catherine Gay, Rose Gorshe, Bernice Wild, Louise Snodgrass, and Marian Foltz. *Rear:* Ruby Sinrud and Pauline Lackman. (*Photograph courtesy of Ruby [Sinrud] Hill*)

The Sullivan Mining Company's electrolytic zinc plant at Silver King, adjacent to the Bunker Hill smelter, as it neared completion in 1928. The smaller buildings at right are a terminal for an aerial tram to the Sidney mine, which supplied ores for testing the process. (*Spokane Public Library*)

Hill's annual reports, and, near the end of 1931, Hecla's board had felt obliged to establish a $500,000 reserve (raised to $625,000 one year later) against future losses in Sullivan. Some directors privately doubted that Hecla should continue to participate in Sullivan. Finally, the board hired Walter Ingalls to report fully on Sullivan's outlook. Ingalls was reassuring, blaming the zinc plant's unanticipated costs on predictable problems of a new plant and temporary limpness in metals markets.

As the bleak months of depression dragged into mid-1932, President Herbert Hoover's term neared its end. In the political campaigns of that summer, marred by the army's callous removal of the lingering veterans of a "bonus army" from the national capital, Coeur d'Alene mine managers found a new cause for alarm with the Democratic party's talk of lowering tariffs to increase revenues. Mining companies feared that lowered tariffs would flood American markets with cheaper foreign metals, particularly from Latin America, Spain, and Australia.

For years, mine lobbyists had defended high silver and lead tariffs as guaranteeing employment for American miners, and Republican administrations had maintained the barriers, but now fifteen million men were out of work in every occupation, and the nation seemed ready for drastic changes. The mine managers squabbled over other political issues, but they were of a single mind about tariffs; they advocated them.

So crucial seemed tariffs that McCarthy convened a "Republican meeting" a few days before the general election, at Hecla's headhouse, "for a discussion of some issues of the presidential campaign" before his morning shift descended into the mine. Mine workmen for years had protested company meddling with their votes—alleging threats. Never had there been such an open, extraordinary entreaty. McCarthy and Donald A. Callahan, who had temporarily set aside mining for a political career, spoke for thirty minutes. McCarthy declared, "You men, your employers, and this community are absolutely dependent on a protective tariff for your prosperity. The Republican party has always been the party of protection."

The Democrats, of course, swept national and state offices. In the year to come, America under President Franklin D. Roosevelt would embark on its New Deal. Preoccupied with bank relief, public works, farm credit, and similar measures calculated to dispel depression, the new administration would not alter tariffs substantially but would enact industrial recovery and silver-purchase measures that directly affected the mining industry.

Although production in the Coeur d'Alenes was nearly at a standstill, Hecla continued to look for other mines. Indeed, this was an ideal time: depressions hatch bargains in mining properties. McCarthy did not give out much information about Hecla's search, disclosing only that the company had turned down the Pilot group and the Mountain Goat. He did not mention, outside the company, that the Federal Mining & Smelting Company inquired about buying the Star (but made no formal tender), and two years passed before he confirmed rumors that Hecla controlled Polaris. Still wary of Polaris, he had waited to see the results of Sunshine's exploration at the 1700 level, presuming the mines to be working the same vein. When Sunshine persisted in rich ore at that depth, McCarthy quickly sewed up Polaris's unissued shares. Weldon Heyburn's cherished mine seemed about to confirm his faith in it, twenty years after his death.

But with Hecla's finances stretched thin, and with uncertainty about national policy, Hecla's board split over funding any work in Polaris. Finally in November 1933, by a five to two vote (Hanson and Kipp voting no), and at McCarthy's insistence, they authorized spending the $90,000 and gave a contract to Joseph and George Grismer to sink a shaft from the old number 2 tunnel.

McCarthy extended the term of a Hecla loan to the president of the Little Sunshine on a hunch that it might be a key to Polaris. When Hecla acquired the adjacent Chester group and nearby Silver Summit two years later, they were consolidated with the Polaris Development & Mining Company as potentially valuable and as likely portals to the Polaris. Hecla would continue to acquire properties in the vicinity.

A cautious Hecla was venturing into unknown and lightly regarded ground. No one could be sure what treasure might lie in the dry belt, now becoming the "silver belt," and speculators—their confidence bolstered by Sunshine—were grabbing whatever ground lay open or could be bought. The silver belt lies between Wallace and Kellogg, south of the south fork of the Coeur d'Alene River, a region of rounder hills and shallower canyons than Burke, green with timber. Here, minerals caught in myriad small folds and faults do not often show as surface outcrops. The veins tend eastward and westward, marked by greenish rock—"bleached," the geologists call it. All of this differs from the rest of the Coeur d'Alene district, where veins tend northward and southward, rise to wisps of weathered mineral on the surface, and dip downward in purplish or gray rock. Given these variances, it is not surprising that managers who knew the Burke and Wardner mines paid little attention to the dry belt. No comprehensive survey of the area, roughly three by seven miles, was begun until July 1936, when the U.S. Geological Survey sent in its men. By then, company geologists had formed private, guarded theories about the vein structure—and speculators had conjured all kinds of guesses to lure prospective buyers of mining stocks. In the midst of depression, only half a decade after the crash in Wall Street, penny mining stocks of the silver belt sang again the siren call of quick riches.

Even in this boom stage, the silver belt impressed such a hardheaded operator as Newmont Mining Corporation, which applied to its erstwhile partner in exploration, Hecla, for a share of Polaris. Sharing did not sit well with the Milwaukee shareholders who had had Hecla to themselves for so long, but they were outvoted. At their meeting on August 8, 1934, the directors agreed—Mayer and Pellette voting no—to offer Newmont up to 200,000 shares (10 percent) of Polaris, at fifty cents a share. Within a few months, William Hanson resigned as a director, perhaps discouraged that his counsel was ignored, and the redoubtable Fred Searls, Newmont's exploration geologist, came on the Hecla board in his stead.

Searls's election as a director closed out the era of Milwaukee domination, which had been waning since Frank Kipp's death and Carl Landsee's resignation. Although this rumpled little man with his oilcloth bow tie joshed them as one of the boys, the other directors were awed by the self-assured Searls. A globe-trotting engineer, he seemed to know every major figure and field in mining around the world. With Searls as a director and his company a stockholder in Polaris, Hecla entered a working, rather than a paper, alliance with Newmont, based on mutual respect and common interests.

For the time being, the key to Polaris was the Silver Summit, with its tunnel that opened near highway and railroad. One of those old small-beer mines that produced occasionally, Silver Summit had been consolidated with several other claims in 1930.

Sales of penny stock financed a tunnel that would reach the vein about a year later. Silver Summit was one of a half dozen mines promoted in a novel way by W. J. Stratton and his wife. They bonded claims and sold "options," using the income from options to develop the property. If they struck ore, holders of options could trade them for stock. The Strattons were considered droll until one of their prospects hit mineral and was quickly taken by the Days, who renamed it Dayrock. The Strattons had formed a company, Stratton's Consolidated, to operate Silver Summit and four others, but they ran out of money.

Silver Summit lay idle for four years until its vice president, Harry Pearson, offered Hecla an option in mid-1935 which Hecla took up, with another on the Chester, in April 1936. Under Hecla's management, Polaris extended the Silver Summit tunnel to the Polaris shaft and built a small mill near the portal.

The mill, designed to be enlarged if ore production warranted (it would not), went up during the numbing winter of 1935–36. The next year, after Polaris's reorganization as a Delaware corporation, its stock was offered on the New York curb. With loans from Hecla and Newmont, Polaris crosscut into an orebody on the 900 level that it would work profitably for six years. The mill was efficient; it recovered about 98 percent of the silver and copper content of the ores to produce perhaps 75 tons of concentrates a month containing 800 ounces of silver and 18 percent copper per ton, but the concentrates were hard to sell because they also contained antimony and arsenic, which impeded processing. During the first six years of operation, Polaris changed smelters five times: East Helena, Tacoma, El Paso, Tooele, and eventually Sunshine, which treated the ore in an antimony plant next to its concentrator.

While Polaris sank a shaft and built a mill, business conditions improved in the Coeur d'Alenes, although the long-range outlook seemed clouded. In an address to the Idaho Mining Association, McCarthy pointed out that, although as much as 65 percent of the nation's lead had for years gone into paint manufacture, substitutes for lead had been making headway since 1925. Furthermore, federal legislation stalled the expansion of utility companies, which reduced the demand for lead as cable sheathing. In 1935, consequently, after five years of production below capacity, the lead industry still faced a surplus.

On the other hand, the Roosevelt administration had restored a measure of confidence in the nation's markets and banks, put thousands to work on public works projects, and, in mid-1934, enacted a silver purchase bill under which the government bought newly mined silver at $1.29 an ounce, creating a steady market for silver. In retrospect, silver, which had been deflated from 1920–33 and hit its lowest world price in 700 years in 1931, took off on an inflationary incline that now would last forty-six years. Sales to the government enabled Sunshine to declare a single dividend of $1.1 million in 1936, the largest from earnings in the Coeur d'Alenes to that time.

On the surge of silver, lead crept upward to its highest price since 1930. All of this helped Hecla: Polaris stock sales returned a profit of $250,000, lent back to the company for development, and Hecla itself calculated a second-quarter net of $265,661 in 1935, compared with $38,981 in the same quarter of the preceding year.

In the hope of reviving the nation's business, the federal government created the National Recovery Administration (NRA)—one of those alphabet agencies of the thirties—calling for industry to regulate itself with codes of fair competition. McCarthy, Easton, Howard Washburn of Federal, and Harry Day represented the Coeur d'Alene mining companies in formulating a Lead Industries Association and writing a code under the NRA. F. H. Brownell and McCarthy served on the code committee. But, sullied by allegations of code violations and charges of abetting monopoly, the controversial NRA would be declared unconstitutional by the United States Supreme Court. Its effect on the business practices of the lead industry had been negligible.

Under the code, however, employees of various mines formed workers' associations. Hecla's men, who had not been unionized since Mace Campbell's day, adopted an employees' representation plan in August 1933, setting out steps for settling any disputes through representatives of workers and management. Under the cloak of workers' associations, the Burke and Kellogg locals of the Mine, Mill, & Smelter Workers Union revived. (The smelter workers union had been formed when the old Western Federation of Miners split into the Industrial Workers of the World and the Mine, Mill, & Smelter Workers, which reaffiliated with the American Federation of Labor.)

Throughout McCarthy's tenure, Hecla managers had prided themselves on their friendly relations with their men. Mc-

Carthy and Hanley kept their doors open for any man who wanted to talk to them. But the Burke union charged that the Hecla workers' association was simply a company union for which the men signed up because shift bosses had said they would be fired if they did not.

Hecla continued to hire through the central employment agency. The union alleged that the agency maintained a blacklist and that the company dismissed men known to belong to a union. Charging that Hecla refused to meet representatives of the Burke Miners Union No. 10 to discuss grievances, the Mine, Mill, & Smelter Workers brought Hecla (and Sullivan and Bunker Hill) before the National Labor Relations Board's regional arbitration panel, which consisted of Philip Ryan, a union spokesman in the Coeur d'Alenes, Donald Callahan, a close friend of McCarthy, and a political appointee, Fred W. Catlett, Seattle. As might be expected, this board ruled two to one that no men had been discharged from Hecla "as the result of their union activities."

A month later, citing the advice of attorneys, Hecla withdrew from the collective bargaining provisions of the code, as did other mining companies. McCarthy issued a statement that his men "are welcome to confer with representatives of the company . . . and a friendly relationship . . . will be continued." Nonetheless, organized labor notched another foothold in the Coeur d'Alenes after a hiatus of fourteen years.

While mining companies could withdraw from the short-lived NRA, they could not so easily negotiate a truce in their controversy over taxes. Idaho's law taxing the net profits of mines had been lobbied into place by mining companies in 1903 as the least oppressive of the measures proposed. But assessed valuations were another matter. With the advent of large-scale lumbering in Idaho, the mining companies bullied counties to shift the bulk of property taxes to the lumber companies, and, in response, the lumber concerns pressed for taxation of mines.

In Shoshone County, one of the principal timber areas of northern Idaho, the mining companies, by nurturing and tormenting local politicians, reduced their proportion of property taxes from 73 percent in 1907 to 45 percent by 1925. In a general way, with the power of Bunker Hill and Hecla in the Republican camp, and the Day family leading the Democratic, the mining companies held a relatively favored position in the county. Lumber companies from time to time supported the formation of new counties, with the expectation that newly employed assessors would reflect their gratitude on the tax rolls.

But mining companies in Idaho could not directly pressure the federal Internal Revenue Department as they did home-spun office holders. When the 1909 federal excise laws were superseded in 1913 by the sixteenth amendment, authorizing Congress to tax incomes, the complexity and impact of taxation abruptly changed. James McCarthy wrote dozens of his share-holders each year explaining that, although the company was arguing with the federals over the company's tax liability, each was individually responsible for taxes on his or her dividends from Hecla. As a result of long bargaining, Hecla in 1926 in-serted a paragraph in its annual report that would be repeated, in substance, in each following report:

> For Federal tax purposes, dividends are deemed to have been paid from most recently accumulated earnings, and all such earnings must be disbursed before tax-free distributions are per-mitted. Under this rule, in the preparation of your individual income tax return, the entire amount of dividends received from your Company should be entered as subject to surtax.

From the inception of income levies, Hecla challenged fed-eral estimates of its tax liabilities. It took the company until 1923 to settle its tax bills for 1909 through 1918. Hecla some-times prevailed, sometimes not. Three barriers blocked easy compromise: a lack of interpretation of tax laws by the bureau or the courts, Congress's proclivity for changing the rules, and the Supreme Court's slow pace—the Court did not rule until 1916 that depletion was unallowable under the 1909 act.

With regard to depletion, the 1913 law allowed "reasonable" deductions for exhaustion of so-called "wasting" industries, such as mines, but limited depletion to 5 percent of gross output, which would not return the capital invested. A 1916 revision continued deductions but distinguished mines from oil and gas wells, limited depletion claims to the market value of one year's product, and tied total depletion over the life of a mine to its valuation on March 1, 1913. The wartime taxes of 1917 imposed excess profit levies up to 60 percent of net income, and a surtax on income distributed six months or more after the end of a fiscal year (except for surplus invested in Liberty Bonds). In 1918 Congress lumped oil, gas, timber, and mining into one depletion rule and, for the first time, stipulated that additional depletion claims could be made for new discoveries.

True, Congress demonstrated progressive liberality toward claims for depletion of minerals, for the mining industry lobbied through the American Mining Congress and badgered congressmen from mining states for favored tax status. But the mining industry was divided. On the one hand, lead producers were exhausting depletion reserves that had been based on 1913 estimates of the total tonnage a mine would produce during its lifetime. They badly needed relief from this "very complex and uncertain process," as McCarthy termed it. On the other hand, the iron companies "have their affairs settled with the tax authorities," he observed, "and are disinclined to see a change."

Boggled by thickets of regulations, Hecla's directors in 1918 had hired Strowger, manager of the Income Tax Company of Portland, Oregon, to advise and represent them in negotiations with the revenue bureau. Sometimes the directors talked of almost nothing but taxes at their meetings. They considered possible actions—reorganizing the company for tax benefits, or paying out all its income to reduce taxes—until Strowger, after launching these notions as trial balloons in Washington, D.C., advised the board that they could not manipulate tax relief by such steps. A year after the board had talked of reorganizing, Strowger reported at a special stockholders' meeting that the federals had agreed on depletion and depreciation, but not on invested capital, so he could not state how much Hecla owed.

Hecla put away thousands of dollars every year as a hedge against potential taxes, usually by investing in government securities that could be turned in for taxes, if need be. Between 1913 and 1925, the company successfully claimed more than $5.3 million in depletion allowances—not all it asked for. And the company tried other ways to cut taxes: it deducted, for example, the costs of suits against Federal and Marsh over the Russell—a claim the revenue people turned down. If the company lost an appeal of this ruling, McCarthy estimated, Hecla would owe between $150,000 and $200,000 in additional taxes for 1926.

Like other companies, Hecla learned to adjust its business to take into account the effect of federal taxes. For day-to-day advice on taxes, McCarthy came to rely on Leo Hoban, a self-made tax expert. Hoban, had come into Hecla as a stenog-

rapher at age eighteen and had worked for the company summers and vacations while he attended Gonzaga University in
Spokane. He had served two years as an army lieutenant in
World War I before returning to Hecla. An athletic, intense man
with a gift for numbers, Hoban applied himself fiercely to any
topic that caught his interest—and, realizing the importance of
taxes to Hecla, he studied the tax system thoroughly.

Hoban had married the boss's daughter, Anita McCarthy,
and doubtless he meant to show that he progressed by worth,
not nepotism. He was an impatient, abrupt man who drove
employees as he drove himself. When dividends were due, for
example, he insisted that stockholder accounts be tallied on one
errorless calculator tape—no corrections allowed. A wrong total could make a grown man cry. By the thirties, Hoban stood
third in an unofficial line of succession. It was more or less
understood that someday Hanley would succeed McCarthy as
president, and that Hoban would follow Hanley. (A story goes
that when someone whispered to Hoban, in a board meeting,
that his daughter had been born, the directors jocularly resolved that the girl's name should be Hecla Polaris. Kathleen
Hoban has been called Polly ever since.)

A voracious reader, Hoban also emerged as as a spokesman
on taxes for the Coeur d'Alene district; he would testify at
congressional hearings and spend weeks lobbying in the national capital. He also, incidentally, applied himself to golf. On
those days when his game soured, his companions drove him
home in brooding silence. When a physician, diagnosing high
blood pressure, advised more recreation, Hoban relaxed in the
same way he worked: he increased his regular round of golf
from eighteen to thirty-six holes.

In the early thirties (after Congress amended depletion rules
in 1924, 1926, and 1932) Hecla reached a stalemate in its dick-
ering over depletion allowances. It filed suit against the revenue bureau. At issue was an allowance for ores found by accident in 1912, ore "unexpectedly encountered . . . within 30
feet of the old shoot," as McCarthy had told the board in 1914.
If this found ore, which sustained the Hecla for a dozen or
more years, could be regarded as a separate vein, Hecla could
claim a separate depletion allowance for it. But the government
contended that the ore, termed an "intermediate" vein to dis-
tinguish it from the original and the east orebodies, was nothing more than a continuation of a lode and refused to approve

the company's claim for it. To represent the company, Hecla turned to the veteran John Gray, who perhaps understood the geology of the Coeur d'Alenes better than any other lawyer, and to the Milwaukee barrister and director Arthur Pellette. These two old-timers carried their suit through the tax courts to a hearing before a board of appeals in Portland in June 1935. Two years later, the board promulgated its finding: Hecla had indeed "made a statutory discovery," meaning that the intermediate vein was separate and warranted its own depletion allowance.

Hecla could collect $189,600 for depletion for this vein—with interest, the amount came to $196,535—and could raise its depletion rate from 1.33 to 1.39 cents a pound retroactive to its 1928 tax. It was a signal victory, that, for $189,000 represented more than twice the company's net for 1932 or, in 1937, more than the dividends from Polaris and Sullivan together. With this, Hecla could count 1937 as the only year between 1930 and 1941 in which it netted more than $1 million.

In the collective memory of Hecla, the depression years were times of near desperation and near disaster, but Hecla never seemed in danger of failing. During those years the company produced income, although its work week was cut back to three days, and in 1932, at the nadir of the depression, the books showed losses for the second and fourth quarters. The company that year managed only a single dividend of $100,000, its lowest since 1904. The directors waived dividends in other quarters, mostly to put money into developing Polaris or to shore up Sullivan. They cashed Liberty Bonds to pay off a $250,000 loan from the Continental Illinois Bank and Trust which had been used to pay earlier dividends.

For the whole district, 1932 had been the leanest year since 1893; Bunker Hill lost more than $1 million, and Federal, $459,000. Business was looking better by November 1934, when Witherspoon argued for cutting Hecla's dividend to eight cents to avoid "the danger of paying out all current earnings on dividends," and the Milwaukee directors, flexing some of their old sinew, voted instead for a ten-cent dividend.

The depression hit hard the working men and merchants as mines cut back or closed. It punctured the pipe dreams of hundreds betting on the penny stocks of puny companies whose bravado exceeded their ore reserves. Yet a feeling seemed to prevail that the mining companies had done the best they could, for the *Wallace Miner* observed, in all seriousness, that "fortunately for the district, the Hecla management and the management of all the other active mines . . . have been actuated throughout the long depression to provide work for their employees, a policy that cannot be too highly commended."

In hard times, the City of Wallace had financed itself with hush money collected by the chief of police from houses of prostitution, gambling places, and speakeasies; the city disguised the take as fines for traffic violations and other misdemeanors. The town apparently raised five or six thousand dollars a year this way until an auditor challenged its bookkeeping. Forty-five persons were indicted for participating in illegal payoffs. The mayor, former mayor, chief of police, and county sheriff were sentenced to fifteen months in prison. The Wallace Board of Trade adopted a resolution, however, condemning Spokane newspapers for their reporting of the trials of "our public officials who have sought to meet the peculiar conditions surrounding the government of a mining community in an honest and open manner," and denouncing headlines that "make it appear that we live in depraved communities."

In May 1935 Hecla gave its men a five-day week, after Bunker Hill and Federal's Morning and Page mines stepped up operations to five days, and Sunshine, to seven days a week—because, said Hanley, "we are not unmindful of the high cost of living and . . . our employees are receiving less work than those of other properties." Hecla could not sell the mineral produced in a five-day week. It would store until the market improved.

Hecla had used the depression years to look for new mines and to develop those it owned, within its means. The Hecla mine, itself, was deepened. Finally lead prices stirred upward, rising from an average of $4.15 in 1935 to $4.82 per hundred pounds in 1936, and consumption of lead increased, reducing the nation's surplus. With a reviving market, Hecla reopened the Star mine in October 1935 after five and one-half years of idleness.

As 1936 approached and men worked again at the Star, "a feeling of optimism spread over the district," exulted the *Wallace Miner*. "There still remain a number of idle mills . . . but the Star program, coupled with increased activities at the Bunker Hill, Hecla, Morning, Sunshine, Page, and other . . . properties points to a better day."

Before it closed, the Star had consigned ore to Bunker Hill's south mill but that plant now worked to capacity with Bunker Hill output. Consequently, Hecla rented the idle Hercules mill at Wallace which had run intermittently as a custom mill since closure of the Hercules mine in 1924. The Day family refurbished their mill for Star ore to produce 400 tons of concentrates a day and leased it to Hecla. Needed as the mill was, Hecla directors thought the rent was too high. (Income from the lease enabled Hercules to declare a modest dividend in 1936.) McCarthy, too, called the rent "excessive," and the partners in Sullivan concluded that rather than continue to lease, they would build the Star its own mill next to the Hecla plant at Burke. This was an oral agreement, incidentally, not confirmed in writing until 1943. On the strength of a handshake, each partner contributed $150,000 toward a new Star mill.

In December 1936 the Sullivan Mining Company—which had required infusions of capital from its beginning and had sucked up another $750,000 from each partner earlier in 1936—paid its first dividend of $179,482. By that time, Hecla's investment in Sullivan exceeded $3.8 million, at least three times the amount anticipated when Hecla went into the zinc company. The electrolytic zinc plant ran at capacity for the first time since construction, the demand for Bunker Hill brand zinc outstripping the 21,000 tons it produced in a year. The plant also produced cadmium, a very new metal on the market, which would make a place for itself for rustproofing steel, fusable plugs, and strengthening copper wire. The Bunker Hill members of the Sullivan board proposed doubling the size of the zinc plant. Hecla's would not go along but consented, instead, to a 50 percent expansion.

The new Star mill was started in the summer of 1937 and the mine closed again to await its completion. Although modern, it was a conventional mill, laid out vertically on the Burke hillside with three operating levels for crushing and flotation to produce both lead and zinc concentrates. It opened in July 1937 and ran continuously at full capacity until February 1938, when lead and zinc prices fell again and the market for Bunker Hill zinc suddenly faded, leaving the zinc plant with more than one-fourth of its annual output unsold. Half of its expanded capacity of 450 cells stood silent, unused, and unneeded.

Metals markets changed with erratic leaps: lead had opened 1937 in demand at $6, advanced to $7.75, and then plunged to $4.75 before Halloween. In a renewed panic that gripped the nation, investors dumped millions in mining shares. Bunker Hill fell from $15 to $13.50 a share. Hecla dropped from $7.25 to less than $5.38 before rallying late in the year to $10 as the brief recession ran its course. Compounding confusion, the federal government reduced its mandated silver price, and profits of silver companies shrank like sodden woolens.

Surprisingly, the 1937 profits of Coeur d'Alene mining companies—riding the crest of shortlived demand in the first half of the year—exceeded even the wartime windfalls of 1917. In 1932 the total net for the district had amounted to $441,610. Now, five years later, Sunshine alone recorded a profit of $7.1 million. Bunker Hill netted $1.9 million; Hecla, $1.5 million; and Federal's old Morning mine, $1.4 million. They would not repeat in 1938. As the companies closed their ledgers on profitable 1937, James McCarthy gloomily forecast that Hecla and Star must cut back again until they sold concentrates in storage.

In a restless and frightened world—Hitler's Germany had just annexed the Rhineland—the price of lead took a further nosedive. By mid-1938, after Germany's invasion of Austria, lead had slipped to $4.25 a hundred; and within months a reciprocal trade agreement between the United States and Canada, which lowered tariffs 20 percent on Canadian zinc ores and slab, drove the price of zinc below $4.00 a hundred pounds. The Sullivan zinc plant, so recently expanded, fluttered to one-third capacity.

Hecla's profits for 1938 would fall to $718,715, half those of 1937. When state and federal governments claimed 18.85 percent of the company's profit as taxes, McCarthy inserted a petulant sentence in his annual report: "Approximately one day's profit out of each week is required to meet the tax levy and before there can be any profit for the shareholder."

The mining business had achieved a monotonous irregularity—open and close, open and close, pay a dividend, miss a dividend, pay and pass. Leo Hoban mailed Hecla's shareholders a glum letter: "The situation is becoming more acute daily . . . not more than 50 percent to 60 percent of the lead output is being sold," and the zinc plant had 7,700 tons unsold on hand.

No matter how dismal the times, however, managers could not let their businesses wither. Through Newmont, Hecla joined in the rebirth of one of the West's storied mining camps, Leadville, the wintry old silver-lead district two miles above sea level in the mountains eighty miles southwest of Denver. Hundreds of prospectors with nothing better to do had begun to comb the old Colorado camps, with here and there a find and rumors abounding. In a depression, jobless men often turn to working old claims. In its boom days, 1880–97, raw Leadville had lured such noted men as Marshall Field, the Chicago merchant, and Meyer Guggenheim, the erstwhile importer of Swiss embroideries who, with his sons, would become dominant in the lead smelting business in the United States. Leadville had showered eccentrics like H. A. W. Tabor with instant wealth, and it had been a bloody field for union warfare as bitter as that in the Coeur d'Alenes.

Mainly because Fred Searls insisted, Newmont had explored old mines, locating promising orebodies. It took options on a large portion of the Leadville district and approached Hecla to invest in its prospects and operate them. There were already a dozen revived mines dewatered and operating again in Leadville—and the Denver mint was busy weighing gold and silver from historic Cripple Creek, Idaho Springs, Alma, and Leadville—in 1939 when the Hecla directors bought stock in the Resurrection Mining Company, named for an old dig about five miles east of Leadville. The camps were, said a writer, a "wondrous hodgepodge of obsolete and modern"—trucks and mules, power drills and picks, weathered buildings occupied again, cobwebs swept away, and windows patched.

For a time, the costs of exploring the Resurrection gobbled most of its income. In 1940, just about the time Newmont applied to list its stock on the New York Stock Exchange, the United States Smelting Company came into Resurrection as a third partner, helping to finance a mill. During fourteen years Hecla would invest $643,000 in Resurrection. Newmont put in a similar amount. In the long run, Resurrection produced a net of roughly $200,000. When the commercial ore ran out, Newmont offered to buy all of the Resurrection stock or to sell its shares. Both Hecla and U.S. Smelting sold their shares to Newmont for $500,000. For Hecla, the selling price represented a book loss, but the company had received $343,579 in dividends over the life of the mine and, as its chief geologist reflected, had gained experience "in reopening and operating an old water-filled, partially caved early-day mine." That experience might be useful in the future.

In the late thirties, James McCarthy occasionally missed a directors' meeting. He was not feeling well. Now in his seventies and beginning to shed some of the obligations of years, McCarthy was a man deeply committed to his company, his community, and his church. He had served on the Wallace School Board and the Gonzaga University and University of Idaho Board of Regents. He had been vice president of the First National Bank of Wallace and treasurer of the Coeur d'Alene Hardware & Foundry, which dealt in mining equipment throughout the West. With Harry Day, he had been a leading contributor to St. Alphonsus Church in Wallace, a member of the committee for a new building in 1926—and had raised Day's hackles by accepting the low bid, not from a Catholic contractor, but from a Mason.

Anastasia McCarthy had died in 1936. McCarthy had taken a long vacation from Wallace after his wife's death and, during his absence, had his house remodeled with the understanding that Leo Hoban, Anita, and their three children, would live with him.

McCarthy's sons, James and Joseph, had attended Gonzaga. Like a number of Catholic men in the mining towns, McCarthy had given money to the university from time to time. Gonzaga awarded him its DeSmet Medal in 1936 as an outstanding Catholic layman, and McCarthy nursed a hope that he could "do something big" for Gonzaga. Consequently, in the spring of 1939, he invited the university's president, Father Leo J. Robinson, S.J., to dine with him at the Davenport Hotel. McCarthy offered Robinson a gift of $25,000, which he had obtained as a personal loan from the Old National Bank. McCarthy's gesture seemed an answer to earnest prayers, for the university, nearly overwhelmed by old debts for construction, was struggling to keep open its doors. The $25,000 enabled Robinson to retire a large portion of old bonds at bargain rates. He regarded the gift as the turning point that saved the school.

By the close of that insecure decade of the thirties, a new Hecla Mining Company was emerging. Arthur Pellette died in 1940, to be succeeded by Wilbur I. Barth, a Milwaukee banker. Someone quipped unkindly that the Milwaukee directors' main chore now was "to bring booze for the meetings." As a matter of fact, the Milwaukee contingent rarely appeared without gifts for the board. As confidence in the stock market returned, many Milwaukee shareholders sold their Hecla stock to put their money in less mercurial businesses.

Hecla's association with Newmont had given the directors certainty that, with perseverance and luck, they could find another mine to keep the company going when the Hecla mine bottomed. Polaris, Union, and Resurrection had eventually repaid their investments with modest profits, but none had proved to be the long-lived mine that would carry the company forward. Neither the Omaha nor the Helene, claims in which Hecla had been interested, yielded commercial ores. In February 1940 the board framed a resolution to be offered for a shareholders' vote at the annual meeting: "Whereas . . . every reasonable effort should be made to prolong the life of the company as an operating enterprise, now . . . the management shall be authorized to continue to search for . . . and invest in properties . . . which are promising."

They intended their resolution to allay fears for the company's future when its principal mine, the Hecla, played out. That could be expected within five or six years. But the directors doubtless meant to declare, as well, that the company would go on with new management, for they knew what most shareholders did not, that the man who had directed Hecla for thirty-seven years lay gravely ill in Sacred Heart Hospital in Spokane.

For decades Hecla had relied on James F. McCarthy's steady hand. Now his stewardship was at an end. McCarthy died on March 6, 1940. He was buried from St. Aloysius Church on the Gonzaga University campus, at a large funeral attended by faculty and students in academic gowns. In their resolution on his passing, the Hecla directors saluted McCarthy's "firmness of character, his inflexible consciousness for the right, and his . . . gentleness and moderation of spirit." Stanly Easton remembered McCarthy as the "perfect Christian gentleman."

7

Hanley

LEWIS EUGENE HANLEY AT SIXTY, FELT HE WAS TOO OLD TO be president of Hecla. But largely because Fred Searls wanted him to, he took the place vacated by James McCarthy's death. Hanley was the son of a one-time sheriff and hotel man, Thomas F. Hanley, and the nephew of Kennedy Hanley, whose long court battle with Charles Sweeny was mining-country legend. A bright graduate of Wallace High School and the University of Idaho, Lew Hanley had joined Hecla as an assayer and bookkeeper shortly after McCarthy. As the company grew, both Hanley and McCarthy had moved to Wallace. Hanley had become secretary when McCarthy was made president and general manager, and then, in 1923, Hanley had gone back to Burke as superintendent of mines.

He was an elemental gear in Hecla's administration throughout McCarthy's presidency. On those afternoons when McCarthy was not visiting Burke, Hanley would come down to Wallace to talk over the day's business. If he and McCarthy ever disagreed on how to run the mine, no one else heard of it. It was not surprising, therefore, that Hanley's eleven years as president would tend to elongate McCarthy's shadow over Hecla, for as president, Hanley would do what he thought McCarthy would have done.

Balding, a little paunchy, with straight features and rimless glasses, Lew Hanley was plain and unpretentious. His mine workers idolized him; he slipped them money when they were broke, got them out of scrapes, nursed them through bad times, knew their families, and understood them. As president, Hanley usually walked to the Elks Club about 11:30 every morning for lunch and pinochle, but he was back at his desk when the miners came off shift so they could drop in to talk—and they did, sometimes grimy from work, sometimes angry, and sometimes merely to pass time.

McCarthy had cared about the men, too, but his innate dignity kept them at a respectful distance. Hanley was an old shoe, chewing on his cigar, in his shirt sleeves, coat draped over a chair. Stories went around about him and his men: one asked to borrow $100 for an abortion because he had gotten a girl pregnant, but Hanley lent him $100 to marry her, instead. The clerks overheard him bawling out a miner who had gone on a spree and punched a policeman. "I don't care if you get drunk and miss a couple of shifts," Hanley was saying, "but you can be a gentleman about it!"

At his first meeting as president, Hanley automatically signed his name to the minutes as secretary, as he had been doing for thirty years. He had to scratch out "secretary" and write "president," and Leo Hoban, who had signed the open president's space, lined that out and wrote in "secretary."

Hanley did not volunteer for committee work in industry associations, as McCarthy had, but he was serious about his responsibility to Hecla. He represented the company in the best way he knew, wherever he went. Mining men learned that he was steady and shrewd. No one had to remind Hanley that his twin challenges as president were to pay dividends and to find another mine. Because he thought he was getting old, Hanley also resolved privately to deliver Hecla intact within a few years to someone else to manage.

Hecla was on the verge of becoming a holding company, as the board acknowledged at its meeting on August 6, 1940. Alluding to surplus funds and "the changing character of Hecla's operations from a strictly operating company to a holding company," they believed Hecla ought to invest some of its money in the stock of other mining companies—solid ones. They directed Hanley to buy shares of stable properties, especially the stocks of Bunker Hill and Newmont, if he could put his hands on them.

On August 8, the German Luftwaffe started nightly bombings of London, preparing for an invasion of England. Nineteen days later the U.S. Congress authorized inducting the National Guard into the armed forces. In mid-September they voted for compulsory military service. Hanley had hoped against a war, with its voracious demand for metals, its government controls, and before long, its incessant draft calls that took away his miners. In World War I, Hecla—like other mining companies—had thrown prudence aside for profit while lead prices were high. Now this war might speed the end of the Hecla mine.

But it did not. Conversely, World War II lengthened the life of Hecla by a few months because the company could not hire enough men to dig it out. Unlike the bonanza months of World War I, this war neither depleted ore reserves nor showered profits on the mines, because no mine could hire enough men to run at capacity after the first eight months of 1942—and because the government imposed price controls hitched ostensibly to "normal" production.

Gaps in the work force had shown in the mines late in the thirties, when skilled younger men had decamped for higher pay with builders holding cost-plus contracts for defense construction. By the end of 1941, machinists, mechanics, and skilled workmen of all kinds had largely deserted the mines for shipyards and airplane factories. Hundreds of others were drafted. A modest influx of less skilled men from southern and midwestern states did not fill their places. On the other hand, when the federal government proposed allocating workers, many Northwest communities refused to accept blacks, electing instead to forego defense projects and putting up with antediluvian artisans.

The Coeur d'Alene mines raised wages in March and again in September 1941 to $7 for miners, $8 for shaftmen, and $8.25 for main hoistmen, the highest paid categories, and promised bonuses when the price of lead rose. But higher pay did not produce many men. By the fall of 1942 Idaho and Washington were among twelve states designated as "critical labor areas," where men in the mining and timber industries could leave their jobs only with permission from a local employment service office.

For a time, soldiers furloughed for ninety days from training camps were assigned to work in mines. Although many were coal miners without hardrock experience, and a number refused to go underground, they "helped materially," Hanley said, "but are not yet full handed." The annual reports of the mining companies for the war years echoed Hecla's for 1943: "The lack of sufficient men and the general inefficiency of what replacements we could get hampered all operations and delayed all construction work." Before long the government resorted to closing marginal mines to release men for larger producers.

Warily, Hecla hired a few women for office work—the first female employees since World War I. Until Ruby Sinrud took her desk on December 18, 1941, the secretaries, switchboard operators, clerks, and everyone else at Hecla had been male. Hecla often hired promising high school boys during vacations, with the idea that some would work their way up through the company. Ruby displaced one of these, Harry F. Magnuson, from the switchboard. On her first morning a foreman from Gem, startled by this unfamiliar voice on the telephone, demanded, "What's the matter, Maggie? You got a cold?" In a time when there wasn't much to laugh at, that gave Hecla a chuckle.

The company had sent Ruby a telegram to come to work— that was customary—and at eighteen, slender, blond, with a year or so of college and a few months in a law office, she became Leo Hoban's secretary, taking her turn at the switchboard. Hoban awed her with his precise manner and quick intellect. He once enjoined her to be more "meticulous" in her work. She had to look up the word. Ruby, considered experienced, was paid $100 a month. Soon nearly a dozen women worked at Hecla, no longer feeling shyly singular, even though male eyes followed them down the long corridor between offices. Hanley put hard hats on them and had them tour the mine, so they would have a better idea what Hecla did.

In general, Hecla men treated the women courteously. Men wore suits with ties, although they usually removed their coats on warm days, and women were expected to wear dresses. They balked only at climbing a ladder to the supply room until Hanley, with his sidewise grin, ruled that those who used the ladder might wear slacks. Magnuson, grumping that all the menial tasks ought not be dumped on women, often took Ruby's place at the paper pulverizer in the basement, where diagrams and reports were shredded daily. A ping pong table appeared in the basement for play during the lunch hour. With Elof Enbom, Ruby conducted a gossipy mimeographed newsletter, the "Heclan," for men who had gone into military service. In such unassuming ways, women changed the once-male ambience of Hecla.

Even with a shortage of miners, however, the Hecla mine inexorably approached its end. Before abandoning the mine,

Hanley ordered extensive diamond drilling, but he found no new ore. "Operations at the Hecla Mine were carried on throughout the year 1943 and will continue on a small output basis for about six months in 1944," he advised stockholders in his 1943 report. "No new ore of any importance was found and only lack of manpower prevented complete removal of ore reserves during the year."

The mine crew hoisted the last tonnage on July 31, 1944. Bottomed at 3,600 feet, Hecla would be allowed to fill with water to the 2000 level, which would be kept open to continue working the Star. In its four decades as a producing mine, the Hecla had yielded 9,050,977 tons of ore, from which the company realized $81.3 million in net smelter returns. Hanley offered a simple, unsentimental statement in his 1944 report: "As predicted in our last annual report, the ore remaining in the Hecla Mine at Burke was worked out during the past year."

As he prepared to batten the Hecla, Hanley reminded the board that the company had "a number of superannuated employees . . . kept on the Hecla payroll although it had been recognized . . . they were not the most efficient type of employees. . . . The Hecla is no longer in a position to give these men work which they were able to do." He recommended pensioning them. The directors approved.

With their mine closed, Hecla turned to another source of ores—approximately four million tons of tailings from Canyon Creek concentrating mills which had been accumulating for forty-one years in the riverbed and on bulldozed flats beside the south fork of the Coeur d'Alene River where its valley widened at Osburn. Here in 1901 the mine owners jointly had built a dam for mill waste, to prevent clogging the river and to blunt lawsuits by farmers who alleged that polluted water harmed their crops and cattle.

Hecla built an Osburn mill, one of the nation's largest for reworking tailings. Designed by Vern Zeigler as an automated plant requiring only five men, it processed 2,800 tons daily by flotation—using a millfeed of tailings that contained about 2 percent lead and 2 percent zinc, delivered by a dumpster that poured eighteen tons into the mill every ten minutes. The $250,000 mill, near the center of tailings deposits on an old range leased from local gun clubs, started up about April 1, 1943. It would run for five years, making a profit each year, from $224,643 in its first, to more than $1 million in 1945.

By extending its field to lower-grade tailings on the edge of the valley, the Osburn plant actually treated more than 3.9 million tons. It was processing the fringes of the dump and was about to be closed when it burned on Christmas night, 1948. For some time, the Gem mill also had been running on tailings. In his letter telling the directors about the fire, Hanley noted that he took "considerable ribbing" from mine managers who pretended to think he burned the plant to be rid of it. Not true. He had leased it, only a few days before the fire, to Zanetti Brothers for one year. The mill stood on Hecla's books as a fire insurance gain of $196,816.

The short-lived success of the tailings plant aside, Sullivan and Polaris generated Hecla's principal income during the forties. While zinc was controlled during the war, Sullivan paid Hecla dividends of $250,000 a year; with controls lifted, Sullivan paid from $500,000 to $750,000 annually. It seemed healthy at last after years of transfusions of capital to keep it going.

On the other hand, Polaris paid only $37,935 in 1942 and nothing the next year, using its money for development rather than dividends. The main orebody had bottomed out at the 2300 level. As early as 1938 Hanley had been talking with Sunshine about extending its deeper workings into the Polaris to see if it might uncover new ore, hoping to lay to rest those old ghosts chattering of shallow veins in the silver belt. To Hanley, to Ross D. Leisk, manager of Sunshine, and doubtless to others, their underground searches confirmed that they all seemed to be working parts of the same vein (later called the Sunshine-Polaris vein system) and they were not sure of its extent or depth. The area is broken by faults, folds, slips, and so on, and the major faults, the Syndicate and Chester, divide along the strike into three segments, the Rambo, Omega, and Rotbart, areas defined by agreements to establish ownership and operating rights. (The names are those of old claims.) When Leisk, a wiry, stooped, slow-talking man who seemed always to squint through round glasses, came up from Arizona to Sunshine in 1936, he had found the company defending one lawsuit and threatened by another alleging trespass. In the early days of the Coeur d'Alenes, costly litigation over mineral rights had bankrupted some companies and cost them their ground. Leisk could envision reenacting the expensive folly of apex suit piled on suit.

Rather than contend, Leisk and Hanley cooperated by establishing an Intervening Area in 1939 to provide for development below the Polaris orebody and between it and Sunshine. By late 1942, Sunshine had extended its 2700 level's east drift and explored the dip extension of the Polaris veins but found only a few insignificant ore shoots. Whispers at the rumor resorts, the Elks Club and Pennaluna brokerage, speculated that Polaris had dug all its mineral. At the end of the year, the Polaris reserves had shrunk to 15,000 tons in the Intervening Area. There was no more.

As a last try—there seemed nowhere else to look—Hanley had Sunshine drive northward to check out the Chester vein, "the last nail in the Polaris' coffin," the seers scoffed, because the Chester had not shown much at upper levels. By intuition or luck, the bore hit spectacular ore, ten feet wide, assaying 24 percent lead and 125 ounces of silver—"dream ore," Hanley chortled. The vein increased in size as the crews drifted on it, until they ran into the lines of Silver Dollar.

Polaris had paid three cents a share in June 1942. Nothing since. Vindicated, in March 1944, the company declared a dividend of ten cents. For the rest of the forties, Polaris would pay Hecla dividends each year, from a low of $189,675 in 1947 and again in 1949, to a high of $379,350 in 1944 and 1945.

To avoid lawsuits, the president of Sunshine, brusque Robert M. Hardy, and its manager, Leisk, worked out agreements with the companies around them to share the costs of mining and the returns from specific areas. In effect, neighboring mines or areas became units of one enterprise operated by Sunshine—Polaris included—and each would pay costs and share profits in proportion to the mineral it owned. (These operating units were unitized in 1958 into the Sunshine Unit Area.) Cooperating also saved the costs of duplicating surface works and mills. Unit agreements would be extended, particularly by large companies, into other crowded corridors of the district.

In the coming years, Sunshine's contracts would take in others, but in 1943 and 1944, when operating agreements were novel, the important contracts provided that Sunshine and Polaris would share the Omega; they, with Silver Dollar (which paid Lincoln a royalty), the Rotbart; and Sunshine and Silver Syndicate would share the Rambo. Hanley described the Sunshine-Polaris compact to his board in November 1943 as fixing "the limits of the area to be mined, under a three-way division of profits, east of the easterly line of the Rambo."

After the discovery of rich ore at 2,700 feet, dispelling finally any suspicion that silver-belt veins were shallow, Hanley urged his board to explore deeper in the silver belt, using the Silver Summit tunnel, and driving the Silver Summit shaft down from 1,500 to 3,000 feet. At that depth, the company could poke out crosscuts like fingers feeling for an orebody. Work on a three-compartment shaft started late in 1945. With a clamshell mucking machine used in shaft sinking for the first time, the Hecla-Polaris crews sank 1,596 feet in eleven months and eight days, an average of roughly 160 feet a month, said to be a record speed. Then crews drove crosscuts north and south from the bottom of the shaft.

Within six months, Hanley sent George F. Mayer a jubilant, barely restrained letter: "We cut a nice-looking vein in the south cross-cut from the Silver Summit. . . . A small amount of ore doesn't make a mine . . . and the publicity . . . has been on the exaggerated side." Mayer could read between the lines: Hanley would not have written if he did not think the strike promising. This was the younger Mayer, who had followed his father, George P. Mayer, into insurance and had inherited an interest in his family's boot and shoe business. He had come on the Hecla board in September 1942, after the death of his father, who was at that time the Hecla director with the most years of service. The elder Mayer, his colleagues recalled, had succeeded Sarah Smith.

Mayer's was the first of three deaths in five years that altered the character of the Hecla board. The Milwaukee banker, Barth, died in February 1946; Clarence Kipp, in October 1947. In Kipp's place, the shareholders elected his son-in-law, Milwaukee attorney Seth Pollard; in Barth's, James McCarthy's older son, Joseph L. McCarthy, who had entered his in-laws' mercantile and lumber business at Orofino, Idaho.

Milwaukee representation fell to two of seven members, the first time since 1891 that Milwaukee directors held less than a strong minority. Mayer voted 2,700 shares; Pollard, 100. The strength of the board passed to Hecla officers: Lewis Hanley, Leo Hoban, and Archibald Witherspoon, the Spokane attorney who was also vice president. Fred Searls missed most of the board meetings: as a wartime consultant on minerals to the federal government, director of a survey of strategic bombing in Europe, then an alternate delegate to the United Nations Atomic Energy Commission, Searls could rarely break away to

Wallace. He became president of Newmont in 1947. When he did attend, he customarily voted with the company's managers, and with Searls's and Joseph McCarthy's votes, management dominated the board.

The spirit of the board was comradely, and Mayer and Pollard were popular members. Their jolly pilgrimages to Wallace usually meant a few days in Spokane where, at Hoban's request, stockbroker Ben Harrison took them to the city's private clubs with slot machines. Mayer and Pollard bought and sold mining stocks through Harrison, as well, and from their small talk the broker learned a good deal about Hecla. His impression was that Hoban "practically ran the company." Hanley worried that he should retire, and Hoban surely could anticipate an invitation to the presidency.

With succession in mind, Hoban privately concluded that Hecla employed few, if any, young men who might manage the company after him. In his decisive way, he chose his own—ambitious young Harry Magnuson, whom he had brought into Hecla out of high school, the bright son of old neighbors. Magnuson went to college, partly during his navy service, and after his discharge, completed a master's degree in business administration at Harvard that he had begun in the navy. Then he came back to Hecla in June 1947. He was clearly Hoban's protegé. Hoban set him to reading files—old letters, balance sheets, and reports—for a thorough grounding in the company. Magnuson was, he would recall, "a sort of assistant to Hoban to learn what I could." And Hoban told him, "Harry, you stay here and study and learn and there's going to be a good role for you."

But Leo Hoban's vision for Hecla would never come to pass. On June 16, 1948, he went to a Pioneer Day picnic at Mullan. Shortly after, he was rushed to a hospital in acute pain, apparently from a long-standing gall-bladder disorder. He died on the operating table, aged fifty-six, after twenty-eight years with Hecla. In a letter to the directors telling them of Hoban's death, Hanley recommended that Ralph W. Neyman, their mine superintendent, replace Hoban on the board.

Neyman, forty-nine, was an innovator. He had learned mechanical and mining engineering by correspondence. After joining Hecla in 1930, he designed specialized machines, including an ore turntable, an automatic-dump mine car, a "side-stepper" transfer allowing cars to pass in tunnels, and an automatic-dumping skip for lowering ore in shafts. He published articles on his inventions in trade journals, attracting notice for his work throughout hardrock mining. Neyman devised timbering suited to the Star's heavy ground, and he supervised construction of Star's underground hoist room. In short, by mechanical ingenuity, he contributed to Hecla's repute as a progressive company. He was also one of Hanley's frequent companions at the Elks' bar.

For Neyman, Hoban's unexpected death meant opportunity: advanced to the board, with Hanley muttering of retirement, he could dare think of himself as presidential timber. For Harry Magnuson, opportunity soured. The directors respected Magnuson's ability and promise, but they thought him too new to the company and too young to step immediately into Hoban's place. Wanting a man who knew mining taxes, they settled on one outside the company: Lester J. Randall, a lean, intense man, proprietor of a Wallace accounting firm with important mining clients. Randall had consulted with Hecla on tax matters, but he was surprised, he would remember, to be invited to come into the company.

On the day Randall's appointment as comptroller was announced, September 1, 1948, Harry Magnuson resigned. With money from his mother, his lifelong confidant and business adviser, he set himself up as a public accountant in an office upstairs from Hecla in the Gyde-Taylor building. Randall attempted to continue his private accounting practice as associate with a Spokane firm, but shortly before Thanksgiving, he offered to sell Magnuson a half interest. Harry's mother again put up the money, and Magnuson became a business partner, pupil, and warm friend of the man whose hiring had prompted him to leave Hecla. The Randalls would, in fact, be godparents to the Magnusons' first child, a daughter.

His first review of Hecla's balance sheets alarmed Randall. Although the company had paid dividends of $1 million, by his reckoning it had actually lost about $400,000 in 1947. Its ore sales and custom milling receipts fell below $300,000. Its major revenue—dividends from Sullivan, Polaris, and Resurrection amounting to more than $1 million—seemed unlikely to go on. Hecla owned 50 percent of Sullivan, 63 of Polaris, and 33 of Resurrection, exercising only limited control over these properties. The stocks of these three appeared on the books as assets valued roughly at $5 million on the market, but Hecla would soon sell its Resurrection at a loss. The tailings mill was ending its run. Hecla lent money to Polaris, and Polaris, to Silver Summit. One of Randall's first recommendations, that Silver Summit be merged into Polaris, was carried out.

Randall worried that, if the zinc market softened, Sullivan might again call on Hecla for substantial cash contributions. He urged Hecla's directors to consider exchanging the company's interest in the zinc plant for Bunker Hill stock to relieve Hecla of potential demands for cash.

The controlling factor in Hecla's financial position was, of course, the lack of a long-lived, large mine like the old Hecla from which the company could regulate production according to the market. The company had certainly looked for new mines but Hanley's reports merely echoed 1942: "New properties are being examined regularly but . . . few have been found that justify development."

Not only were good mines hard to find but other companies competed for them. With the end of wartime price controls and production quotas, and with the extension of federal silver purchases, a mild boom puffed the Coeur d'Alenes, not a flourish of lone prospectors combing the hills as in the old times, but of large companies stalking smaller to seize. When Hecla's directors voted a dividend in November 1946, they put on the record their "due regard for the fact that the Hecla is carrying on a vigorous campaign to purchase or discover new mines."

While rumors went around that this big national company or that one was scanning the district for prospects, most of the ferreting in the Coeur d'Alenes fell to "the big five," as a newspaper writer called them: Bunker Hill, Sunshine, Day, Federal, and Hecla. They searched by underwritten subsidiaries, by co-operative exploration projects, and by advances in exchange for stock in small companies that had exhausted their treasuries. The district had spurted after the war. There were now thirty-four concentrating mills (all flotation), a third of them less than four years old, and twenty-four active mines with an aggregate net in 1948 of $10.4 million, more than double that of 1946. Prices were up and men more plentiful, although dam construction on northwest rivers siphoned off some of the most skilled.

The expansion of mining stretched the towns at their seams. New residential districts sprang up at Silverton, Pinehurst, Elk Creek, and the Sunnyside addition to Kellogg.

Before McCarthy's death, Hanley, Pellette, and Witherspoon had settled a contract with Atlas, a cluster of fifty-nine claims and a millsite south of Mullan. Hecla took an option on 51 percent and agreed to explore. (McCarthy had stayed out of negotiations because he owned stock in Atlas.) The Atlas president, W. Earl Greenough, had formed the company in the twenties by consolidating four old mines; he had driven a tunnel by assessments and in 1933 had held control despite a stockholders' revolt against continued assessments. He wanted Hecla to come in, he told his people, because "the Hecla management is honest and has ability and experience . . . [and] large financial resources."

During 1940 Hecla had sunk an 800-foot shaft from the Atlas tunnel but, after running 1,300 feet of crosscuts, found nothing and gave up its option at the end of 1941. Greenough, an attorney turned mine operator, left the district for employment with a federal agency during the war, so Hecla watched over Atlas as caretaker. With wartime shortages of equipment and supplies, the idle Atlas took in a few thousand dollars by selling its cable and salvaged equipment. A lessee found some commercial ore above the tunnel, renewing hope that Atlas might still warrant developing. When Greenough returned, he spent the $8,000 or so realized from equipment sales, busied himself writing a history of the district, and died in June 1947 without resuming Atlas operations. His brother, Roger W. Greenough, taking the company reins, consented to a new contract for deep development of the Atlas jointly by Hecla, Newmont, and New Jersey Zinc, who together agreed to invest $1 million in their search.

They doubtless shared the growing sentiment that ores lay at great depths along the Coeur d'Alene River valley. Nearly 550 new claims had been filed in the area. Asarco, with Day Mines, had gambled with a 3,000-foot thrust downward from the old Galena shaft—renamed the Vulcan—west of Wallace. But the fickle Atlas again yielded nothing. Newmont pulled out. So did New Jersey Zinc. And Hecla, after years of trying to show that the property would make a mine, dropped Atlas again.

On the other hand, Silver Cable, on the Montana side of the Bitterroot Mountains about eight miles east of Mullan, contained known orebodies. The mine had been located by prospectors trapped there by forest fires in 1910. Painfully burned, they walked out across smoldering hillsides after the flames passed. Hecla leased the Silver Cable in 1942 from its owners, Montana investors and the widow of James Corbett, once Missoula County sheriff. Although the Silver Cable was snowed in and unworkable for three or four months each year, it produced ores for the Gem mill during most of the forties and returned a modest profit before it was worked out.

And there was the Blue Moon in California, a small mine leased by Hecla that showed small profits as long as it lasted. Such properties sometimes came to Hecla as the result of conversations at mining conventions—like blind dates. If a prospect sounded inviting, the company would ask its chief geologist, Robert E. Sorenson, to look at it. The Blue Moon, with a relatively shallow shaft, showed good ore at 385 feet, and Hecla invested $293,637 in advances and stock.

After a couple of years of production, however, the mine caved in. It had virtually repaid its costs and was not worth reopening. Hecla abandoned it.

Because the notion lingered that rich ores lay undiscovered under their noses, the mining companies of the Coeur d'Alenes rooted on the fringes of the district. Geological theory suggested that the Osburn fault, the major structural feature, had shifted twelve to fourteen miles in eons past. If this were so, an easterly extension of the silver belt might lie about as far from Mullan as Sunshine from Bunker Hill. This reasoning had led to the Atlas exploration. But perhaps—maybe—Hecla had not looked far enough. After months of negotiations, the company in 1946 acquired 131 claims and took options on others in the Rock Creek drainage a few miles southeast of Wallace, seven miles east of Polaris and Silver Summit. Rock Creek, at six square miles, was one of the largest fiefdoms of one company.

"One of the biggest deals in recent years," the *Wallace Miner* said of Rock Creek, adding that the area was "believed to be the eastern extension of the silver belt, practically undeveloped territory." Hecla formed a subsidiary, Rock Creek Mining Company, with 3,000,000 shares, of which 1,500,000 went to former owners for their ground. Hanley warned his board that a Rock Creek dig would "cost considerable," but they could not disregard the tantalizing chance that Hecla might rouse another Sunshine sleeping under the piney hills.

To explore the treed, brushy inclines and sharp ridges that

drained into Rock Creek, Sorenson first rented a bulldozer to break a seven-mile road and jeep trails so that his men would not need to hike from two to four hours, carrying packs, to reach work sites. Then, to save costs, he prospected the surface with an eleven-foot bulldozer mounted to an International crawler tractor, cutting just below the brows of ridges and trenching likely slopes—gouges eight- to twelve-feet deep in most places, and in a few, twenty-five feet deep and forty-feet wide, to bare the bedrock where geologists could study structure and sample mineralization.

In two summers, the roaring bulldozer chewed fourteen miles of roads and nearly six of trenches at a cost of less than $13,000. Behind it tramped the geologists, correlating what they found in trenches with showings in a tunnel driven roughly parallel to one of the main ridges. On the basis of Sorenson's observations, Hanley reported to Hecla's stockholders that "mineralization is stronger on the tunnel level than it is on the surface," raising hope that mineral might improve with depth. "The results" he added, "compared favorably with similar developments at shallow horizons in the Silver Summit," but before tunneling further, his men would use the bulldozer and diamond drills for more analysis of the surface. At this point, the end of 1948, Hecla had gambled $378,467 in loans and stock for the Rock Creek Mining Company.

Although surface samplings implied mineral somewhere below, the costs of underground exploration would be high. "Excessive," said Fred Searls when he sat with the other directors, after Hecla had burrowed for two years along Rock Creek, to consider what they might do next. Searls looked carefully through the tunnel and stalked over the trenches. While he did not disparage Rock Creek, he said bluntly that perhaps Hecla should invest in mining stocks "rather than to continue speculative development at the present high prices." If Hecla proposed to continue searching in Rock Creek, Searls recommended that it go back to the Atlas and use that shaft for deep exploration.

Searls's opinion carried weight. The bankers and attorneys among Hecla's directors were hesitant to challenge his opinions of mines. Hanley pointed out that Richard N. Hunt, chief geologist for the United States Smelting & Refining Company, was sending two geologists to inspect Rock Creek. If men of international standing were interested, it seemed too soon to give up on Rock Creek. Hecla offered Newmont and New Jersey Zinc shares of Rock Creek to come in as partners. Neither accepted. By the end of 1950, Hecla had sunk more than $408,000 in trying to find an easterly extension of the silver belt, and the Rock Creek subsidiary was out of money. No commercial ore had turned up. Five years later, Hecla would sell its six square miles of Rock Creek at a loss.

For most of the forties, the Sullivan's dividends accounted for the largest part of Hecla's income. Bunker Hill was also looking for new mines. As it assessed zinc sources for the Sullivan plant, Bunker Hill was intrigued with the Pend Oreille Mines & Metals Company in northeastern Washington which worked large deposits of low-grade zinc. Pend Oreille was the child of two immigrant Danes; its president, Lewis P. Larsen, and secretary-treasurer, Jens Jensen. Opinion varies to this day whether the two were promoters or miners, although Hecla's people would come to believe that neither man possessed more than a rudimentary knowledge of geology—and neither could read a balance sheet.

Larsen, a farmer, had learned his mining by working in the Coeur d'Alenes for several years beginning in 1897. He prospected the relatively untouched hills of northeastern Washington where in 1906 he located the Josephine claim, adding others as time went by. He had no practical means of exploiting his prospects until 1909, when the Idaho & Washington Northern Railroad reached the vicinity. The railroad's president, F. A. Blackwell, bought Larsen's rights to clay, lime, and shale deposits for a cement factory at Metaline Falls.

Larsen borrowed money to explore and build a small mill for the Josephine. Jensen was also employed as an occasional agent for the purchase of white-pine stumpage for the Diamond Match Company. In 1926 the two organized the Pend Oreille Lead-Zinc Company, selling about $400,000 worth of preferred stock, and giving common to buyers of preferred or peddling it on the Spokane exchange for about thirty-five cents a share. Two officers of Consolidated Mining & Smelting Company of Canada bought stock expressly to enable the two Danes to renovate their mill.

Few people had heard of Pend Oreille until February 1928, when manipulators on the Vancouver Stock Exchange picked Pend Oreille as the Judas goat for a stock-kiting scheme, whispering that Consolidated men bought because Pend Oreille was unexpectedly rich. (Neither Larsen nor Jensen was involved in the manipulation.) Pend Oreille's stock rocketed to five dollars in days and soared on to $25 a share in one month. A Canadian mining journal guessed that Pend Oreille "seems to have been engineered by the same gang that worked the market for Coast Copper . . . hoodwinking the public with the high standing of Consolidated Mining & Smelting," and demanded a provincial inquiry into "the manner in which Washington and Idaho stocks have been boomed on British Columbia markets."

The common stock that Larsen and Jensen had given away now changed hands in frenzied trading. Within weeks, majority holdings of the two founders reached a paper value of more than $5 million. Larsen took the opportunity to buy an English colonial home on five acres in Spokane for $30,000. By the time the manipulation ran its course, Pend Oreille Lead-Zinc was well known, if not favorably so, in the mining markets. The next year, Larsen and Jensen changed its name to Pend Oreille Mines & Metals.

When zinc fell on hard times in the thirties, the company barely stayed afloat. It netted less than $20,000 in 1933; in 1938, only $15,435. The Danes reorganized the board, naming Archibald Witherspoon vice president. They shipped ores, part of them to Bunker Hill. Thus the Bunker Hill people became familiar with Pend Oreille ores, estimating that they generally carried about 5 percent zinc, and as metals revived in the forties, they recommended to Hecla that Sullivan buy a substantial interest in Pend Oreille.

Hecla's geologist, Sorenson, went over the Pend Oreille ground carefully in 1945. The next year, Bunker Hill, Hecla, and Sullivan all bought Pend Oreille stock on the open market and started quiet bargaining with Larsen and Jensen. Immediately Pend Oreille stock commenced to rise from about $2.35, and Hecla stopped buying. "But by that time," Hanley growled, "it seemed to be common knowledge in Spokane that a deal was on for Pend Oreille."

Negotiations with Larsen and Jensen went on for two years, during which they acquired 59.41 percent of the Reeves MacDonald mine on the Canadian side of the border. Finally the two agreed that Sullivan would acquire one-third of their company's stock: 200,000 shares for $1 million at signing; 200,000 more for $1 million more in May 1949; and 400,000 for $1.5 million in 1950, although, Hanley explained to his board, Bunker

Hill and Hecla would actually buy the stock "on account of possible substantial tax savings." Larsen and Jensen would stay on as officers, and Witherspoon as a director on a board with three Pend Oreille and three Sullivan representatives. Vern Zeigler would design a new mill. When the contract was signed May 4, 1948, Hanley fumed, "Rumors of the deal, even to the number of shares and the price, have become street talk" in Spokane. On Spokane's clubby exchanges, there seemed to be no secrets.

Hecla continued to buy Pend Oreille stock "without crowding the market," as Hanley put it. By mid-1949 it owned 41,195 shares bought for an average price of $4.013 through Pennaluna & Company, the Wallace and Spokane brokers. The company would continue to add Pend Oreille stock by small purchases calculated not to excite the market.

With its investment in Pend Oreille, a half interest in the now-profitable Sullivan, and participation through Polaris in the silver belt, Hecla seemed stable if not flourishing. Its income in 1949 amounted to more than $1 million; it paid dividends of $1 million; it owned stocks of Sullivan, Resurrection, Polaris, Rock Creek, and other companies worth more than $5.7 million in the marketplace, and counted an earned surplus of more than $9.2 million. In 1950 its income rose to $1.2 million, largely from dividends, and the value of its investments, to $5.9 million. Again it paid dividends of $1 million. The prices of lead and zinc advanced. True, Hecla had not found another big mine—it was virtually a holding company—and its quests for mining properties had been mostly disappointing, although at that time Rock Creek seemed still a possibility.

Lew Hanley concluded that he had done what he could for Hecla. He had been with the company forty-seven years, nearly all his working life. He might have retired sooner if Leo Hoban had lived. By 1950 Hanley was worn and ailing. He gave his board time to look over candidates before the annual meeting on May 24, 1951, when he retired. The stockholders gratefully created the post of chairman for Hanley and kept him on the board. Eighteen months later, he died in his sleep in the home Hecla had bought for him.

Before Hanley retired, the board had argued for months over his successor, split between two candidates, Sorenson, the geologist, and Neyman, the inventor and manager of mines. Even before becoming open rivals for the presidency, the two disliked one another intensely and publicly—Sorenson, the office politician, personable; versus Neyman, tall, domineering, defensive because his training had been by correspondence rather than a university. No matter which man the board chose, the company faced a potentially damaging rift in management. Hanley had mediated between Sorenson and Neyman, keeping them apart and at work, and he apparently expressed no preference to the board.

Since they could not agree, the directors asked Archie Witherspoon, the vice president, to take over temporarily. Witherspoon accepted, knowing that as an attorney and banker, he was simply buying time for the board to settle on a new president. But he was flattered. A large, boastful man, Witherspoon had no doubts that he could run the company. He bragged, at times, that he was a director of seventy-five companies, a man of standing, a man of accomplishment. Fortunately for Hecla, he knew his limitations as a mining man.

The board rented Witherspoon an apartment near the Hecla offices and he commuted weekly from Spokane while the directors debated a new president. For some time, the board talked of appointing a general manager first, but Searls and Witherspoon got together in New York and agreed that a president should be named before a general manager. Thus, after seven months of an interim presidency, as the directors convened in Milwaukee, Searls rattled their long table and protested, "This is no way to run a company! I will support Les Randall for president." Witherspoon chimed his agreement. Then, so did the others.

In this manner, Lester Randall, thirty-nine months with the company, became the compromise choice as Hecla's seventh president. His appointment took effect on December 1, 1951. The board elevated Neyman to general manager and Sorenson to vice president, and they elected John R. Matthews to succeed Randall as secretary-treasurer.

8

Renewal

LES RANDALL HAD REASON TO FEEL MIGHTY PLEASED. THIS fresh April morning in 1966 marked his last stockholders' meeting as president, and he could tell the sixty or so who came that the first quarter's income had been the highest in the company's history. If metals prices did not slip, this would be another record year.

The company that had fallen on hard times and netted only $361,834 or thirty-six cents a share in 1954 now owned producing mines that brought in more than $5.8 million or $2.48 a share. Hecla had paid dividends of more than $2 million in 1965—the first $2 million dividend in thirty-nine years—and would pay as much or more in 1966. Randall waved aside acclaim for his role in reviving Hecla, but he took credit for—bragged about—spotting the men he called his "management team," who, during his fourteen years as president, had reversed Hecla's slide following exhaustion of the original Hecla mine.

Randall had surmounted personal catastrophe, too—had bounded back from a near-fatal heart attack three years earlier that kept him away from Hecla for months. On Fred Searls's advice he went to a San Francisco physician and learned, Randall declared, "I am not nearly as bad off as I had been led to believe." One of his team, William H. Love, steered Hecla while Randall was convalescing and, in those months, magnified the impression within the company that he was next in line after Randall, an impression confirmed on this April day in 1966 when Randall moved up to chairman and Love, to president.

Fourteen years earlier Randall had come into the presidency determined to change Hecla's management structure and style. He could not be another Hanley who, after a lifetime with Hecla, sometimes ran it like a country store. Hanley knew every ware on the shelves, and his afternoons were devoted to his miners. As an accountant, Randall demanded precision and tidiness;

he was impatient with chitchat and at home with facts and numbers. Throughout his presidency, reports and balance sheets would be detailed and thorough.

Perhaps Randall remembered a letter he had received as comptroller from a small stockholder in New York who sold his wife's stock because the company's reports did not impress him as "sufficiently revealing to shareholders." Randall even insisted that the duties of the office be clearly stated in the bylaws before he became chairman. And because he could not be another Hanley, Randall would rely on Gus Voltolini to talk to the men. Down to earth, outspoken, Voltolini talked the miners' language, and the men trusted him. When he took early retirement in April 1982, Hecla employees would give Voltolini a plaque in recognition of his "consideration of his fellow men."

As comptroller, Randall had concluded that the Hecla's subsidiary companies cost it money and needless staff effort. For example, Polaris paid income taxes and when Hecla received Polaris dividends Hecla paid taxes again on the same money. Many of the same men met as directors of a subsidiary—Polaris, Silver Summit, or Chester—who solemnly reported to themselves as directors of the parent Hecla. In one muddled transaction later (which strengthened his view), Randall, as president of the Chester Mining Company, signed a contract with himself as president of Hecla.

His letters and memos counseled that Hecla not "put all its eggs in one basket," but rather invest in sound stocks of other companies, and, without abandoning its primary mission, diversify into other businesses. He judged that Sullivan was a drain on Hecla's resources and, even before he became president, recommended that Hecla buy out of Sullivan.

Randall prodded his team to cut costs—savings he could reckon on a profit and loss statement. Surrounded by lawyers, bankers, and merchants on his board, he wanted mining men, and occasionally he met one whom he recommended as a likely director. When in doubt, Randall looked to Newmont as a model. He recommended, for instance, that Hecla's employee retirement program, begun in 1947, be revised along the lines of Newmont's. Randall, himself, resolved to retire when he reached the appropriate age. He thought privately that McCarthy and Hanley had worked too long, possibly discouraging younger men, ambitious to reach the top, from staying with the company.

Angular and exuberant, with a quizzical expression, his dark hair graying, Randall had a lock that fell boyishly across his forehead. He never wholly shed the misgiving that he was a provincial from Wallace mixing with noted men in business. Occasionally he dined in New York with Bernard Baruch, adviser to presidents, because Baruch liked to talk about mining. On his home ground, Randall's manner was businesslike and fair minded; he sometimes concentrated his thoughts so wholly that he walked unseeing past old friends. As a listener, head cocked, so tenaciously did he fasten on a topic that he was almost intimidating. He asked pertinent questions. Bill Love, explaining a technique for mining, remembered Randall, the nonminer, saying to him, "Bill, you haven't thought this through."

One of his first moves was to merge Silver Summit into Polaris, pointing out that this would "save the double tax on dividends as profits are passed from one company to its parent." Some dissident shareholders held out for a higher value on their stock—the basis was one share of Polaris for each two of Silver Summit—but, as Randall remarked later, "They gave up and sold their stock on the open market when they found we were not willing to pay more than the market price." Whenever practical, Randall would pull Hecla's properties into the company to simplify managing, to save money, and to pool their depletion credits for taxes.

Sometime after unitizing, the Spokane stockbroker, Ben Redfield, who had promoted the Chester—"It'll send your sons to college," he would assure prospective buyers—decided that Chester had leased too cheaply to the unit area. Randall asked an old friend from Moscow days, the Spokane attorney Horton Herman, to work out a new deal that would satisfy Redfield. Herman and Redfield renegotiated the Chester lease—and then Redfield decided again it was not enough. Randall, resignation in his tone, telephoned Herman to try again. When he sought a board member later, Randall would remember Herman's role in Chester and nominate him.

Freeing Hecla of the albatross Sullivan took four years. Bunker Hill had incurred further expenses for a plant to extract sulphuric acid as a by-product, and the zinc market had tumbled again. Consequently, Randall had to write his board that Sullivan was short of cash once more, its dividends diminishing (down from $1.2 million in 1951 to $1 million in 1952 and heading toward $250,000 in 1953), and it was "practically impossible" to guess what might happen next.

He and the other Hecla men on the Sullivan board demanded that department heads spend nothing until the company reduced its $1.4 million inventory of unsold zinc. Although the zinc plant processed about the same tonnage in 1953 as in 1952, its gross income for comparable four-month periods fell from $9.3 million to $5.7 million. Because Hecla, at the time, depended almost wholly on income from Sullivan and Polaris, a fluttering Sullivan beat ominously for Hecla.

The market did not improve. The zinc plant continued to lose money and Randall guessed the company would make enough to pay its bank loans but not a dividend. (Actually, it paid dividends of $15,000 in 1954.) He began talking with Bunker Hill about trading Hecla's interest in Sullivan for Bunker Hill stock, but the proposal stalled when Bunker Hill's stockholders insisted that the company increase its stock to raise money for new properties and exploration.

In the meantime, Seth Pollard badgered Randall about Pend Oreille. When would it increase dividends? He raised his questions at directors' meetings and in letters, asserting that for the money invested in Pend Oreille stock, Hecla should be collecting large dividends. Vern Zeigler converted the Pend Oreille to trackless mining to reduce costs but that was not enough, Randall acknowledged, because "the grade of ore mined during the past months has been decreasing." By the end of spring 1953, Sullivan shut down Reeves MacDonald, but held off closing Pend Oreille because it needed zinc ores and because "once we lost the crew it would be very difficult to get the men to return because of competition from government projects in nearby districts"—dam construction. Nevertheless, Randall warned, Bunker Hill and Hecla were "very concerned over the marked decline in the grade of ore."

Continuing losses convinced Randall that Sullivan and Pend Oreille were dragging down Hecla, that Pend Oreille's earnings did not justify the $4 paid for its stock. He conferred with Jens Jensen, the Pend Oreille vice president, about the grade of ore, saying that "it certainly was lower than originally anticipated." The round little Dane responded logically that "a shortage of labor at the Pend Oreille makes it impossible for them to carry on a proper developing program." With development, the mine might have selected only better grade ores for the zinc plant. Randall dispatched his bickering department heads, Neyman and Sorenson, for a reappraisal of Pend Oreille—but he had more than half made up his mind that Hecla should get out.

Consequently, he offered to sell Bunker Hill both Hecla's half interest in Sullivan and its stock in Pend Oreille. Now, Bunker Hill was receptive—perhaps weary of Hecla's carping. Hecla would exchange its 50 percent interest in Sullivan for 275,000 shares of Bunker Hill common, and would sell to Bunker Hill its 494,696 shares of Pend Oreille for $4.25 a share, or $2.1 million. With this transaction, Bunker Hill wholly owned Sullivan and held 26.2 percent of Pend Oreille. Randall got an irate telephone call from Baruch, who had invested in Pend Oreille, complaining that news of the deal depressed the market for his stock.

Stockholders of both companies approved the exchange, which gave Hecla a 17.37 percent interest in Bunker Hill, making it Bunker Hill's largest shareholder. Bunker Hill contracted with Hecla for continued operation of Star, for a fee of $30,000 a year and a rental of $70,000 for its shaft, tunnels, and mill. Six years later, the companies would revise this agreement to drop the fee and rental and give Hecla, instead, a 30 percent interest in the Star's production.

The unpredictable Sullivan had been carried on the books as Hecla's biggest asset at more than $4 million; Pend Oreille, at $1.7 million. With those erased, Randall also sold off the bleak Rock Creek claims, book-valued at $409,285, taking the loss rather than sink more money there. Thus, in a few months Hecla cut away part of its web of extraneous boards and managers. But those untenable balance sheets continued to vex Randall. He summoned Neyman, Sorenson, and Matthews to a "policy meeting" to decide what to recommend to Hecla's directors. Hecla had $905,620 tied up in new mining projects, and they realized that its "financial picture justifies only limited additional commitments for other ventures. . . . All present agreed that Hecla could not put all its eggs in one basket."

But its eggs were virtually in one basket: Bunker Hill stock (300,000 shares) valued at more than $5 million, supplemented by a 55 percent interest in Polaris, $301,217. And the future of Polaris was doubtful. Sorenson predicted that Omega and Rotbart would play out within seven years. The grade of ore declined, offering little alternative but to continue searching.

After judicious snooping among his acquaintances, Randall suggested that Hecla contract with the neighboring Coeur d'Alene Mines Corporation to explore its old Coeur d'Alene mine and the Rainbow (51 percent owned by Coeur d'Alene) through the Silver Summit shaft. This would be "a limited additional commitment" for as much as $490,000, and Randall warned that "this represents virgin ground in the Silver Belt that has never been previously prospected." He proposed exploring, he acknowledged, largely because a shaft and mill were already there, adding, "We readily admit that the possibility of encountering ore in either of these projects is largely a gamble."

The gamble lost. After three years and more than 13,500 feet of drifting and crosscutting, Hecla conceded that the Coeur d'Alene-Rainbow was still "little more than a prospect." Hecla pulled out. The Coeur d'Alene corporaton would sue, alleging that Hecla had failed to keep its surface plant and mine in good repair, asking half a million dollars in damages. Randall explained that the suit arose "from a difference in interpretation" of their contract, but a court—after five weeks of argument, 164 exhibits, and 2,900 pages of testimony—awarded Coeur d'Alene Mines $129,129.

Faced with ebbing reserves, Sunshine, Hecla, and Silver Dollar resolved to expand exploration in the properties around Sunshine. Sunshine and Hecla had earlier agreed, on Fred Searls's counsel, that Sunshine would mine the Intervening Area between Sunshine and Polaris. (Incidentally, Searls soon dropped off the Hecla board. He had been taken ill from a train at Missoula, Montana, with what he thought was stomach upset. His ailment proved to be a blood clot in his lungs, and, on his doctor's advice, he cut back his activities.) With the Hecla-Silver Dollar contract as a model, Sunshine had written similar agreements with smaller companies whose properties could be reached by crosscutting from its shaft. For an expansion, Sunshine sank its number 10 shaft, which connected to the Jewel shaft at 3,100 feet and eventually would reach a depth of 6,000.

Then Hecla, Sunshine, and Silver Dollar unitized the Rotbart, Omega, Intervening Area, Polaris, and American (the westerly part of the New Purim Area) on January 1, 1958. Each owner would thereafter receive income from the unit in proportion to its ground—Polaris, 33 percent. At the time, Polaris showed reserves in the Omega and Rotbart for less than two years but seemed likely to yield more ore below the 4000 level.

With unitizing, Randall again urged a merger of Polaris into Hecla, sweetening the offer to induce Polaris stockholders to accept, on the basis of six shares of Polaris (market value seventy-nine cents) for one of Hecla ($9.25). To exchange Hecla stock for 1,032,120 of Polaris owned by minority shareholders would cost 173,000 shares of Hecla.

Hecla shareholders would be asked, at the same time, to authorize an increase in capital stock from 1,000,000 to 1,500,000 shares, the first increase since reorganizaton of the company in 1898.

Merging with Polaris and unitizing the Sunshine area would reduce costs of management and exploration but would not necessarily produce new income. For some time, the board had talked of investing Hecla's surplus, and perhaps even working capital, in the stock of other solid companies. Carroll Searls, an attorney who succeeded his brother Fred as Newmont's man on the board, had telephoned Randall at 6:30 one morning to urge that Hecla buy preferred stock of Tennessee Gas Transmission. Randall put half a million into it. The directors formed an investment committee of Searls, Randall, and Richard Hunt— Hunt had come on the board, at Randall's suggestion, in place of Witherspoon. John Matthews studied the market, picking International Nickel and Newmont as likely investments. Ross Leisk, who had left Sunshine to consult and had come on Hecla's board, and Matthews both wrote thoughtful memoranda outlining suggested investment policies for Hecla. With these as guides, Hecla dipped into the stock market, acquiring modest holdings in such companies as American Metals Climax, American Smelting & Refining, American Zinc, Anaconda, Atlas Consolidated, Cerro, Copper Range, St. Joseph Lead, and Standard Oil of New Jersey, buying stock that seemed undervalued and selling when a profit could be turned. A wary, unhurried buyer, for the most part, Hecla increased its income by a few thousand dollars a year playing the market.

Randall inclined to think that Hecla could diversify, as well, into manufacturing in Seattle or Spokane if it established business connections there. He frequently suggested that Hecla open offices in cities where its scouts could run down rumors of business opportunities and meet business people. Once he suggested that Hecla "explore other industries such as the manufacture of detergents" using Bunker Hill sulphuric acid, adding that a consultants' report "might be turned over to the chamber of commerce in Spokane as inducement to encourage industries into this area that use sulphuric acid."

Diversification was in the air. Business newspapers were full of reports and rumors of conglomerates and diversifying—old, well-known companies spreading their risks beyond their primary fields, big fish ingesting small (and occasionally, the opposite) and reshaping the nation's corporate landscape. Corporate mergers mirrored, in a larger glass, the congealing of interests in the Coeur d'Alenes as the "big five" bought—or merged—penurious companies with promising prospects. Perhaps with unconscious irony, Randall observed that stock in the Bunker Hill seemed "too large an investment by Hecla in a company whose income is almost completely dependent upon favorable lead and zinc market conditions." That had been precisely Hecla's position since the company started business.

Forbes magazine advised mining companies to diversify in the face of oversupplies of lead, zinc, and copper and widespread searching for new deposits that might glut the market more, remarking acidly that "apparently the lead and zinc industry had become too accustomed to government intervention and indirect subsidy to function profitably on its own." Randall mailed copies of this article to his directors.

One company virtually fell into Hecla's lap: Accesso Systems, Inc., a struggling Seattle manufacturer of movable ceiling panels for offices. Stanley Sorenson, brother of Hecla's Robert Sorenson, had invented a system for hanging false ceilings in a way that allowed easy shifting of recessed lights. The ceilings had been sold to buyers as distant as Tennessee and Alabama, mainly by the enthusiasm of Seattle architects. Sorenson and Matthews analyzed Accesso, reporting the company seriously handicapped by lack of capital or sales organization. Accesso sounded as if it might have a big future, and Hecla's directors, on Randall's recommendation, authorized a loan (through Polaris, as it happened) of $255,000 to Accesso. Randall favored Accesso, he told the board, because Seattle might be an advantageous location for Hecla to pick up other building materials interests and perhaps to open an exploration office.

Acquisition of a 73 percent interest in Accesso also pointed a way out of Randall's frustration with Neyman's and Sorenson's fierce rivalry. Randall valued both men but was forced to discount their advice as partisan. Sorenson, sensing how fragile his tenure with Hecla might be, was willing to resign and to manage Accesso and, incidentally, to open a part-time exploration office in Seattle.

Almost as Sorenson was moving, Neyman resigned angrily, protesting that his counsel was ignored. He mailed each board member an irate five-page letter recapitulating his career with Hecla, charging that mining properties he had recommended "have been turned down without proper study," and declaring, "I cannot believe that . . . the Hecla Mining Company will be able to perpetuate itself through its present geological and exploration department," a direct attack on Sorenson.

Thus Hecla lost two competent men who could not get along, the congenial Sorenson and the inventive, intractable Neyman. The company threw a retirement party for them at the Shoshone Country Club.

Accesso would not sell widely. After two years, Hecla bargained away its interest, but Sorenson did not return to Wallace. He retired to Edmonds on the Washington coast, where he died in 1969. Neyman went to Federal Resources Corporation, a uranium mining company in Salt Lake City, as its president. He retired in 1961 to work as a consultant, living at his Priest Lake (Idaho) home, where he died in 1977.

Randall had a chance to test his notion that affiliations in Spokane could lead to new interests when Edward A. Coon, vice president of the Spokane & Eastern Trust branch of Seattle-First National Bank, tipped him off that L. J. Borjessan was considering the sale of Ace Concrete Company with a plant and offices about two miles east of Spokane. The Borjessans, dairy farmers, had taken over the floundering Ace in 1949 and by hard work built it into the second largest (of three) aggregate and pre-mix concrete suppliers in the Spokane area, earning about $70,000 a year. Borjessan now was ill, ready to sell, and his wife proved a stubborn, shrewd bargainer. She reluctantly accepted Hecla's offer of $700,000, then asked for more for spare parts, land (81.5 acres), and other assets, retreating unwillingly toward Hecla's bid.

Finally the deal was closed. Hecla took over Ace on August 31, 1959. "This investment cannot be considered as a bonanza," Randall warned the directors. "It does offer us a reasonable return . . . and a base in Spokane from which opportunities may later develop." James H. Hunter, a Hecla engineer since 1943, moved from Wallace to manage Ace while Borjessan worked beside him for a few weeks. (Two years later, oddly enough, Newmont would get into concrete: with Cerro Corporation, it would consolidate small cement companies in the East as Atlantic Cement Company.)

Hecla didn't understand, at first, that the concrete business was primarily marketing, not manufacturing, or that William M. Murphy's family, proprietors of Central Pre-Mix, had no intention of letting someone exceed them. Although it never paid a dividend, Ace did a steady business, expanded into prestressed and precast products, opened another plant at Moscow, Idaho, and remained a factor in the region's construction industry for seventeen years longer. By 1976, when Ace was coming off its worst year—a net of $24,000—Hecla had sunk $1.6 million into it. Acme Concrete offered to buy it. Hecla sold for $2 million. Bill Love would be president then; he figured that Hecla realized roughly a 15 percent return on its equity, and concluded ruefully that the company had learned a lesson—"to stick to our knitting. We're miners, not marketers."

For all his pains to diversify, pare costs, cut away encumbrances, and invest prudently, Les Randall knew from the start of his presidency that his first goal had to be finding a new mine. He must gamble on other men's judgments. He favored limited risks, musing that a hundred prospects washed out for every one that became a producer. Randall publicized a standing offer of $20,000 cash to anyone outside the company who brought Hecla a mine. Looking back in this light, Ralph Neyman's vendetta had been tragic; it had sapped his contribution to the company. Randall probably should have chosen early between Sorenson and Neyman—but he had not, and Neyman could feel put down and unappreciated. Neyman had done a lot for Hecla.

Neyman had operated nearly every Hecla property since 1940. Under his supervision, the Star counted spectacular savings in operating costs: between 1945 and 1957, the expenses of labor, supplies, and power for mining rose approximately 80 percent. Neyman held the Star to 43 percent. With smaller drill holes and bits tempered in oil rather than coke furnaces, he reduced drilling and blasting costs one-third; his dump-car system reduced haulage costs; he introduced scrapers to muck stopes, raising production 30 percent a shift; and on and on. Neyman's Star was widely recognized as a model of efficient mining.

Neyman also conceived a crosscut 8,500 feet from the Burke

dump directly into the Star at the 2000 level, to eliminate ore transfers, pumping, and shaft maintenance for the route through the old Hecla, saving $1.7 million over a seven-year period. It is indicative of the directors' wariness of Neyman, however, that they approved this practical new way into the Star only on condition that Fred Searls sanction it. He did, and Neyman opened the new tunnel in mid-1954, on schedule despite water flows and ventilation problems caused by Asarco's closure of the Morning in 1953.

Although Rock Creek had not panned out, Neyman saved Hecla thousands of dollars there by driving an exploration tunnel 4,483 feet in 213 breathtaking days, devising a "cherry picker" to lift cars from tracks so others could pass, and outfitting an armored car with fans to clear fumes and smoke quickly from blasts. The U.S. Bureau of Mines issued an information circular describing his time-saving equipment and methods at Rock Creek.

But on occasion, Neyman had embarrassed Randall. Early in 1954 Hecla, and every other operating mine in the district, had cut back from six to five days when the price of lead fell, reducing the average miner's pay from $385 to $300 a month, "hardly a living rate for a family man in this district," Randall told the board. Bunker Hill had offered its unionized men a raise of seven cents an hour. Neyman had deliberately planted a rumor that Hecla would pay a bonus for increased production, raising output in a five-day week to nearly what it had been in six—and forcing Randall to scramble to satisfy the men.

And Neyman found a way for Hecla into uranium mining. From his first days as president of Hecla, Randall had been nagged about uranium, about the company's place in the frenzied prospecting that churned the Colorado Plateau. Most major mining companies held uranium prospects or were trying to find them—Fred Searls had fifteen or twenty men in the field for Newmont, "trying to get a foothold"—but getting into uranium was like a runaway boy catching his first freight train: it moved awfully fast; he wasn't sure where to catch on or what to do if he got on. Seth Pollard, convalescing from a heart attack, had time to write urging Randall to act. Randall could only reply, "We are still watching it."

Randall scouted Utah's uranium districts in person, conferred with Hunt, chief geologist for United States Smelting & Refining—and they agreed that "because of the great promotional activity," neither U.S. Smelting nor Hecla should "attempt to compete with promoters who are prepared to offer almost anything," or the oil company scouts "willing to offer up to a quarter of a million dollars . . . before any development work has been done," Randall told Pollard.

Herbert E. Harper, a Hecla geologist, confirmed these views. "The boom activities in the Plateau region have now reached such proportions that it is unlikely that any areas exist that have not been flown or examined in at least a superficial way," he reported after several weeks in uranium country. The Atomic Energy Commission drilled likely areas, holding them for leases to high bidders, and Harper counted "some 300 applicants" for ten or twelve leases available. All around the producing mines— Steen's, Happy Jack, and Pick's—"local people and speculators quickly locate large areas," whether or not they found any indications of mineralization. Harper thought Hecla's chances for quick entry into uranium were slight "under terms which are reasonable or commensurate with the cost and risk involved in exploration." He predicted, however, that the "wild speculation will subside within a few months," and then Hecla might get its chance.

Those were days when mining companies, as one manager said, had to "take a stand on uranium," and most of the larger Coeur d'Alene companies had stakes in uranium. Randall suspected that other operators considered him laggard—he had heard "already some local criticism that Hecla is not more active." And when Newmont bought into Dawn uranium, on the Spokane Indian Reservation barely 120 miles from Wallace, Fred Searls chided Randall for overlooking a uranium prospect so close by. Randall tried belatedly to deal with Midnite Mines, proposing to operate the Dawn project, but Midnite turned down Hecla's tender of $1.2 million.

Forwarding Harper's report on the Plateau, Randall declared to the directors, "Hecla can't afford 100 gambles to find the one property." And yet, he confided to Joe McCarthy, "I think we could be quite severely criticized by our shareholders if we didn't maintain contact with a hotspot" like Utah's uranium fields. And so, even though it was moving awfully fast, Hecla stretched for a handhold on the uranium rush.

On the advice of bankers in the uranium district, Randall planned to open a small office, perhaps at Grand Junction, Colorado, so that prospectors looking for financing could be referred conveniently to Hecla. Meanwhile, through friends Ralph Neyman found U & I Uranium, Inc., a coalition of six companies united by Lester Harrison, a longtime attorney and mining man at Kellogg, Idaho. Harrison's U & I owned two bright prospects: the Radon group of ten claims and, westerly and adjacent, the thirty-five Hot Rock claims, in the north end of the Big Indian Mining District, about thirty-five miles south of Moab, Utah. Because the Kellogg company needed financial assistance, Harrison would be willing to give Hecla an interest in both groups for funds, installing a surface plant, and mining the ore.

Randall sped to the directors, explaining that U & I, "pestered" by others, was eager to deal. A working agreement was hurriedly signed on December 7, 1954. Hecla shelled out $97,882 to reimburse U & I for its exploration work. Hunt wrote Randall approvingly that Radon might "excuse a little haste. It is a very attractive prospect."

Some shareholders were not enthused by Hecla's jump into uranium. Matthews, in a typical response, attempted to be reassuring: "Your management feels that its venture into the uranium field has a better than even chance of producing a substantial profit for the Hecla shareholders. . . . It is true that the mining of uranium is not a cinch for profits. . . . Your management is doing its utmost to give Hecla more than one basket from which to draw its income."

To manage the Radon, Hecla chose the man who had been directing the Atlas exploration, thirty-year-old Bill Love, an engineering graduate (with honors) from the Montana College of Mineral Science and Technology, who joined Hecla after two years as a metallurgist at a pilot flotation mill. Neyman hired Love in 1948, set him to installing an underground compressor and then, to changing ore-handling methods in Star—all fine, but Love really wanted to operate a mine. When Hecla contracted a second time to explore Atlas ground, Love demanded that assignment. "I was pretty blunt," he would recall. A firm man with unwavering blue eyes, articulate (he corresponded briefly for *Mining World*), Love could be obstinate. Sorenson backed Philip M. Lindstrom for Atlas, but Neyman, in his insistent way, wedged Love into the post, where Love performed with distinction. As the man at Atlas, he got to know Les Randall for the first time. Randall was impressed with this comer; he marked Love for bigger things with Hecla.

Consequently, Love was dispatched early in 1955 to southeastern Utah to start a mine in desert hills pocked with prospect holes. At Moab, a town of about 900, he rented a used trailer for an office and a house as temporary barracks for his men. Until a camp could be built at the mine, they commuted over dusty trails by bus.

Radon quickly became a model of planning and speed. "If careful pre-planning will help pave the way for future profits," *Mining World* declared, "Hecla . . . is off to a flying start." Love crowded construction office, warehouse, and water wells near the mine, while crews drilled thirty-one more holes to outline the orebody. Uranium deposits in the Big Indian district are generally shallow and flat, like pancakes, in host rock of sandstone and mudstone which collapses easily when wet with drill water. Some companies worked there by open pits. By June 20, with a 75-foot bolted steel headframe in place, Love's four-man shaft crews worked around the clock, seven days a week, driving and timbering a 692-foot shaft in 65-1/2 days to reach the ore horizon, and sending ore from the shaft to a mill.

Dick Hunt drove down from Salt Lake City to look. He wrote Randall of "a good showing of high grade ore with shaley layers above and below it. . . . Bill Love is to be commended for excellent progress and a shipshape shaft and plant—all in five months' time. His record of 10.3 feet per day in the shaft is making an impression on the district and should help Ralph Neyman in any negotiations for future operating contracts."

The rich Radon, an orebody 2,150 feet long averaging five feet thick, would have to be dug out completely to realize the full value of the mine. To extract the ore, Neyman and Love adopted "long-walling," a method from European coal mines never before used in an American metal mine. They would take out the mineral in slices across the orebody's full width (400 to 700 feet), working from the far end back toward the shaft, allowing the mudstone to cave in behind them as ore caverns were emptied. German-made telescoping steel props supported tunnels beneath the treacherous mudstone. In its first year of production, Radon paid back Hecla's development money, approximately $880,000. Love estimated that uranium cost about $10 a ton to extract; it sold to the government for $70. The Hot Rock was mined by crosscuts from the Radon shaft, after exploration with financial aid from the federal Defense Minerals Exploration Administration. It was not as rich.

In a nine-year life, Radon and Hot Rock yielded 536,853 tons assaying .686 percent uranium oxide which paid Hecla a net income from uranium approaching $9.3 million.

A geological barrier called the Lisbon fault marked the boundary of the Big Indian "ore channel." Love and Doug Bell, a Hecla geologist, urged Hecla's directors to let them explore north of the fault, even giving their project a name, Shoshone, and seeking to option several square miles. Love staked ground without asking for board approval, but the directors would not go further. A Newmont geologist's report and Dick Hunt dissuaded them. Hecla gave up the Shoshone which later made a mine for Rio Algom of Canada.

Bill Love had paused in the office on a fall day in 1956 when the radio telephone called his name. A radio telephone uses a loudspeaker. This was to be a conversation Love would have preferred to carry on in private. A changing shift straggled past and the staff worked at desks as Randall's voice boomed, "Bill, you know that Neyman's leaving, and the directors and I have decided we want to offer that job to you." Love demurred; he had just started long-walling and wanted to see it through. And Randall boomed again, "Don't be reluctant. We'll make you manager of mines and pay you $15,000 a year." He agreed, however, to give Love a few days to consider. From the beginning, Love had seen Radon as a springboard to a bigger job, and Randall's offer nearly doubled his salary. Negotiating for everyone to hear, he returned to Wallace as manager of mines, transferring Lindstrom to Radon to finish there.

The departures of Neyman and Sorenson had afforded Randall the opportunity to form the executive team he wanted. With Love as manager of mines and Harper as chief geologist, Randall placed their offices next to his, so the three could confer on exploration, and he and Love could consider operating decisions together—although Love would aver that Randall "gave him a free hand." Each man respected the other's knowledge and integrity; their exchanges were forthright and friendly, and Love and Harper agree that Randall rarely made a decision they could not endorse.

Without question their most significant decision was to buy the Lucky Friday, a mile east of Mullan, a mine with as shabby a past as Long John Silver. For more than half a century, the Lucky Friday group, six claims staked between 1899 and 1906, had been worked sporadically by greenhorns and it uniformly abused them. B. P. Potts, for whom an ephemeral town, Potts-ville, was named, sold his one-fourth interest for $750. A company worked six years trenching the site, until the sheriff sold them out to satisfy $2,000 in unpaid workmen's claims. Another company, discouraged by twelve years of tunneling, declined for nine years even to pay annual taxes of $15. Mining professionals ignored the Lucky Friday because it lay between two faults and showed nothing on the surface, and amateurish trenching and tunneling revealed only wisps of vein. In the opinion of most, the Lucky Friday was another of those forlorn claims that seduce tyros, a false hope high in the hills rising easterly toward the ridge of the Bitterroots. Hecla had nuzzled this ground: Silver Mountain lay east and Atlas, south of the Lucky Friday, and Hecla had not found commercial ore in either.

Yet Lucky Friday whispered sweetly in another ear: John Sekulic was a Mullan gas station proprietor enchanted with tales of the claim from an old miner. In 1938 he leased, with option to buy, the six deserted claims for $15,000. He hired miners out of work to pull down rotting timbers and clear the caved tunnel while he sought a big company to back him. None would.

On March 30, 1939, Sekulic, with the help of attorney Charles E. (Chase) Horning, organized Lucky Friday Silver-Lead Mines as an Idaho corporation with 1,200,000 capital shares, conveyed his lease to this new company, took an office upstairs from Hecla in the Gyde-Taylor building, and doggedly sold about 270,000 shares at 2.5 cents to pay for sinking a shaft 100 feet in the footwall nearest the best vein showing. Most of the stock sold to Sekulic's personal friends who put in a few hundred dollars each. Sekulic paid for labor and supplies with more stock, when workmen or merchants would take it.

The vein looked better at 100 feet, and on that slight promise, Sekulic, Horning, and Judge Albert H. Featherstone persuaded Golconda Lead Mines, Inc., of which Featherstone was president, to write a series of contracts to sink to the 300, then the 500, and next the 600 levels. Sekulic also gave Featherstone 155,000 shares for personal funds the judge put into development. Sekulic and Horning, at one juncture, each lent the company $5,000 to pay its current bills. The vein looked better as miners went down. Short shoots of silver-lead ore yielded enough income for the company to pay back its cash advances, sink to 1,400 feet in 1948, and deposit $62,500 in its treasury. Lucky Friday had shipped its first ore, 478 tons, to the Golconda mill in January 1942. Nine years later, the company paid its first dividend.

Sekulic determined to list his company's stock on the New York Stock Exchange; he asked Randall to allow Herb Harper, the Hecla geologist who had occasionally moonlighted for Lucky Friday, to write the geology section of an application to the exchange, and Randall agreed, on condition that he see the report. Sekulic also tentatively engaged Vern Zeigler and his brother-in-law Lou Grant to design a 750-ton mill for Lucky Friday.

Lucky Friday was earning nineteen cents a share—and had mapped enough ore to justify sinking its shaft to 3,000 feet— by mid-1953 when Randall read Harper's approving report. Randall recommended that Hecla buy 25,000 shares at $2.10, "with the thought of selling for a profit at some future date," for the mine showed unmistakable promise. Even the often pessimistic Sorenson considered the mine's prospects "rather good," and its stock likely to appreciate. The board approved the buy. Soon Lucky Friday looked even better, but Sekulic, who had paid himself $200 a month as manager, would not see the mine's great years; he died in 1956. His ashes, as he had requested, were buried above the Lucky Friday portal.

Sekulic's friend and advisor, Horning, general counsel for Hecla, took over as president and general manager of Lucky Friday. (His only pay as attorney for Lucky Friday had been one $500 check in 1946.) Although the directors' meetings had previously been held in his or Judge Featherstone's offices, Horning formed a habit of convening his board in the Miners Club, a Mullan bar, whose proprietor gave Horning a key that he wore on a huge chain—"a chain you could tie a bulldozer with," Gus Voltolini chuckled. The directors met to vote dividends, helped themselves to food and drink, and left money on the bar to pay. Horning locked up after them. Any miner fired from Lucky Friday collected his last paycheck at the Miners Club.

In the five years after Hecla bought its first Lucky Friday stock, the mine steadily advanced. Between 1954 and 1958, it produced ores averaging 17.2 ounces of silver and 8.6 percent lead a ton, increased net income to thirty-eight cents a share, and paid dividends of more than $1,568,000. Randall began to think that Lucky Friday might be the new mine he had been seeking. Chase Horning's close friends, seeing predatory glances toward Lucky Friday, begged him to keep it in local hands. Consequently, Horning and John A. Featherstone, son of the late judge and now president of Lucky Friday, both large shareholders, offered Hecla their stock and that of friends. Randall took an option at $7.50 a share to buy the Horning and Featherstone stock and proposed to Hecla's board that they make the same offer to all shareholders of Lucky Friday.

But acquisition stalled when a contest erupted inside Golconda over the number of shares belonging to the Featherstone family. For some years Golconda, with 110,000 shares acquired for financing the Lucky Friday shaft, had more or less steered Lucky Friday. Now Golconda's vice president, Harry Magnuson, with a group of other shareholders, contested ownership of additional shares given the Featherstones for money they had put into the mine. Randall's term of option dribbled away while Golconda claimed the Featherstone shares. Magnuson threatened court until Featherstone returned 45,000 shares of his family's stock to Golconda. With that settled, Featherstone and Horning extended Hecla's option.

As Hecla's counsel and a Lucky Friday director, Horning felt himself in an awkward position. He favored acquisition by Hecla but could not, in good conscience, make a better bargain for himself than for the shareholders; he therefore insisted that he "not get anything out of this that any other shareholder doesn't get." Horning's scruples effectively blocked Hecla from buying shares below the option price.

As a printer's deadline passed without delivery of a letter explaining the offer to Lucky Friday shareholders, Randall learned to his dismay that a majority of his directors opposed buying the Lucky Friday. With a long face, he called Love and Harper aside one afternoon to break this news. Both men were stunned. "It was a bargain, and we knew it was a bargain," Love would remember, "and we couldn't understand the board turning down an opportunity like that."

The board's objection was money. Some thought the price too high. Lucky Friday had sold for ten cents only a few years earlier. And they feared that if all of Lucky Friday's 1,306,479 shares outstanding came in at $7.50, that could cost Hecla more than $9.7 million. Hecla did not have that much money. Not counting its investments in stocks of other corporations or its physical plant, Hecla's liquid assets totaled less than $7 million. Randall wanted the company to issue an additional 37,500 shares (authorized at the time of the Polaris merger) to cover the Lucky Friday purchase but, even so, several of the directors saw the offer as risky.

Disheartened, Randall telephoned Fred Searls in New York to brace his own confidence in Lucky Friday. Searls flew to Wallace the next day and, with Harper and Love, donned a slicker and miner's cap to stride through the Lucky Friday, muttering, "This isn't right." and, "I've never seen anything like this!" Love and Harper were thoroughly dispirited when they emerged from the mine, but Searls turned to them and Randall to declare, "In spite of everything I've seen, it's a nice little mine. You tell your board that Newmont will take every share of Lucky Friday that Hecla doesn't buy. You go tell your directors that."

Randall convened his board for a special meeting and, this time, with Newmont's guarantee that "it would protect Hecla's cash position in the event more stock was offered than Hecla could afford," the directors approved buying Lucky Friday— "on the ground that if it was good enough for Newmont, it was good enough for Hecla," Randall would say later.

On December 12, 1958, Hecla bought 184,000 shares at $7.50 from Featherstone, Horning, and their wives and friends. Three days later Hecla tendered an offer to buy other Lucky Friday stock at the same price. Even now, the purchase did not go smoothly. Some Hecla shareholders protested that Newmont's participation had been hidden from them. The most consequential of these was Joseph H. Hirshhorn, a "substantial stockholder" in Hecla through Callahan Mining Corporation, of which he was the major shareholder. A flamboyant promoter of Canadian mines and oil wells, Hirshhorn complained through attorneys to the American Stock Exchange—until 1959, the curb—that Hecla's application to list 37,500 additional shares was defective because it did not reveal Hecla's understanding with Newmont, and that letters to Lucky Friday shareholders were "patently misleading. The omission of any reference to the Hecla-Newmont agreement made it falsely appear that Hecla alone was purchasing" Lucky Friday.

Hirshhorn's complaint, at its root, was an attack on Newmont's position as a large Hecla stockholder with representation on Hecla's board. Hirshhorn protested that the "transaction bears all of the earmarks of a studied plan" to deny Callahan its rightful voice in Hecla's affairs. "For years, Newmont has been the dominant stockholder of Hecla," Hirshhorn's complaint asserted. "Its representatives apparently feel that their position may be challenged" by Callahan's acquisition of a large block of Hecla.

Hirshhorn withdrew his complaint on an attorney's advice but Randall was obliged to mail another letter offering to return stock to sellers "if the fact that Newmont Mining Corporation was a party to the deal may have affected their decision." Only a handful asked for the return of stock.

In all, 644,058 shares came in, roughly 49 percent of Lucky Friday's outstanding stock. Hecla bought 453,664 for cash—$3.4 million; Newmont bought 190,394 and shortly after exchanged 50,000 of these for the newly issued 37,500 of Hecla. Thus Hecla became the major owner of Lucky Friday (38 percent). As a condition of the sale, Lucky Friday stipulated that Hecla make places for two of its people, Dave Elder and Gus Voltolini. As we have seen, Randall made Voltolini his personnel director to talk to the miners. But Hecla had not heard the last from Hirshhorn or Callahan.

9
Investing

PURCHASE OF THE LUCKY FRIDAY, IN RETROSPECT, WAS HE-
cla's turning point, the fulcrum that restored Hecla as an operating company with prolonged life. Most of the company's
other mines since 1944 had been short term, although Radon's
profits had helped buy Lucky Friday, and the Star had tested
its mining methods. The Lucky Friday would be mined by cut
and fill, backfilling with mill tailings pumped back into the mine.
"When we went into the Lucky Friday," Bill Love would explain, "we had developed mining techniques that we needed
to really make the Lucky Friday go, right from the beginning,
without fumbling or stumbling. So all that work at the Star
paid off."

Lucky Friday may have been a supreme stroke of good luck
for Hecla, but it was also the deserved outcome of hard work
and good sense. With thousands of risks to be taken, Hecla's
management had bet on the right one.

Randall acknowledged later that Lucky Friday was bigger than
he realized when he recommended buying it. "None of us ever
dreamed that it would become the great mine it is," he said.
Hecla built a new 700-ton Lucky Friday mill near the portal
within a year of buying the mine, increasing production substantially over the Golconda mill. With the mill, they built new
surface buildings, installed a new conveyor from mine to ore
bins, a new hoist, and a new ventilation system. True to form,
Randall called for merging the Lucky Friday into Hecla, cal-
culating hypothetical balance sheets to show the resources,
working funds, and income possible with merger.

The Lucky Friday stockholders expected Hecla to make money
for them and if there were a merger, to reward them hand-
somely. Many of them had purchased their shares for dimes
to help out John Sekulic, a few had almost forgotten they owned
shares until the mine paid dividends, and some friends had
given a railroad engineer his Lucky Friday stock as a gag birth-

day gift. Now Lucky Friday sold at inflated quotations, sometimes beyond $30 a share.

With income from Radon and Lucky Friday, Randall could
finance his next steps. He intended to accumulate a reserve
that would allow Hecla to pay dividends in lean years as well
as good ones, to continue to invest in other companies, and to
expand Hecla—to make it more visible to potential investors
and possible partners. On dividends, he wrote the directors,
"I don't think it's fair to shareholders to cut dividends because
we have a bad year," adding, "Hecla stock has been quoted
somewhat higher over the years than . . . the stock of other
mining companies of comparable size. I have been told that the
basic reason for this has been our policy of maintaining uniform dividends. . . . Hecla is one of the few mining stocks
held by trusts and individuals who depend on dividends."

His reason for investing in other companies was oblique.
"Hecla's principal objective is not to establish an investment
account solely for the purpose of developing income," he declared. "The principal objective of our investment program is
to find new properties through the development of associations with other companies." This was an adaptation of Searls's
policy for Newmont. Randall and Bill Love once listed the names
of smaller western mining companies "who might at some time
need help from Hecla," with the notion of investing a little in
each "because such investment might lead to a joint participation and development project." They had not made the investments, but in Randall's scheme, investment went hand in
hand with new properties. Randall would plant listening posts
in the mining industry by investing.

To find new properties, Randall also proposed opening Hecla offices in cities such as Vancouver, Challis (Idaho), or Grand
Junction, where mining men gathered. He confessed that "for
the past eight years, practically all of my spare time has been
devoted to close scrutiny of operating problems, with very little time devoted to making contacts for new properties." He
regretted that "too much time has been devoted to investigation of prospects referred to us by unreliable people." He suggested to the board that Harper direct an exploration office in
Spokane and that other geologists open Hecla offices in other
cities "to spend their entire time toward acquiring new prospects." When Idaho amended its laws in 1957 to tax the dividends from domestic corporations paid to state residents, Ran-

dall fretted that the law would cost Hecla upward of $46,000 a year and snapped, "We could move our general office to Spokane and hire four or five geologists for what it will cost us to remain in Wallace!"

Randall's assumption that mixing with the mining crowd outside the Coeur d'Alenes would bring Hecla new properties seemed to pay off. When Hecla sallied into western mining camps, its celebrity from Radon eased negotiations. It also eased the bargaining with Harry Cranmer's New Park Mining Company, Salt Lake City, to manage and operate the Mayflower mine, north of Heber, a gold property with lead and silver values that sent small consignments of ores to Midvale. After testing the Mayflower and Pearl veins to assess reserves, Hecla contracted to build and operate a 400-ton plant and to extract ores by a sandfill system, now a familiar Hecla technique. Hecla was to recover its costs before dividing profits with New Park. Randall's team estimated that production would pay for the mill in twenty-eight months. They brought in a new chief, Gordon Miner, a tall man who had turned down professional football for mining and had managed the mines at Moab for Homestake Mining Company for eight years.

Mayflower cost $1.8 million before it produced ore, about half a million more than anticipated. Over an eleven-year life, however, its net income surpassed $11 million, divided between New Park and Hecla. One year it was America's fifth largest gold producer. The two companies closed the mine at the end of 1972, although it might have lasted a few more months, because it appeared that Utah's tax on net mine proceeds would exceed income. As they cleaned up before closing, they hit a limited streak of rich gold just as the market rose—a nice bonus. For their competent performance at Mayflower, Bill Love marked Miner and another engineer, George Wilhelm, for bigger roles with Hecla.

About the time Hecla went into the Mayflower, it also took over operation of the Ruby Hill, a gold, lead, and silver property in the historic Ruby Hill district at Eureka in central Nevada. Gold and lead had been discovered there only five years after the storied Comstock rush of 1859, but five more years passed before smelterers could coax metal from the stubborn ores. Then nineteen smelters sprang up. Local boosters bragged that Eureka would be "the Pittsburgh of the West," and in the district's heyday, 1871–88, they boasted that Ruby Hill controlled the lead markets of the world. When mines dug too deep to pay, the district faded, and in 1905 the last furnace shut down. Richmond and Eureka Consolidated, the largest operators, had clashed over underground rights in the nation's first major apex suit, in which the U.S. Supreme Court enunciated the so-called broad lode precept—broad lodes or zones being orebodies not defined by distinct veins.

After 1905, lessees tried to work the old claims from time to time, but waterflows at depth drove them out. A Canadian promoter, Thayer Lindsley, who started there in 1919 and stayed three decades, sank the Fad shaft 2,240 feet before water gushing from a fissure into a crosscut flooded his workings in 1948. The two old companies, Eureka and Richmond, had been purchased by U.S. Smelting, which, with Newmont and Cyprus, formed the Ruby Hill Mining Company to consolidate a number of properties, including the Fad shaft. Hecla had advanced Eureka money to buy into Ruby Hill. Consequently, in 1962 Hecla was invited to operate the property for a 5 percent share of profits. (Under a revised agreement, Hecla eventually acquired a 20.5 percent interest.)

Ruby Hill challenged the engineers to shut off water deep in the earth. Hecla drilled from the surface into the crosscut, reversed the flow from the fissure by forcing huge volumes of water down the shaft, and finally, by pumping 32,000 sacks of grout through its long drill-hole, slowly sealed the fissure. In the last weeks, however, drilling crews lost the drill string in the long bore, rousing fears that they had stopped grouting too soon and that flooding would resume, but the seal held. Hecla's men, asserted one, were "fiercely proud" of their technical achievement. With the water shut off, the Fad shaft was pumped out and drifting begun on the orebody. "Substantial ore reserves" were there, Randall said, but assays indicated they would not return the costs of taking them out.

Hecla reported in 1966 that "the economic evaluation does not support a program for bringing the property into production," estimating the cost at upward of $13 million. Its crews pulled the pumps, let the shaft fill with seepage water, and put Ruby Hill on the shelf. Hecla gained increasing respect in the mining community for adroitly sealing the Ruby Hill shaft and for its association with one of the giants, Cyprus Mines Corporation.

During the Ruby Hill work, Hecla received flattering attention in business newspapers and trade journals. In one story, Randall was quoted as telling shareholders: "Hecla is now sufficiently well financed to compete with most major companies in its search for new mining opportunities." In another: "Hecla's corporate success saga is just beginning."

The big reason for Hecla's better financial position was its merger with Lucky Friday. Randall had advocated combining the companies from the time Hecla took control. Leisk and Hunt, detailed by the board to compare the market worth of Hecla with Lucky Friday, were advised by a New York investment firm to merge Hecla into Lucky Friday "to overcome unrealistic Lucky Friday market values," and later to change the name of a united company back to Hecla. (Hecla never seriously considered that.)

Randall was willing to sugarcoat an exchange of shares to win over any reluctant Lucky Friday stockholders. Leisk calculated an exchange at 1.03 Hecla for each share of Lucky Friday. "In order to solve the problems between the two companies," Randall told the directors, "I would consider a merger at 1.18 to 1," although that would require Hecla to increase its outstanding stock. Hecla thus followed a familiar path in mine financing: increasing the stock to cover the costs of new ventures. And his board regarded new issues as an acceptable means of financing.

This was a different board from earlier days. The directors in 1964 were Marcus D. Banghart, vice president of Newmont; John Grunow, president of Newmont's subsidiary cement company; Harry Magnuson, who represented Golconda's strong interest in Lucky Friday; Hunt, the retired geologist; Leisk; Love, elected a director in 1960; and Randall—in sum, a directorate of men experienced in mining finance and mining, precisely the kind of board Randall wanted.

Hecla's directors went about the merger with Lucky Friday warily. "A formidable obstacle to a realistic and equitable merger has been created by the fact that Lucky Friday shares are overpriced and Hecla shares are underpriced on the stock market," Leisk had warned. Lucky Friday shone as a cinderella stock— and indiscreet jockeying might puff its inflated quotations. Moreover, 61.8 percent of Lucky Friday remained outside Hecla's control. Randall and Magnuson, with leave from Hecla's board, huddled with key Lucky Friday shareholders to learn their views toward merging. They found opposition and uncertainty.

Eventually, a merger was proposed on the basis of 1.5 Hecla for each share of Lucky Friday. Hecla shareholders would be asked to increase capital stock by 1,000,000 shares to 2,500,000, of which 1,212,145 would be exchanged for Lucky Friday. After stormy deliberations, directors of both companies approved the proposition and on March 5, 1964, stockholders also voted for it, Lucky Friday balloting 82.2 percent in favor, Hecla, 81.4 percent. On April 1, 1964, the merger was consummated, retroactive to January 1, increasing Hecla's assets virtually overnight from $16.6 million to more than $28.4 million. Its income from ore sales rose from $8.8 million in 1963 to more than $18.8 million in 1964. Hecla's net income nearly tripled from $1.8 million in 1963 to more than $5.1 million the next year, "attributable to the merger of Lucky Friday Silver-Lead Mines Company into Hecla," said the annual report.

The Lucky Friday, however, was not quite home free. In their proxy statement on the merger proposal, the Hecla directors felt obliged to mention the pretensions of Joseph W. Greenough who, in the name of Atlas, had staked three claims over Lucky Friday orebodies on ground patented to Lucky Friday's predecessor in 1926. When a state court barred Greenough from the ground—Hecla's board labeled his action "nothing more than an attempt to steal the property"—Greenough went to federal court, which remanded him to district, and the district court ruled for Lucky Friday. Greenough next appealed (on procedural grounds) to the state supreme court; he lost, but he would sustain his claims for five years before giving up.

Furthermore, Lucky Friday miners belonged to the United Steelworkers of America (CIO). With McCarthy and Hanley in charge, Hecla employees had been slow to join unions, although twenty years of confrontations between the International Union of Mine, Mill, & Smelter Workers and other companies had abraded Hecla's operations, and Hecla's presidents customarily sat in strategy meetings with other managers. Unionism, once stifled by hiring hall and blacklist, had returned to the Coeur d'Alenes in the guise of NRA employee associations. The old Mine Owners Association had given way to the Sixteen Operators, a coalition of managers represented in union dealings by the Wallace attorney, Harold J. Hull. In the decade after World War II, the Sixteen Operators shrank with mergers and closures until, by the mid-fifties, only three large unionized companies remained: Bunker Hill, Asarco, and Day Mines. During the labor-hungry forties, Mine-Mill had parlayed the need for men into substantial gains, eliminating "no strike" clauses, and instituting health and welfare plans. Not until 1949 could Hanley report that "for the first time in eight or nine years, all properties have full crews."

Elsewhere, Mine-Mill was embattled. The Congress of Industrial Organizations (CIO) expelled Mine-Mill in 1950, alleging that the union was dominated by communists. The Coeur d'Alene mine operators saw the expulsion as a lever to rid themselves of the union. Helped by discontented local officers, and with war in Korea, they launched a patriotic campaign against Mine-Mill. Mayors of Wallace, Kellogg, and Mullan proclaimed Anti-Communist Weeks, with speeches, radio programs, and a seven-mile auto caravan winding through the district. Dissident workers got up a Miners' Education and Organizational Group with the purpose of "eliminating communist influence from local unions," and brought in professors from Gonzaga University to lecture on communism and labor tactics.

Mullan locals, which had refused to honor Mine-Mill strike calls in 1949 and 1951, broke off to form new locals with CIO backing "to free us from the red-dominated Mine-Mill." The United Steelworkers of America started recruiting in the district's mines. A National Labor Relations Board (NLRB) election demanded by upstart unions, however, in January 1953 resulted in a general victory for Mine-Mill—except at Mullan where Lucky Friday workers voted 17 to 5, and Morning, 131 to 105, for CIO locals.

The campaign preceding this election had been conducted noisily on radio and in newspapers, but the mine workers themselves had been singularly noncommittal. As they balloted in dry-houses coming off shift, they stalked away without conversation, eyes downcast. In their minds, the issue was wages, not communism, and most believed that Mine-Mill could deliver higher pay and improved benefits. There could be no doubt that a lingering specter of management suppressing labor, as in the past, and a social chasm between managers and workers, contributed to the result of the voting.

Even so, nothing seemed settled. Conflicts between management and unions sharpened in the months after the 1953 election. Mine-Mill closed the district with a six-month strike in 1955, longest until then in the Coeur d'Alenes, and struck again for seven and one-half months in 1960. (Hecla took the precaution of raising wages seven cents an hour, to $18.50 a day for miners, during the strike.) To end the 1960 walkout, Bunker Hill formed the Northwest Metal Workers, a company-sanctioned union, and narrowly won decertification of Mine-Mill. Day Mines' men switched to the Steelworkers. A subversive activities control board examiner declared Mine-Mill "a communist infiltrated union," ineligible to represent miners under federal law. The locals for Lucky Friday and Sunshine, consequently, affiliated with the Steelworkers.

This turbulent patrimony settled on Hecla with its acquisition of Lucky Friday. Now, Randall's team was seasonally preoccupied with contract negotiations which Randall left largely to Love and Voltolini. The latter joked that contract talks meant "trying to get a nickel out of the men for the company, and a nickel out of the company for the men." Even though the men came willingly to Voltolini, who spoke up for them, the intrusion of the union hindered the personal contact between managers and men that had been a Hecla hallmark.

To its dismay, Hecla learned that Bunker Hill was playing a lone hand in union bargaining, without even "neighborly advices permitting some discussion prior to drastic action." With the unity of management temporarily dispelled, the Lucky Friday men struck, staying out twelve weeks until Hecla concluded a three-year contract with Steelworkers Local 5114—the only unionized workers in Hecla.

Randall was disconcerted by one more kink in the Lucky Friday merger: the Securities and Exchange Commission (SEC) accused his friend and former partner, Harry Magnuson, of using "inside" information—as a director of Hecla and vice president of Lucky Friday—to profit from the merger, and of failing to report stock transactions. The SEC alleged that Magnuson, learning that the ratio for exchange of stocks differed from their market values, sold and bought, and advised Golconda to sell Lucky Friday and buy Hecla, profiting by $28,405.

As an accountant and financial advisor to mining companies, Magnuson had become a director and officer in several. Furthermore, he had invested regularly in Golconda stock, buying shares when he could, as his accounting practice grew. Astute, personable, Magnuson came from pioneers of the district. His maternal grandfather, Louis Sala, had been imprisoned in the aftermath of union riots until the Western Federation of Miners secured his release. As an accountant, Magnuson prospered, buying waterfront on Lake Coeur d'Alene and real estate and stocks as investments, some in the names of family members. He owned 37.5 percent and his friend, Ben Harrison, 62.5 percent, of the Pennaluna brokerage. Ben managed Pennaluna's office in Spokane and was secretary of the Spokane Stock Exchange.

Magnuson wrote Hecla directors personal letters to tell them about the SEC charges, and Randall followed with his own. "In my opinion, the . . . SEC contention is somewhat ridiculous," Randall said, pointing out that the boards of Lucky Friday and Hecla had hesitated to merge, one Lucky Friday director had "violently opposed" combining, and Leisk consented "reluctantly" only a day before it was agreed. Randall argued that the merger had been so uncertain, until the last moment, that he did not see how anyone could have taken advantage of it.

The SEC found in Golconda's minutebooks, however, that Magnuson had assured Golconda's directors sometime earlier that the merger was "inevitable." Magnuson acknowledged that he believed it would happen and that he traded in stocks, but he denied "inside knowledge." His attorneys, after five years in the courts, would acquiesce in a consent decree: Magnuson admitted no violations but agreed to pay $5,746—and Golconda, $41,346—to a trustee who would distribute the money to persons showing that they had been "defrauded" by the transactions.

With the Lucky Friday merger, Randall reviewed Hecla's standing in the marketplace, uneasy that the company's stock was undervalued. Despite its listing for forty-nine years on the American Stock Exchange, Hecla was little known outside the western hardrock mining community and the investors who favored its regular dividends. Hecla was eligible, however, for listing on the prestigious New York Stock Exchange (NYSE) on the basis of minimal criteria: earning capacity, publicly held stock, and outstanding shares. Listing among the 1,240 companies on NYSE would presumably boost the quotations for Hecla's stock, give it wider notice, and eventually broaden its base of 6,632 shareholders. Only two companies in the inland

Pacific Northwest were then listed on the "big board," Sunshine Mining and the Washington Water Power.

On application, the New York Stock Exchange accepted Hecla for trading beginning December 21, 1964. Traditional social obligations surrounded the entry of a new firm into the exchange: the directors and their wives would attend the opening of trading, Randall would be expected to buy the first 100 shares, and the Hecla people would be guests of the exchange president at a cocktail party and luncheon where there would be publicity pictures and welcoming words. Randall, Love, Magnuson, and William J. Grismer and their wives attended; Randall bought his shares at $33.37 (Hecla had closed at $33 on Amex the previous day) and spoke briefly, declaring that "listing on the New York Stock Exchange is an important milestone in the growth of Hecla."

In its report of the day, the *Spokesman-Review* recalled that Hecla's "fortunes had dimmed somewhat until 1951. During a reorganization that year a talented comptroller, Lester J. Randall, was handed the presidency. . . . Randall and the shrewd management team he developed began an uphill fight . . . [and] boldly invested in many mining ventures where others failed. For Hecla the real turning point came in January 1959. Randall offered $7.50 per share for 600,000 shares of Lucky Friday."

Randall recognized that Hecla's increased prosperity and recognition might make the company a target for takeover. He and Love had been jittery about predatory darts for some time— hardly new, for James McCarthy had regularly scanned market summaries to detect any unexplained stirring of Hecla stock. So had Hanley. Randall had been jumpy about takeover ever since Callahan Mining Corporation bought Hecla stock a few years earlier, particularly because Joseph Hirshhorn used Callahan as a vehicle for oil and mining promotions. Today Hirshhorn is remembered for donating a national museum of art with a sculpture garden, but in the fifties he was a canny, restless speculator in oil, real estate, gold, copper, and uranium in the United States and Canada.

Hirshhorn had risen, Horatio Alger style, from janitor to trader. He had pulled out of the market just before the 1929 crash and thereby profited in millions. For his audacious tactics—a Canadian journal, *The Northern Miner*, called him "the daring mine maker"—scrupulous investors dealt with him at arm's length. In the late forties, Hirshhorn had bet $30,000 on a geologist's hunch in the Algoma Basin, north of Lake Huron, and with an elaborate charade of fake prospects to put off rivals, had locked up Canada's richest uranium field—1,400 claims covering 56,000 acres, worth perhaps $8 billion. As in business, so he was in art collecting. A curator compared Hirshhorn to Mellon—"the morality of the great white shark."

Short (five feet, four inches), volatile, Hirshhorn's way was pungent and explosive; he "dominated every group," the *New York Times* would say, with "verbal karate." To think that Hecla might be one of Hirshhorn's targets chilled Randall. Callahan had been a pioneer of the Coeur d'Alene district, long shepherded by brothers, James and Donald Callahan, until its stock control had gone to New York buyers in 1936. Hirshhorn moved on Callahan with a purchase of 770,000 shares in 1954 and as its chairman shaped Callahan as a U.S. counterpart to his International Mines Service, Inc., which diversified from Canadian mines promotion into oil, natural gas, and manufacturing. Under Hirshhorn, Callahan ranged across six states and Alaska with interests in Canada.

Callahan had begun to buy Hecla stock unobtrusively in 1957. With its purchase of 49,500 shares in March 1958, it displaced Newmont (with 45,300) as Hecla's largest single stockholder. Shortly after, Randall braced Hirshhorn at lunch in New York. Hirshhorn denied any intention of seizing Hecla but a few months later, Callahan's president—suave, quick-witted, rotund Joseph T. "Jo" Hall—asked for a list of Hecla shareholders. Because this might signal proxy solicitation for control, Randall refused to give Hall the list. Hall explained that Callahan merely wanted to identify owners of large blocks, to buy from them rather than through the exchange. Randall again demanded to know if Callahan aimed to take over Hecla. Hall denied such a purpose, but Hirshhorn's repute—the white shark—was not reassuring.

But Hecla recognized Callahan's holding by electing Hall to the board in 1958, on Pollard's resignation, and the next year, naming Hull, attorney for the Sixteen Operators and vice president of Callahan, to a directorship in place of Charles A. Tilford, who did not stand for reelection. At the end of 1959, consequently, Hecla's board of seven consisted of Banghart and Grunow (Newmont men), Hall and Hull (Callahan men), and

Randall, Hunt, and Leisk. Leisk had succeeded Joe McCarthy, who resigned when he sold his businesses in Orofino to accept appointment as Idaho commissioner of finance.

Randall's worries about takeover were, in one sense, futile. Any major company, taking the notion, could have digested Hecla without burping. Randall had looked to Newmont to defend Hecla, but with the retirement of Fred Searls as president of Newmont in 1954, relations between Newmont and Hecla drifted from benevolence toward business association. Plato Malozemoff, who had joined Newmont after World War II as a metallurgist and financier and had been instrumental in turning Tsumeb copper in South Africa into a bonanza for Newmont, became president. Searls took the title of chairman. Russian-born Plato, however agreeable, did not share the goodwill dating back to James McCarthy's time, and Randall could no longer be sure that Newmont, if Malozemoff sensed a better deal, would stand like Horatio between Hecla and an attacker.

As Randall got to know Jo Hall, his fears of Callahan abated. Hall had been with Sunshine until 1936, when he joined the new Callahan that New Yorkers fashioned. A Yale man exuding personal charm, Hall knew his way in the labyrinths of the market and mining finance. As a Hecla director, he learned that Hecla was uncomfortable with its 19 percent holding in Bunker Hill, and not long after coming on the board, Hall asked Randall if Hecla wanted to sell Callahan its Bunker Hill stock. Randall freely admitted "a feeling of uneasiness about Bunker Hill policy and . . . management," but did not think Hecla should sell "unless we could get some investment equally as good."

Uneasiness with Bunker Hill harked to Sullivan days, when Hecla had occasionally scuttled Bunker Hill schemes to balance its lead and zinc capabilities. But since, Hecla had been put out when Bunker Hill abruptly raised its smelter charges. When Stanly Easton retired in 1954, the chummy directorate of Bunker Hill had chosen John D. "Jack" Bradley as president. Bradley, a mining engineer, son of the late Bunker Hill president Frederick Bradley, had married Easton's daughter Jane. He had been a Bunker Hill director since 1938. A San Franciscan who commuted to Kellogg, Bradley had exasperated the other managers by dealing with unions on his own. A good many of his peers felt that the Bunker Hill began to slide when Bradley allowed his executives to commute to Kellogg from lake homes. Traditionally, managers had lived in a compound of company houses near Kellogg, where the perquisites of rank were precious and a new general manager's wife was expected to redecorate the best house with a prodigality that confirmed her husband's rise to the top.

By 1958, with lead mining in a depressed cycle, most mines had reduced their work weeks to four days, and Bunker Hill had stopped paying dividends. Wanting a stronger voice in Bunker Hill's management, Hecla asked for more representation on its board. Bunker Hill seemed indifferent, however, and Spokane stockbroker Harrison muddied Hecla's campaign with his proxy solicitation to elect Spokane directors to Bunker Hill. Harrison asserted that 42 percent of Bunker Hill's 5,188 stockholders lived in northern Idaho and eastern Washington, holding 35 percent of its outstanding stock, while six of seven directors lived in San Francisco. If he could rally enough proxies, Harrison declared, he would nominate Harry Magnuson and Horton Herman to the Bunker Hill board. Randall, he said, represented Hecla, not the area's stockholders.

Harrison attracted only about 650 proxies for 200,000 shares (of 1,583,000), but Bunker Hill, sniffing restiveness, enlarged its board to nine members, adding Kinsey M. Robinson, president of the Washington Water Power Company, and Ross Leisk to the new seats. Whatever headway Randall may have made with Bradley toward improving Bunker Hill management was lost, however, when Jack and Jane Bradley died in an auto collision on the Sacramento freeway on Thanksgiving night.

After Bradley's death, Randall and Hall worked out a trade: Hecla would exchange 68,000 shares of Bunker Hill common with Callahan for 77,000 shares of Hecla on condition that Callahan buy 32,000 additional Bunker Hill from Hecla for $11 a share—a bargain. This would erase Callahan's holding in Hecla and would reduce Hecla's Bunker Hill which, as Randall made plain in a press release, was "deemed out of proportion to Hecla's total investment in its other assets." Hecla's shareholders approved the trade. By prearrangement, on May 6, 1960, Hall and Hull quit as Hecla directors and Love and Magnuson replaced them. Hecla could now breathe easier about Callahan and Joseph Hirshhorn. But Randall was appalled to learn that Hecla had contracted its accounting to the Bunker Hill's computer. He ordered that stopped.

Hecla would further reduce its Bunker Hill holding to approximately 6 percent by paying a fourth-quarter dividend for 1965 in Bunker Hill stock and then closing out its interest in Bunker Hill entirely by selling back to Bunker Hill all its remaining shares, 99,421, for approximately $2.5 million in 1966.

A few months before Hecla applied for listing on the New York Stock Exchange, Marcus Banghart mentioned, in a directors' meeting, that Newmont was seeking funds for what looked like a truly major undertaking, Granduc, a copper prospect in the desolate, glacial Alaskan Range of Northwest Canada. Both Randall and Love spoke up, asking if Hecla could come in. Bang backed away, explaining that, uh, Newmont was talking right now, you know, to Canadian companies. A few days later, Randall wrote him a letter: "This is to advise you that if others do not materialize, Hecla would like an opportunity to participate" in Granduc.

Granduc had wallowed in heavy weather for a decade, but Malozemoff's "imagination had been fired by the challenge," according to Newmont's historian. Granduc had been spotted originally from helicopter by a geologist for Granby Consolidated Mining, Smelting & Power Company investigating reports of claims staked in the area. Granby, which had been associated with Newmont in a nickel property, did not have the resources to exploit Granduc and had invited Newmont to come in as an equal partner. (The name Granduc is a combination of Granby and Leduc, the river and glacier nearby.) Exploring, limited to short, frigid summers, had cost $500,000 or more annually, and the partners had sunk $6 million in drilling without fully outlining the orebody. It looked big—but Granby, discouraged by costs, dropped out.

Malozemoff offered to sell Hecla $10 million in cumulative preferred stock of Granduc Mines, Ltd. Randall was pleased to tell his board, "Frankly, I was quite surprised to find that we should have little difficulty in financing Granduc," based on projected costs and income.

Love investigated Granduc for Hecla. He was not enthusiastic, concluding that "if Hecla were to hold its share as an investment throughout the entire operation of Granduc and [if] the profitability of the mine was no better than indicated, it is not an attractive venture." He predicted that Hecla's return from Granduc would be realized from future sales of appreciated stock.

Granduc was thus equivocal—a prospect of unknown dimensions in an appalling location from which Hecla might profit if its stock rose on the market. The board voted, nonetheless, to accept Malozemoff's offer. With Hecla's $10 million in hand, Malozemoff raised $10 million more by a long-term ore sales contract with Asarco and $30 million by first-mortgage bonds to Bankers Trust Company of New York.

Granduc, at the foot of glaciers, lay 31.5 miles in a straight line from the hamlet of Stewart, the closest port, about 60 miles above Prince Rupert, British Columbia. A reasonably direct land route from Stewart, which was to be home base for workers and shipping point for concentrates, required tunneling through intervening mountains. Crews started to drive a 10.5-mile tunnel in late 1964, while others set up a work camp at the mine site to begin the surface plant, shaft, and adits. In February of the following year, an avalanche wiped out the camp, killing twenty-six men. Survivors perched on blades of bulldozers cutting trenches in the snow to search for victims. They found one, buried three days under a helicopter pad, who had heard search planes taking off but could not signal them. As the avalanche roared across the camp, some men clawed themselves free. "Horrible," recalled Love, who flew in to inspect the tragedy. "That wasn't a large mountain and it didn't look dangerous . . . but weather conditions were just right and the whole side of that mountain came down. Terrible." The last bodies could not be removed before June. By then, the turnover among workers had reached the staggering rate of one quitting of every three.

Furthermore, Malozemoff had revised upward his forecast of the cost of getting into production. Now it stood at $80 million—too rich for Hecla, and Hecla converted to a 16 percent stock interest rather than put in more cash. Newmont thereupon organized a new wholly owned subsidiary, Granduc Operating Company; leased the Granduc claims to the new company on a royalty contract; brought in Asarco as a partner in the lease; and cancelled its own stock in Granduc Mines, which had the effect of raising Hecla's interest to 35.4 percent of the shares outstanding. The tunnel would be holed through (after hitting water and battling collapsing shale) in December 1968, and the concentrating mill would treat its first ores in November 1970—while deficits piled up. Copper content in the concentrates ran below estimates because the sublevel caving method of extracting ores diluted them.

Granduc would betray Malozemoff's hopes. Within three years, the copper market faded, forcing Granduc to halve production. Hecla exchanged some preferred stock with Granduc Mines for unsecured notes on which it would receive only partial payments against the principal. The mine suffered a net loss in 1977 of more than $17.7 million. By then, Newmont and Asarco had given up hope that copper markets would revive. They marked down Granduc to a nominal value of one dollar, wrote off their investments, gave up their lease, and salvaged some underground equipment. Hecla, which had recovered part of its costs from royalties, would similarly write off its remaining investment, $5.5 million, but would retain its stock interest: all of the preferred and 35.4 percent of the common stock.

Despite Hecla's ventures outside northern Idaho, Lucky Friday remained its principal property and a focal point for potential competition. Day Mines, Inc., had "picked up everything that was loose" around Lucky Friday, in the words of a Hecla manager, including the Hunter Ranch, immediately west of Lucky Friday.

For years, Hecla and Day had regarded each other with a coolness nurtured by competing cheek by jowl in Burke canyon, one always suspecting that the other plotted to invade this vein or that one. In earlier times, McCarthy and Harry Day had cooperated in the Mine Owners Association, but McCarthy accommodated Asarco, the smelter trust, while Day abhorred it. Both men were loyal to the town of Wallace, but McCarthy was a Republican and Day, a leader in the Democratic party. In those days, Wallace had both a Republican and a Democratic newspaper, a Republican and a Democratic bank, and so on.

McCarthy had been angered by Eugene Day's bid for the Hecla with Sarah Smith, as well as by Harry Day's siding with the Marsh against Hecla. For his part, Harry Day had been outraged by McCarthy's selection of a Missoula Mason to build a new Catholic church in Wallace. Relations had been so chilled, for a time, that when Harry's son, Henry Lawrence Day, stopped by the Hecla offices to see Hanley, he was said to be the first Day in twenty years to visit Hecla. The office staff gaped openly as Day, in yellow sweater and baggy corduroy trousers, marched through the long hall to Hanley's office.

Day Mines and Hecla had usually set aside their differences in favor of a business deal. McCarthy, for example, had joined

Eugene Day in buying the Coeur d'Alene Hardware & Foundry Company. Now, the Day interests in properties embracing the Lucky Friday offered an opportunity to deal. Randall and Henry Day negotiated to develop the Hunter Ranch through the Lucky Friday shaft and to split costs and profits. As they talked, Day mentioned that he might sell a substantial block of Day Mines stock to diversify his interests and lighten his responsibilities, for he was now sixty-three with no male heir.

Randall proposed to his board that Hecla buy 400,000 or more shares of Day partly by exchanging 3.6 Hecla for one Day and partly by paying cash at $7.75 a share. "Obviously, a purchase of Day Mines, Inc., stock at . . . $7.75 cannot be justified on the basis of a past history of earnings," he acknowledged. "However, from a long-term viewpoint, we believe it would be a good investment." Randall did not say the obvious: that controversy over ore rights loomed unless Hecla and Day worked together. Moreover, Day Mines operated the Dayrock mine and held several promising properties in the Coeur d'Alene district—12 percent of Rainbow, worked by Asarco as part of the Coeur unit project, 25 percent of Asarco's lease of the productive Galena (a Callahan mine), 41 percent of Abot Mining Company, and a long-term lease on Independence Lead Mines, both with claims near Lucky Friday. Day also owned gold mines near Republic, Washington, and 4 percent of Pend Oreille Mines & Metals. Day's net in 1967 was $1.2 million, 41 cents a share, roughly one-third of Hecla's earnings per share.

Love worked out an agreement to trade 78,000 shares of Hecla and to pay $914,360 for 403,509 shares of Day Mines, approximately 14 percent of the outstanding stock. To quiet speculation, Randall said publicly that the Day acquisition was simply an investment, disavowing any intention of taking part in the management of Day Mines, even though Hecla was now Day's largest stockholder. To his directors, however, Randall remarked, "We would not plan on taking control for at least one year hence and possibly two years." Quotations for both stocks rose following announcement of Hecla's acquisition.

In connection with the Day deal, Randall had suggested to his board a cooperative exploration beyond Lucky Friday into prospects owned by Day and associated companies. These companies now agreed to unitize their properties as the "DIA Area"—Day for Day, I for Independence Lead, and A for Abot—with Hecla advancing all the funds for exploration, taking all income until its expenses were repaid, and then dividing profits 60 percent for Hecla and 40 percent for the others.

While talks with Day were going on, Randall sent Love to bargain for the old Morning mine with J. C. Kieffer, general manager of Asarco's northwest mining department, acting on Love's assurance that the Star and Morning could be mined deeper profitably. Except for salvage in the upper levels, Asarco had closed the Morning in 1953 after sixty-four years of virtually continuous production. Rumors had circulated then that Hecla might buy the Morning.

Now in 1961, eight years after the mine had been closed, Love concluded a lease on the Morning for a royalty to Asarco and assigned 70 percent of Hecla's interest in the lease to Bunker Hill to conform with a revised 30–70 division of Star operating profits, superseding the management agreement of 1955 when Hecla sold out of Sullivan. Calling the Morning and Star the "Star Unit Area," Hecla mined the Morning through the Star.

Hecla soon realized that the mines would have to go far deeper to profit, and concluded that Hecla must own the Morning to deepen it. "Income over and above cost is contingent upon economic mining of deep level ore reserves," the company's 1965 report said, "and present plans (which would not have been considered feasible without purchase of the Morning property) call for major underground installations to facilitate extraction of ore from deep levels of the Star-Morning Unit."

Hence, Love approached Kieffer again in 1966. "That was the first really serious negotiation I got into," Love would recall. Kieffer did not want to sell, but the decision would be made in New York. "Joe Kieffer was a tough guy. We talked and talked. It took me a year."

Apparently because the Morning mill had burned in 1957, and the home office refused to sanction further expenditures for deep mining—the Morning was said to be the world's deepest lead mine at 6,600 feet—Kieffer finally reported that Asarco would sell. In the meantime, Randall had warned his board that, alone, the Star would have to be abandoned in two years, "unless steps are taken immediately to improve Star mine facilities." With the Morning, however, Randall's team believed the Star Unit "might operate profitably for years to come."

The Morning was one of the district's oldest mines, worked since 1889, and even in its last feeble year of operation by Asarco, it had been the sixth largest producing mine in the Coeur d'Alenes. As the outcome of an apex suit concluded in 1921, the Star and Morning shared an endline set by the court, an arbitrary division of the single orebody both worked. It was common opinion that the judge located the endline out of sympathy for E. W. Moffitt, who had explored the Star for years, driving parallel to a vein and only thirty feet from it, without striking commercial ore. Over the years, thirteen distinct veins had been mined through sixty miles of tunnels in the Morning. Several openings connected the Star and Morning for ventilation and pumping. The Morning depended on the Star for air—even chilled air under pressure could lower temperatures only to 87° at 6,600 feet—and the Star depended on the Morning for pumping, since Star's water tended to run off into the deeper Morning. After 1948, when Hecla bought some houses in Mullan, some Star men came to work through the Morning. Their conjunct orebody narrowed with depth and seemed to tilt toward deposits below the Star's lowest level.

Ownership of the Morning combined with unit operation of mines near Lucky Friday would establish a Hecla corridor from Burke to Mullan, a zone of contiguous mines. This corridor lay in a complex geological belt north of the Osburn fault. No telling what might still lie hidden in those convoluted folds.

Asarco sold the Morning to Hecla for 25,230 shares of Hecla stock (roughly $747,400) on February 12, 1966. Almost immediately Hecla started sinking a new central shaft capable of reaching the 9100 level, beginning at the 2000 level and using an older shaft for the first several thousand feet. Furthermore, Hecla negotiated a new agreement with Bunker Hill for the Star providing that on May 1, 1981, the companies would terminate royalty payments to Hecla on Morning ores and would divide the property equally between them. The Star Unit Area, with the strictest control over costs, would yield profitable ores for seventeen more years (until 1982).

And now it was the spring of 1966, approaching the time Randall had set to retire as president, confident that his retirement would encourage younger men to see careers for themselves with Hecla. So would a stock option plan for key employees adopted by the shareholders at their 1964 meeting. Randall would remain as chairman, transferring daily management of Hecla to one of his team, Bill Love.

Randall could be satisfied with his fourteen years. The company's net for 1966 would be "an all-time record" of $6.8 mil-

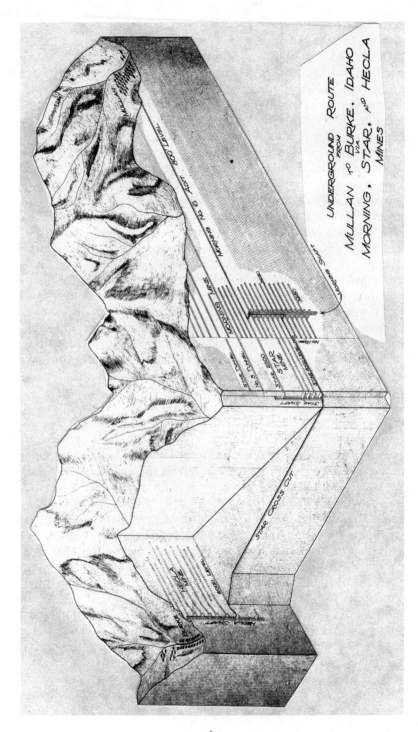

UNDERGROUND ROUTE
FROM
MULLAN TO BURKE, IDAHO
VIA
MORNING, STAR, AND HECLA
MINES

160

lion. He had done nearly all he set out to do: He had put through internal changes for orderly management—on Grunow's suggestion, he had begun an "agenda book" for each director with detailed statements of items to be discussed, so that meetings could be precise and brief; set specific dates for directors' quarterly meetings; and initiated ratification of the board's actions by shareholders—blanket approval, to be sure, but until 1966, shareholders had not been invited to confirm the directors' decisions.

Hecla was now considerably better known in the industry and in the marketplace, its stock traded on the New York Stock Exchange, and exploration offices opened in strategic centers: Tucson, Reno, Salt Lake City, Vancouver, and Toronto.

Randall had acquired mines to carry Hecla forward—mainly Lucky Friday and, with a shorter predicted life, the Star Unit—and had erected protective barriers around them by lease, purchase, or unit agreements. And he had maintained steady Hecla dividends through lean as well as fat years.

Randall had come into the presidency of a company unsure of its future. He would leave it strong and confident. He could afford a smile of satisfaction as he called to order his last shareholders' meeting. After that, Love would be president of Hecla and its destiny would be in his hands.

10

Lakeshore

THE SONORAN DESERT EXTENDS FROM MEXICO INTO SOUTH-
western Arizona. It is a land with little prospect, one of the
most arid basins of North America, cupped by low mountain
ridges and dotted with the baleful beauty of saguaro (a giant
cactus), cholla, mesquite, and ocotillo—the kind of land conferred on Indian tribes, where now live the Papagos, whose
word for "little spring" gave Arizona its name. There are about
7,500 Papagos on roughly 2.8 million dry acres, trying to farm
and raise cattle on soil that, it is said, "will not support a cow
to an acre." Impoverished, teeth ground down by sand in their
food, the Papagos cluster in hamlets at water holes or at Sells,
the reservation headquarters. Sells was named for Cato Sells,
commissioner of Indian affairs in the administration of Wood-
row Wilson, who, if he had had his way, would have given
each Indian a plot of land "to work out his destiny" without
any help from the government.

Roads here, unpaved and unmarked except for weathered,
hand-lettered signs pointing toward Indian villages, have been
a route for drug and illegal immigrant traffic from Mexico. Because the area was split off from Mexico by the Gadsden Purchase, many Papagos have relatives across the border. Most
speak a native tongue laced with Spanish and English terms.
They have been largely Catholic from Spanish times. About
1968, Mormons started to proselytize the Papagos, creating re-
ligious and political schism on the reservation.

One hundred miles or so to the southeast, at Bisbee, copper
has been mined since 1880. And about the time Bisbee was
starting up, copper claims were staked on the northern reaches
of the Papago reserve, then abandoned, relocated, and sporadically mined. After World War II, the U.S. Bureau of Mines
explored there by drilling. On the basis of that work, a local
company, Transarizona Resources, Inc., consolidated old claims
to mine by open pit, but went into receivership in 1962. Four

years later, El Paso Natural Gas bought a half interest and during exploratory drilling found a larger deposit—an orebody bigger than it cared to handle—offering to share with another company that would take the remaining half of Transarizona and operate a mine, giving the place the unlikely name, in that desert, of Lakeshore.

Hecla was among those that bid for the Lakeshore project. In the fall of 1968, Hecla's president, Bill Love, sent its chief geologist, Herb Harper, a solid, deliberate man, to look at El Paso's copper on the Papago reservation. Harper had visited Transarizona's mine six years earlier and had come away unimpressed. But now he reported that El Paso had a major discovery on its hands, and Love determined to bid for half of it. Hecla's by-word for the next decade was to be Lakeshore.

Lakeshore loomed so large, like one peak towering paramount above foothills, that it dwarfed Hecla's other ongoing business: the deepening of the Lucky Friday and Star-Morning, the new copper venture in northern British Columbia, talk of merger, a hazard in silver futures, and internecine struggles for stock control. Bill Love came into the presidency bent on maintaining the momentum Randall had given Hecla. He planned to free the company from its sole dependency on silver and lead, and to fend off raiders.

One of Love's first steps was to emphasize exploration. He and Harper agreed they would concentrate on known districts in the western United States and Canada and attempt to participate in joint ventures; they would look into copper, uranium, and other properties. The board raised the exploration budget to $1.5 million, and would increase that in succeeding years because, as Chairman Randall pointed out, "Our chances are limited . . . and [we] have therefore materially increased our budget and efforts" to find new mines. In 1967 Hecla spent almost as much for the fixed costs of outpost offices as its annual expenditure for exploration between 1962 and 1965. The main exploration office was returned from Spokane to Wallace.

One frigid prospect, Liard Copper Mines, northeast of Granduc, would require hauling ores 100 miles by truck to tidewater at Stewart. Discovered in 1957, Liard was so remote that the original company put off exploring until a provincial highway reached the area. Then Asarco optioned Liard but gave it up when drill holes showed an average grade of ore below expectations. Independent tests of the samples, however, indicated a deposit of 200 million tons of 0.4 percent copper with recoverable values in molybdenum, gold, and silver, which seemed encouraging. A former Asarco man, Phil Conley, in Hecla's Vancouver office, leaped at Liard when Asarco backed out, and through a Canadian subsidiary, Hecla Operating Company, Hecla contracted to explore and develop the property for a 70 percent share of profits.

Seven drill holes, outlining an orebody one by one-and-one-half miles, persuaded Hecla that Liard was "the most attractive of Hecla's exploration endeavors in Canada," and that the low-grade copper could be mined profitably by open pit. That was, Bill Love would remember, "the heyday of copper optimism." Copper prices had been rising steadily on the world markets for half a decade.

Hecla would hold on at Liard for nearly eleven years, expand into adjoining claims—Paramount, Schaft Creek—and watch the copper market stumble and fall. In the end, Liard yielded no copper for Hecla. The electrical generation of northern British Columbia then proved inadequate for large-scale mining, and an ambitious provincial government imposed new taxes on gross royalties—a tax the Mining Association of British Columbia unsuccessfully attacked as "unconstitutional," but operators did not dare flout it, for the law allowed confiscation for failure to pay. Yet a consensus prevailed that the copper market would recover, and when Hecla concluded in 1978 that Liard "was not a good project for Hecla . . . now or in the near future," it sold its 70 percent to Teck Corporation of Vancouver for a net profit of more than $632,000, retaining a 5 percent interest in any future profits. (To date, there have been none.)

Despite Hecla's investment in Liard and its exploration offices throughout the West, Love was careful to tell shareholders that "the principal emphasis in our search for new ore is in the Coeur d'Alene district." And in the district, the owners of small mining companies, some virtually dormant for years, realized that their best chance lay in developing their claims from the shafts of Hecla or Sunshine. Small companies could not finance deep shafts, and to the managers of bigger ones, sinking competing shafts seemed a waste of money. For its part, Hecla foresaw a likelihood of conflicts over mineral rights when veins ranged beyond the boundaries of its mines.

Consequently, the time was ripe for further unit agreements, and in Love's first full year as president, 1967, Hecla wrote five of them: the DIA Area, unitizing properties northwest of Lucky Friday; North Abot, unitizing Abot and Day properties to be explored from Lucky Friday; West Independence, to be entered at the 7300 level from the Star-Morning; Consolidated Silver, nine prospects south of the Osburn fault to mine from the former Silver Summit; and the Nine Corporation, a consolidation of 225 claims owned principally by Hecla and Day Mines in the Dobson Pass section north of Wallace.

These would take three to ten years for drilling, shaft construction, equipping, and crosscutting before the extent of mineral, if any, could be determined. Not all would pan out: the Nine Corporation, for one, would be shelved after three years of geochemical analysis and drilling showed no mineral worth digging for. Consolidated Silver, formed in 1967, would deepen the Silver Summit shaft; it absorbed Silver Summit and leased the unitized ground to Asarco which, in turn, conveyed a one-fourth interest in its lease to Hecla to operate the project. After three years, when no significant mineral had been found, Asarco terminated its lease, leaving Hecla to find other partners.

Con Silver would be suspended until 1980 when Hecla, Coeur d'Alene Mines Corporation, Silver Dollar, and Sunshine joined to resurrect it with Hecla, holding 64 percent, as managing operator. (Silver Dollar's interest was absorbed in 1981 by Sunshine.) As the Consolidated Silver Venture, it would produce 27,584 tons of ore in 1981 averaging 12.2 ounces of silver and .26 percent copper a ton but as silver prices fell, would suspend production again. It would be 1983 before the shaft reached its intended depth of 5,524 feet and exploration of prospective ores to the east began. Three years later, Con Silver would be put on the shelf again to wait for better silver prices.

Even while they were deepened, the Lucky Friday and Star-Morning continued to disgorge ores—the Lucky Friday about 185,000 tons and the Star-Morning about 280,000 a year—although a shortage of skilled men reduced output from the Lucky Friday in 1969 and 1970. Moreover, a flow of underground water delayed sinking the number 2 shaft for Lucky Friday, requiring nearly a year to dam with grout. In the Star-Morning, construction of a new shaft and installation of the Scot hoist consumed more than four years.

The hoist, built by the Scot firm of Fullerton, Hodgart & Barclay, noted for hoists in deep South African mines, had to be manufactured in sections that could pass through eight-by-eight passages, to be assembled in a hoist room carved at the 2000 level. This was the hoist that would reach to 9,100 feet if ore persisted at that level—potentially the deepest mining shaft in North America.

"The Lucky Friday makes the single most important contribution to Hecla's earnings," Bill Love remarked on the occasion of Hecla's initial listing for trading on the Pacific Coast Exchange in San Francisco in September 1967. Silver regularly accounted for more that 40 percent of Hecla's income. (In 1968, silver brought in 58.9 percent; in 1975, 62.3 percent.) The silver market had turned "volatile," to use Love's term, after the Treasury stopped selling at $1.29 an ounce, although the government maintained a ceiling price until 1972. On occasion, massive Treasury sales temporarily depressed the price but, in the long run, silver rose more or less steadily for forty-five years, starting with Treasury purchases in 1933 and appreciated 7,568 percent by 1979. Those were years when silver miners rode jauntily at the crest of the market.

During 1968, certain that silver would continue rising, Hecla's board bought 224 silver futures contracts that would mature in one to two years, placing $1.2 million with brokers as margin. A good many silver producers were buying bullion or stockpiling or buying on margin. "We thought silver was going up—Les and I agreed on this," Love recalled. "We were producing silver, so we took the position that as long as we could deliver silver, we could use futures contracts." But the frisky market dipped and by year's end, Hecla had lost $600,000. (Love and Randall had also invested personal funds in futures.) "We did what everyone else who gets into the commodities market will do if he doesn't know precisely what he's doing: we continued to buy when the market went up and when the market went down," Love went on, "and by the time we got out, we lost money." Hecla's losses ran to nearly $2 million. Looking back, Love said ruefully, "We made a mistake—and we had to eat it."

In its 1970 report, Hecla's management acknowledged its error, noting that it had renewed silver future contracts as they matured, compounding its losses. A Spokane attorney, Thomas D. Malott, who owned stock, and another Spokane shareholder, sued Hecla claiming damages for the market loss. The court denied their petition, decreeing that Hecla's directors, "acted in good faith within the authority of the articles of incorporation . . . solely for the best interests of Hecla Mining Company." But by chance, the judge's clerk neglected to file the judgment, and the case went to an appellate court on a technicality—that the lost document prevented an appeal within thirty days as required. The appellate court, in a split decision, declined to review the case.

One advantage to listing on the Pacific exchange was that, due to the difference in time zones, Hecla stock could be traded for more hours each day. That suited Love and Randall's purpose: "to reflect the Company's growth in recent years by increasing the number of shares outstanding and to effect a market price range . . . more attractive to the investing public," and to encourage stockholders to ratify an increase in capital stock to 6,000,000 shares.

With the increase, each shareholder received one additional share for each share owned, a stock split on June 7, 1968. In effect, the distribution doubled dividends to individual shareholders, for despite lower net earnings (due to a union strike of Lucky Friday from October 1967 to June 1968), dividends per share which had been sixty cents in 1967 before the split, amounted to sixty-five cents in 1968 and seventy cents a share in 1969. With the split and trading in San Francisco, Hecla asked the Spokane exchange to de-list its stock, a request the exchange's directors ignored. Then Hecla sent an emissary to Spokane to suggest that the exchange stop circulating "crazy, wild stories" about Hecla and its business. The exchange ignored that request, too.

Meanwhile, the costs of mining and smelting crept upward. Lucky Friday miners had negotiated a wage increase of forty-five cents an hour, bringing the average pay to $22.98 a day in the first year of a three-year contract. Between 1972 and 1977, the average cost of mining and milling one ton from the Lucky Friday would increase from $23.16 to $41.08, and at the Sunshine Unit Area, from $30.66 to $102.72. During the same period, by sending richer ore to smelters, Hecla raised its average net smelter return to $102.18, and Sunshine, to $110.68. Twice in these years, the Bunker Hill smelter would arbitrarily increase smelting charges, and with the second increase, Hecla complained that the smelter "unilaterally changed the terms

. . . and eliminated Hecla's profit" from the Star-Morning, submitting its protest to arbitration. An arbitrator held for Hecla.

As Hecla's mines continued to make money, the danger of takeover loomed in Love's and Randall's minds. Whether Hecla has ever been in actual peril of takeover seems an open question. For one, Henry Goldberg, a New York investment broker and Hecla specialist since 1916, detected "no danger of anyone taking it over." Nonetheless, an apprehension of takeover influenced Love's actions as president. His foreboding magnified with a raid on Bunker Hill in February 1968. With conglomerates—companies that combined diverse businesses under one management—swallowing quarry right and left, Hecla could no longer expect a raid solely from within the mining industry.

When it pounced on Bunker Hill, Gulf & Western (not long before, a small manufacturer of automobile parts) had also gulped New Jersey Zinc, then Paramount Pictures. It was aiming at Armour. Too late, Bunker Hill's directors realized their vulnerability. They were not prepared to defend the company. After losing millions in a long strike in 1960 which depressed its stock, Bunker Hill had paid off its debts and launched an expansion program; it owned untapped high-grade silver in the Crescent mine, 22 percent of a Nevada gold mine, and tracts of Idaho forest. But Bunker Hill's stock, recently bought by easterners willing—perhaps intending—to turn it for quick profit, meant that no large blocks belonged to loyal owners who might thwart a raid. Hectic days: Charles E. Schwab, Bunker Hill's president, telephoned hurriedly around the country seeking a friendly buyer—Homestake, Utah Construction & Mining—and the directors sifted proposals from companies willing to merge. None could move fast enough.

Gulf & Western came within hours of acquiring Bunker Hill before Gulf Resources & Chemical of Houston outbid it with a tender of $56 a share for 700,000 shares, $10 higher than Bunker Hill ever brought. Gulf Resources sucked up 500,000 shares in one day—arbitrage stock plus 50,000 thought in "friendly" hands. "The game was over," Schwab acknowledged. Gulf Resources had grabbed 36 percent of Bunker Hill's outstanding shares in a few weeks. He telephoned Robert H. Allen, president of Gulf Resources, to confirm the takeover.

On June 6, Gulf Resources & Chemical's logo went up on

exchange boards in place of the familiar BH. Allen witnessed the first trading on the New York Stock Exchange. Telling his story, Schwab was candid with Love and Randall. He had been dismayed by the speed of the raid and how little he could do to combat it. Of course, his story made Love and Randall more wary.

Like the mugging of a neighbor, Schwab's encounter set the Coeur d'Alene mining community on edge. Hecla's directors asked investors and legal consultants how to prevent a take-over, and Randall summarized their advice: One warned that a "typical takeover target has decreasing dividends, so we should raise dividends"; a lawyer recommended splitting stock—"we have done this"; good relations with stockholders; purchase of Hecla's outstanding stock—"doesn't seem practical for Hecla"; and a counteroffer to any tender—"we should seriously consider this." Randall concluded that Bunker Hill might have fended off Gulf Resources with a counteroffer "if they made prior arrangements for a line of credit, and we should look into this."

With raiders much on his mind, Bill Love was unsettled by Herb Harper's report of a breakfast meeting in Wyoming ostensibly to talk about uranium prospects with Tim Collins, a Denver investment broker who represented Herbert F. Korholz's Susquehannah Corporation, a diversifying uranium mining and milling company. Korholz was notorious for take-overs and, remarked Harper, Collins had seemed "a lot more interested in Hecla in general than in uranium." Shortly after, Love was shocked to learn that Harry Magnuson had sold his personal stock in Golconda—118,225 shares—to Korholz through Collins. Love felt an ominous chill, for Golconda with 13 percent was among Hecla's largest shareholders.

An urbane Hollander who had come to the United States to make his career, Korholz set traps with small companies to snare bigger ones, "raising a very American storm in U.S. business," *Forbes* magazine asserted. In a "particularly bitter stockholder dispute," Korholz had taken control of Susquehannah, said *Forbes,* and with it "outmaneuvered" other raiders to grab Atlantic Research Corporation. Earlier, using a Colorado insulation company with annual sales of $100,000, he had gulped a $6-million insulation manufacturer and moved on to American Gypsum Company.

Moreover, Susquehannah had raised $22.5 million in twenty-four hours with a public offering of convertible debentures—money to settle debts and acquire new interests. And Susquehannah, by a tender offer, had snatched 38 percent of Pan American Sulphur Company. It then offered to exchange up to $2 billion in Pan American securities for control of American Smelting & Refining, "one of the largest transactions in the history of U.S. business, if completed," reported the *Wall Street Journal*. Although Asarco's officers refused even to acknowledge Korholz's telephone calls, in December 1968 Asarco split its stock and announced it would buy back substantial amounts to head off raiders.

Magnuson professed to sense no threat to Hecla. He had simply jumped at his chance for "more money than I'd ever dreamed of," he would say, when "the roof blew off" the stock market. He and Collins met at a silver seminar and set off together to talk about Golconda over a drink. They were men much alike: a little heavy from too many business lunches, boyish, each head of his own company, each daring. Collins, known in Denver as a hustler, had helped Great Western United acquire Shakey's Pizza Parlors and was involved in negotiations for a takeover of Denver's First National Bank. Through Collins, Korholz paid Magnuson $18.50 a share for his Golconda stock. At that price, 188,225 shares brought more than $3.4 million. Elected to the Golconda board, Herbert Korholz seemed a threatening presence to Love and Randall.

Love and Randall flew to Washington, D.C., to meet Korholz. Returning to the airport, as Love rode with Korholz in his limousine, Korholz demanded a place on Hecla's board of directors. Love refused, saying that Magnuson represented Golconda, but that if Magnuson got off, Korholz might come on the board. Korholz "flew into a rage . . . said all sort of things," Love remembered. When he rejoined Randall at the airline, Love grunted, "Next time, you ride with Korholz!"

Hecla's concern for friendly shareholders had led to conversations about possible mergers, joint ventures and acquisitions with a number of companies during 1968, including Newmont, General Tire, Standard Oil, Kaiser, and Asarco. Dick Hunt acted as broker for a proposed marriage between Hecla and U.S. Smelting, Refining & Mining Company. Randall thought their "mining operations could be very effectively combined," and proposed exchanging one share of U.S. Smelting for a combination of a Hecla debenture with a face value of $50, one share of Hecla common, and a warrant to buy one-half share of Hecla at a price to be set later.

"In management's opinion, this proposal could well be a great benefit to Hecla's shareholders and has sufficient merit to warrant very serious consideration," Randall wrote the directors. Under NYSE rules, Hecla and U.S. Smelting had to make their negotiations public. Consequently, a printed letter went to Hecla shareholders describing the proposed merger. Hecla would absorb U.S. Smelting's mining operations in a transaction that the *Wall Street Journal* guessed at $156 million.

A financial writer in the Spokane *Spokesman-Review* predicted that a merger would "cause a new churning in the delicate power balance in the Coeur d'Alenes" and force Hecla to move from Wallace, leaving Sunshine and Day Mines as "the last of the big ones" with main offices in the mining district.

But Hecla and U.S. Smelting mutually dropped their plans to combine, "for the time being." Neither amplified a brief announcement. Hecla was caught up in a bigger prospect, its largest mining venture, one that might double or even triple its assets and income—Lakeshore, the vast copper deposit on the Papago Indian Reservation in the Sonoran desert of southwestern Arizona.

Harper, Hecla's chief geologist, had kept watch on Lakeshore through his friend, John Reynolds, El Paso's geologist, whom he saw often at mining conferences. (Reynolds had once been stationed in Spokane with the U.S. Bureau of Mines and was widely acquainted in the Coeur d'Alenes.) To turn back: Harper had visited Lakeshore when Transarizona had it. He considered Transarizona's experiments with copper extraction "a little scary" then. The U.S. Bureau of Mines and University of Arizona were also trying, without success, to develop a process using coke, salt, or another agent to get out the copper. Four years after Transarizona went into receivership, Narragansett Wire, a fabricator of copper wire, acquired it, paid its debts, and traded off a 50 percent interest to El Paso Natural Gas as operator. El Paso enlarged the mill, renegotiated Transarizona's compacts with the Papagos, and commenced drilling to determine the extent of the orebody, intending to mine by open pit. El Paso acquired Narragansett as an outlet for copper in 1967, and thus, all of Lakeshore.

In its drilling, Harper knew, El Paso "started picking up long intercepts of oxidized ore. Then, in some holes, they got down into sulfides which gave the first real indication" that Lakeshore was bigger than they had guessed. Analyzing fifty-three drill holes, El Paso estimated perhaps 471 million tons in three layers, like a club sandwich, a top one of disseminated oxide ore averaging 0.71 percent copper, a middle of disseminated sulfide, 0.7 percent, and a bottom tactite sulfide zone, smallest but richest, somewhat south of the others, averaging 1.69 percent copper. At 1968 prices Lakeshore, as one of the largest copper deposits in the United States, might produce ores worth $3.7 billion.

When he considered these forecasts, Harper was not surprised that El Paso decided to look for a partner experienced in hard-rock mining to operate Lakeshore, for El Paso's experience lay with petroleum. As the first petroleum company to diversify into mining (open-pit coal and uranium), El Paso had stubbed its toes. Its major effort then centered in New Mexico where, in December 1967, it had exploded a nuclear device deep underground to open a gas field. Harper passed the news to Bill Love in October 1968 that El Paso would solicit bids from prospective hard-rock operating partners.

To Love and Randall, Lakeshore beamed as a lodestar, a timely opportunity to extend Hecla's productive life indefinitely, release the company from its sole dependence on lead and silver, and triple its assets and income with one momentous dare. This, they decided, was the challenge that Hecla's inventive staff had been building up to meet. They resolved to go after Lakeshore, although Hecla had not been among the twenty or so mining companies initially invited to bid. A number were known to be interested. Lakeshore would demand a giant stretch of Hecla's finances, and it was a gamble. About the risk, Randall was frank: "Copper prices are cyclical—and thirty cent copper could give us trouble." Others also sounded warnings about the risk. But at the moment, nearly everyone expected copper to hold its relationship to prices of other commodities.

The Hecla bid called for a relatively quick payback from Lakeshore, three and a half to four years to bring the mine into production. Love at first considered open-pit operation until his review of the orebodies showed that would not be feasible. Hecla then determined to run two long declines beneath the orebodies for stoping and to design a metallurgical plant to produce pelletized cement copper precipitates from the oxide ores and electro-won cathode copper pig from the sulfide—a milling process dictated partly by environmental regulations and partly by the nature of the ore deposits.

Hecla would offer El Paso 1,000,000 shares of Hecla stock, roughly a 17 percent interest. Overnight El Paso would become Hecla's largest stockholder as well as its partner in Lakeshore, an offer not only financially attractive but one intended to place enough shares in friendly hands to minimize chances of a raid—to exorcise Herbert Korholz.

The metallurgical scheme was, in large part, the design of William A. Griffith, a forty-six-year-old metallurgical engineer who had joined Hecla a few months earlier after a decade as director of research and development for Phelps Dodge Corporation's largest branch. Griffith had come to Hecla with the recommendation of Gordon Craig, Hecla's mill superintendent, to help solve Ruby Hill's metallurgical puzzles. (These are not resolved yet because Ruby Hill's ore, says Hecla, will not pay the costs of mining it.) Griffith applied at Craig's invitation and Love created the post of research director for him. "He had a lot of experience with copper," Love would recall, "so when we got interested in Lakeshore, I brought Bill into the picture." Griffith took the ideas of Hecla's people and devised a flow sheet "in a way that nobody had ever put it together before," said Love. "We showed it to El Paso and they loved it because we were getting everything but the squeal out of that pig."

Griffith's design called for conventional concentration of sulfide ores, then sulfate roasting of the concentrate to produce leachable (dissolvable by percolation) copper calcine and by-product sulfuric acid. The calcine would be leached, recovering its copper content, which would be electro-won to produce salable copper cathode. The by-product acid was used to leach oxide ore in a vat system; the dissolved copper was precipitated as cement copper, pelletized for sale to smelters. The sulfide-concentrate residue from leaching was manufactured into sponge iron. "It was a great process, really," Love enthused. "We had nobody else in the organization with the knowledge" to design that process—novel enough that Griffith and those working with him would patent elements of it.

At the January deadline for Hecla's bid, a few of the office staff typed the proposal and colored the maps almost to midnight while a taut Love and Harper hovered by, their bags packed for the flight to meet El Paso's men. Automobile-door

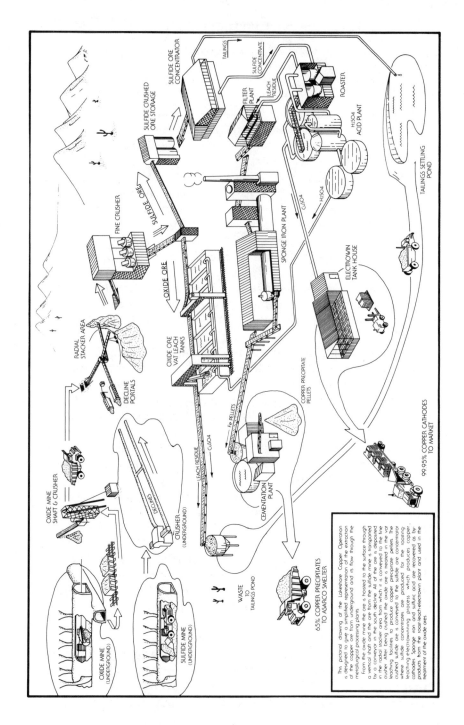

OXIDE MINE (UNDERGROUND)

SULFIDE MINE (UNDERGROUND)

OXIDE MINE SHAFT & CRUSHER

CRUSHER (UNDERGROUND)

DECLINES

RADIAL STACKER AREA

DECLINE PORTALS

FINE CRUSHER

SULFIDE CRUSHED ORE STORAGE

SULFIDE ORE CONCENTRATOR

SULFIDE ORE

OXIDE ORE

OXIDE ORE VAT LEACH TANKS

LEACH RESIDUE

CuSO4

SPONGE IRON PLANT

H2SO4

TAILINGS

SULFIDE CONCENTRATE

FILTER PLANT

LEACH RESIDUE

ROASTER

H2SO4 ACID PLANT

CuSO4

H2SO4

ELECTROWIN TANK HOUSE

TAILINGS SETTLING POND

Fe PELLETS

COPPER PRECIPITATE PELLETS

CEMENTATION PLANT

WASTE TO TAILINGS POND

65% COPPER PRECIPITATES TO ASARCO SMELTER

99.9% COPPER CATHODES TO MARKET

This pictorial drawing of the Lakeshore Copper Operation is designed to give a simplified representation of the extraction of the copper ore from underground and its flow through the metallurgical processing plants.

From the oxide mine the ore is hoisted to the surface through a vertical shaft and the ore from the sulfide mine is transported by a conveyor in the south decline. All of the ore is deposited in the radial stacker area from which it is conveyed to the fine crusher. After being crushed the oxide ore is treated in the vat leaching facilities to produce copper precipitate pellets. The crushed sulfide ore is conveyed to the sulfide ore concentrator where sulfide concentrates are produced for the roasting-leaching-electrowinning process which produces copper cathodes. Sponge iron and sulfuric acid are recovered as by-products from the roast-leach-electrowin plant and used in the treatment of the oxide ores.

174

locks froze, and Love and Harper went into the parking lot to thaw them.

But when the terms of the informal bid reached Hecla's directors ten days later, there was a colder blast. Harry Magnuson would not hear of issuing 1,000,000 shares to El Paso. The directors were astounded. They had studied reports and projections for four months and now were meeting in Los Angeles to close the deal while El Paso's negotiators waited nearby at the Hyatt House. But Magnuson balked. Sometime earlier, when Magnuson had also resisted an increase in capital stock, the board had amended its article 6 to provide that stock could be issued for property only by unanimous vote of the directors. Now, with Magnuson refusing to yield, Hecla could not deliver the stock it had promised El Paso.

Magnuson's was no trivial mutiny. With Love and Randall, he was one of Hecla's executive committee. He certainly knew the company's circumstances. Six directors perceived Lakeshore as Hecla's best chance in years for expansion and long life. One stood against them. In the following weeks, angry accusations broke out of the boardroom. Magnuson publicly chided Hecla for its haste and privately accused Love and his staff of protecting their jobs by buying a friendly shareholder. Love and Randall asserted that Magnuson had conspired with Korholz to seize Hecla, quoting testimony from a Texas courtroom where Korholz described Hecla as "an ideal vehicle" for "a financial restructuring of Asarco using a smaller company as the vehicle."

Resolved that Magnuson would not plunder Hecla, Randall enlisted a large stockholder, Howard R. Short, a retired Idaho mortician (said to have won his Hecla stock initially in a card game), to stand for election to the board in Magnuson's stead and to vote in favor of the stock issue to El Paso. By himself and through his family, Short owned 54,300 shares of Hecla, more than the other directors combined. The board dropped Magnuson from its slate of nominees for the coming annual meeting. For his part, Magnuson, with the counsel of Witherspoon's old firm, solicited proxies to keep his seat, while his Seattle attorneys sent letters to the Securities and Exchange Commission and the stock exchanges challenging Hecla's authority to issue additional shares.

Love was sure that Magnuson was somehow involved in a takeover—that this might be the most consequential threat to management since the attack by Sarah Smith and Eugene Day forty-eight years earlier. For some months, Hecla had relied on Joseph H. Flom, the New York attorney who was building his company—Skadden, Arps, Slate, Meagher & Flom—into the nation's foremost consultant on takeovers. "An unprepossessing man with a genius for crafty arguments," *Fortune* called Flom. Now, at Flom's direction, Hecla maligned Magnuson, mailing shareholders copies of a district court decision in an SEC case quoting the judge as saying of Magnuson that "a clearer record of flagrant, persistent, and callous violation of the law would be hard to find." Later contrite, Love would acknowledge that the personal attack "wasn't necessary and we didn't feel good about it," but Hecla retained Flom for his skill in blocking takeovers and felt obliged to follow his counsel. Hecla also hired a Wall Street firm to help solicit proxies.

Magnuson contended that Washington state's Uniform Business Corporation Act of 1933 conferred cumulative voting rights on shareholders, even though Hecla's amended articles of incorporation expressly barred cumulation. By cumulative voting, a shareholder could cast ballots equal to his shares multiplied by the number of nominees for director. Golconda proposed to cast its 691,000 votes all for Magnuson. And in Golconda's name, Magnuson sued in Spokane County Superior Court, both to enjoin Hecla from dealing with El Paso and to require cumulative votes.

Hecla did not print Magnuson's views in its proxy statement on Lakeshore, contending that they arrived by mail too late for inclusion. Only six days before the annual meeting, Judge William W. Williams released his memorandum opinion that Hecla shareholders could not vote cumulatively.

Two weeks before the annual meeting, Magnuson had resigned from Hecla's board, but he remained the center of dissent as the shareholders gathered on May 29 at the Ridpath Hotel in Spokane. For Hecla's meetings, the high-ceilinged ballroom was cut in half with a tan fanfold partition and at one end a platform was set up for officers and directors. Shareholders and spectators sat in folding metal chairs facing the platform; they whispered among themselves during the proceedings and made apologetic forays for coffee and rolls on tables at the back of the room. A cluster of employees and regular attendees offered the motions and seconds to keep the business moving. On this day, with revolt in the air, the ball-room was three-fourths full, the conversation, edgy.

But the meeting was decorous. Presided over by a resolute Randall, gaunt from recent illness, it heard the customary reports of operations. When nominations were called, Wray Featherstone offered Harry Magnuson's name as a director and a short time later moved that shareholders be allowed to vote cumulatively. On voting, Randall ruled Featherstone out of order, citing "past practices" and the recent opinion of the Spokane court.

When Lakeshore came up for discussion, Magnuson distributed and read an eleven-page typewritten statement opposing the project. He spoke for seventeen minutes into a microphone facing the directors, declaring that Lakeshore would dilute shareholders' equity and "doesn't fit corporately. . . . The size and risks are too great . . . a radical departure from long-standing Hecla policies." He denied any scheme for a "Golconda-Magnuson takeover." After questions and answers about Lakeshore, Randall adjourned the meeting until the next morning to allow election referees time to count proxies and ballots.

On the following morning, the referees announced that the company's slate of directors had been elected—Magnuson had not—and more than 2,837,000 shares, roughly 57 percent, favored Lakeshore.

Thus Hecla quelled its Magnuson revolt, but hard feelings remained. Magnuson's cronies, who formerly lunched with Hecla people at the Elks Club, switched to The Mint, a town restaurant—an alienated faction reminiscent of the days when the Bank Street crowd had avoided the Cedar Street and Wallace was polarized by lawsuits and politics. Randall was quoted in *Forbes*: "I did what had to be done. I won, but I'm sorry to say not without leaving a few bloody noses. One was obviously Magnuson." To its board, Hecla would add a former governor of Arizona, John R. "Jack" Williams, for his knowledge of state politics, and later, W. Burney Warren, retired president of the El Paso Company.

Yet, Randall and Featherstone arranged a truce of sorts: Golconda dropped two suits in return for Hecla's promise to explore the southeast part of its ground. A year later, Golconda would sell off its Hecla stock. But Golconda did not withdraw its suit for cumulative voting. In March 1972, the Washington

Supreme Court would rule that Hecla, having "availed itself" of the state's corporation laws, must allow cumulative voting for directors. At the 1972 annual meeting, cumulative votes would elect Harry Magnuson a director of Hecla again.

Hecla started work at Lakeshore with exultant haste. For a week or more, Love constantly took congratulatory phone calls. "Almost every major copper company" had bid for Lakeshore, *Forbes* reported, and Hecla had won because "it came up with a deal that emphasized exactly what El Paso wanted: quick payback." It went on: "Randall had, over two decades, rebuilt Hecla so that its bid was backed by human resources."

Hecla's project manager, curly-haired, square-jawed James Hunter, toiled patiently in a battered trailer near the old Transarizona plant, three and one-half dusty miles by washboard road from the blacktopped state highway to Casa Grande, thirty-two miles north. Casa Grande was a sprawling, torpid, cotton-farming town of fewer than ten thousand where most of Lakeshore's workers would bunk.

As the new operator, Hecla had to come to its own agreement with the Papagos. Hunter found himself awash in bureaucrats and intrigue. Thomas A. Segundo, the tribal chairman (who held a civil engineering degree from California and had studied law at Chicago), was miffed that the Papagos had learned of Hecla's part in Lakeshore from newspapers. Flooded with calls, Segundo could only tell his people that he "knew nothing about it." But to Hunter, he was nonetheless cordial and forthright. The tribe, he explained, wanted to be sure that Hecla did not delay, would exploit all the ore—not merely the richest layer—and would train Papagos as miners. Segundo suggested that Hecla advance royalties to the tribe.

In contrast to Segundo's candor, others used oblique tactics to divert some of Hecla's El Paso payments to the tribe—manipulations that Hecla imputed to Edward B. Berger, a smallish, assertive Tucson attorney who represented the Papagos. Prominent in Tucson legal aid and economic development, Berger had once led a grand jury probe of South Tucson and was later elected magistrate for the town. Hecla's men learned about Berger's terms for the Papagos piecemeal: a Hecla attorney, Robert W. Mullen, picked up some during a chance meeting in a coffee line; Hecla's secretary and treasurer William J. Grismer eavesdropped on a telephone conversation, concluding that Berger and Addison Smith, the Papagos's mining advisor, were "looking for some blackmail."

The Papago Tribal Council acted with agonizing slowness, but, grumbled Bill Love, "The real problem was that the Indians had a mining engineer . . . and they had a lawyer—the mining engineer was bad enough, but the lawyer was impossible." He resented Berger's smug appraisal: "I get criticized a lot, but I laugh all the way to the bank." Papagos who opposed the tribal leaders alleged that Berger received $100,000 above his $179,000 retainer for negotiating the Hecla contract and that he had collected more than $1 million from the tribe for special services over three years.

At last two leases—one, a mineral lease covering 4,180 acres for ten years, and a second, a business lease for surface plant covering 6,325 acres for twenty-five years—were signed with the Papagos in mid-September. Hecla might encumber the leases to borrow capital. It agreed to train Papagos to mine. The tribe's royalties, adjustable after five years, were to be 10 percent of net smelter returns for precipitates, and 6.14 percent of cathode copper sales.

Four months later, Hunter's machines and men had cleared portal sites to begin driving the twin 7,500-foot declines that would run (at a 15° slope) under the orebodies to mine them. One slope would be initially a roadway for huge Wagner ST-8 load-haul-dump diesel vehicles (with six-foot tires and front end buckets that scooped eight tons at once) and then fitted with a belt conveyor for ore. The other slope, with a skip (gondola) on railroad track, would lower men into the mine and haul out waste.

Tragically, as the project took shape, Thomas Segundo died in an airline crash. Hunter began the diplomacy of establishing trust with a new tribal chairman—and a new attorney, for Berger had resigned under pressure from a faction of the tribe, to be replaced by William Strickland, a Tucson attorney who had headed Transarizona.

Now, Hecla needed large sums. The directors suspended dividends to conserve money for Lakeshore, paying instead 2 percent annually in stock. But Hecla needed more than its own resources. By the end of 1971 the twin declines extended beneath the orebodies—nearing their full length—and miners were taking out sulfide ore. Hecla let a contract to the Parsons-Jurden Corporation, New York—to assess the metallurgical process devised by Griffith and produce a comprehensive report to impress bankers from whom Hecla would seek loans—and built three experimental plants to test Griffith's design. Love would mail each director a chunk of copper from the pilot electro-winning plant—99.93 percent copper—as a memento, writing: "Perhaps you can use this as a paperweight." (Griffith had done more than design the process; he had run discounted cash-flow studies on Lakeshore, using lower copper-price projections, to reach the appalling conclusion that the enterprise was financially doomed. Too late to pull out, Love redoubled his resolve and pushed ahead.)

Shortly before Christmas 1972, Love and Grismer concluded a credit agreement allowing Hecla to borrow up to $42 million in revolving loans from four banks: Chase Manhattan, New York, the lead bank, Manufacturers Hanover, Seattle-First National, and Valley National of Arizona. The terms of the loans precluded cash dividends. With an initial loan of $9 million, construction started on a full-scale metallurgical plant, to be completed within four years.

Love had hoped to have Lakeshore in production in three and one-half years, but the project fell steadily behind schedule: contract negotiations with the Papagos had been drawn out; with federal price ceilings, Hecla could not obtain some machine parts—it sent three men to scout dealers for them; then Hecla had to supply its own electricity from secondhand generators when the local cooperative could not handle the demand; next, before resigning, Berger, to exploit the power needs of Hecla and other companies, had persuaded the Papagos to form a Papago Tribal Utility Authority (PTUA) to provide current—but Hecla had to lend the tribe money to build its transmission line and to connect with Arizona Public Service; and at 5,700 feet, one decline suddenly spurted steaming water, flooding the tunnels and the decline within hair-raising inches of electrical switching gear before it could be sealed with cement grout at considerable cost and loss of time. By the end of 1972, Love, piloting his plane to Arizona, was demanding speed to get Lakeshore on schedule.

Hurry intensified the danger underground—Wagner scooptrams racing through tunnels, unreasonable quotas for shifts. When he saw his shift boss "with a wild, irrational look," miner Stephen M. Voynick later wrote, he knew another order was out to speed up. At one underground site, he said, crews carrying high-ampere electric torches waded knee deep in water to weld a steel frame for grouting. Perhaps Voynick exaggerated, but to the miners everything seemed hurried, makeshift, temporary.

The Hecla crew swelled to 1,131, a mixture of newcomers and old hands, one hundred sixty Papagos, a dozen or so women demanding equal opportunity, and several Chilean refugees who had fled mines expropriated by their country's Marxist government. In general, the Papagos learned to be competent miners despite their hesitation, at first, to go underground. In the manner of miners everywhere, workers hired on and quit constantly, and each new-hire got a briefing on Lakeshore, a map of the workings, and a safety lecture before descending in the skip as part of a team of eight or ten to toil in the clangorous, sweltering tunnels.

When desert temperatures rose above 100 degrees daily from May through September, the tunnels oozed wet heat, despite the best efforts of a young engineer from India, Kuldip Khunkhun, to cool them. Determined to become an American citizen, Kuldip saw his job—ventilation engineer—as his ticket to staying in the United States. With its usual preference for new technology, Hecla used Robbins 81-R drills, the largest then built, to smash circular shafts through the rock for ventilation, fitting the shafts with 96-inch fans that nearly deafened workers passing beneath them. But, as the miners griped, ventilation meant numerical criteria to Kuldip. To the engineers on the surface, the mine was "environmentally advanced." To the men underground, Lakeshore was stifling, humid, dirty, and dangerous.

Miners were issued self-rescuers, canisters with filters to be placed over mouth and nose as short-term protection against carbon monoxide from a fire. Hecla used stench alarms that sent a skunk smell through the noisy tunnels to signal fire. The self-rescuers were mandatory at Lakeshore in the aftermath of a tragic accident at the Sunshine mine in Idaho on May 2, 1972, where carbon monoxide killed 91 men working 3,700 feet underground. Beyond its horrifying warning, the consequences of the Sunshine fire for Hecla were $545,000 in rescue and rehabilitation costs as participants in the unit area, and the loss of income from Sunshine in a rising silver market at a time when Hecla desperately needed money (and was losing in silver futures). Shortly after Sunshine reopened, a four-month strike there cut off Hecla's income from the unit area again.

Only fifteen months after the Sunshine fire, Lakeshore billowed smoke; 110 miners wearing self-rescuers walked safely out. A Wagner driver, nearly buried in cascading muck, had fled for his life, leaving the diesel engine running. The overheated engine then exploded, setting mine timbers afire and trapping two miners who dashed into a dead-end tunnel. Futile rescue operations drew scores of news reporters to Lakeshore for a week until the fire was out and the bodies were found. The state mine inspector played poker with rescue teams during their rest period—learning directly from their chatter how the rescue attempts were going. For a developing mine, lashed to produce fast, Lakeshore's safety record would be remarkable: including the two killed in the fire, six died during Hecla's tenure there.

Treacherous underground, harried on the surface—managing Lakeshore was like wrestling a mean bear. In his impatience now with interruptions, Randall asked the Ridpath Hotel to stop posting lobby notices of directors' meetings—"occasionally something comes up when it is not too good to publicize that we are having a meeting." Copper surpluses piling up were depressing world prices. Developing nations—Zaire, Zambia, Peru, and even calamitous Chile—manipulated copper as a political weapon, as others used oil. While long strikes closed U.S. copper mines and smelters in 1974, the federal government sold its stockpiles. Randall, talking to shareholders in 1970, had predicted that growing electrical demand would increase the use of copper; now, Bell Laboratories announced new alloys that would reduce copper in electrical devices. Plumbing went plastic.

Bill Love had estimated that producing Lakeshore copper would cost initially about eighty cents a pound, and that production would get cheaper. Everyone assumed that copper prices would rise or fall in step with the prices and costs of other commodities. That copper would maintain its relationship to the prices of other lines seemed a reasonable assumption. A Merrill Lynch study of the copper situation appeared to confirm this; it forecast copper prices of seventy-five to eighty cents, perhaps even one dollar by the end of 1974. Love expected Lakeshore to start commercial production in the middle of 1975. On the second day of 1975, Phelps Dodge, Kennecott, and

Magma cut their selling price for cathode copper to sixty-eight cents. The unthinkable had happened. Copper was falling by itself, out of step.

Confident that the market would recover its balance, Love and his managers decided to mine Lakeshore's higher grade ores first—a tactical error, Love later realized, because these tactite sulfide ores presented special problems. The tunnels caved. The plan for mining them had to be revised. ("Poor ground conditions," the annual report called this.) Power interruptions stalled work. Operator-errors by men learning the new metallurgical process marred leaching. Copper pellets ran lower grade than expected.

And all this while, Lakeshore's voracious hunger for money chewed at Hecla's finances. Love and Grismer renegotiated bank loans to raise Hecla's ceiling to $48 million, then to $53 million. In December 1975, Love warned his board of "impending cash problems." Lakeshore was running toward $190 million, 25 percent above forecasts, and not yet producing. Start-up had been moved back eight months to early 1976.

Lakeshore began commercial production on January 26, 1976, with Love goading his managers to cut costs. (For financial reporting, the mine was deemed in production on April 1.) As the integrated mine and plant gathered speed, efficiency improved and costs started downward—21 percent lower in the mine and 19 percent in the plant—and the work force was trimmed to about 1,500. But with copper prices detached from their normal relationship to other commodities, prices of everything but copper shot upward.

From a technical view, Lakeshore was a success (although it was initially plagued by snags—high summer temperatures affected concentration of sulphuric acids until additional cooling capacity was added, and quality control was erratic). Mining confirmed estimates of the orebody, and the electro-winning process worked as designed, using energy efficiently. The plant met environmental standards. At Lakeshore, Hecla had advanced the methods for mining and processing copper ores. In cooperation with Southwire Company at Carrollton, Georgia, Hecla was the first to produce copper cathode of a quality to be converted directly into rod without the intermediate step of electro-refining, a method broadly adopted since.

But as fast as Hecla reduced costs, copper prices fell, hovering near seventy cents. "The average price for copper should have been between 90 cents and 100 cents a pound," Love told the shareholders, but as the market stood, Hecla's net loss from Lakeshore had risen to $10.2 million by the end of 1976.

In April 1977, Lakeshore produced copper above its designed capacity and made a small profit, its best month. Almost nothing else went well. In the Coeur d'Alenes, strikes at Bunker Hill and Sunshine forced stockpiling and cut off expected income. The company wrote off Granduc. Hecla was sinking in a morass of falling income and rising debts. In August, major U.S. producers dropped the copper price to sixty cents. Early in September 1977, with operating losses in Arizona at $45.9 million, Love shut down Lakeshore and laid off 1,500, thinking the closure temporary. He kept 130 key men ready to reopen when the market improved.

Love's message in Hecla's 1977 annual report began, "The worst year in the copper industry since the 1930's, in terms of market price as related to production costs, resulted in Hecla Mining Company's poorest year since its incorporation in 1898." He had gone back to the banks to raise the loan limit to $55 million and defer payments on principal, and he scouted for another company to put new money into Lakeshore.

Large world surpluses of copper and low prices had punctured Hecla's great expectations. A decade of struggle was lost. Until copper prices rose dramatically, Lakeshore would sleep.

I I

Two Plus Two Equals Five

BILL LOVE PUT THE BEST FACE ON HECLA HE COULD MANAGE in his 1978 report to shareholders: "I assure you that Hecla Mining Company is a viable, healthy company at this time, and I think the earnings which the Company achieved during the fourth quarter of 1978 will attest to that fact." Hecla had made money in the fourth quarter, a net of $3.2 million, including $632,000 from the sale of its Liard properties.

But 1978 overall had been a year of bloodletting. Hecla's net loss for the year ran to $96.8 million—$96 million of it, a non-cash write-off of Lakeshore. Money flowed out for debt service and holding costs at Lakeshore. Love cut deeply with broad strokes: Herb Harper, Jim Hunter, and Gordon Miner retired early; the 130-man cadre at Lakeshore was reduced to a custodial fifteen; everyone who could be spared above or below ground in Arizona and Idaho was let go. The exploration offices in Vancouver, Reno, and Denver closed.

For Gordon Miner, Love's wholesale dismissals were especially joyless, for Miner had had aspirations to succeed Love as president of the company. He had risen from manager of operations to one of two senior vice presidents (Griffith was the other) in the Lakeshore years, and he had more or less run everything else while Love struggled with Lakeshore. If anyone at Hecla was blameless for the Lakeshore debacle, it was Miner. He had stood apart; he refused transfers of his people to Lakeshore to keep Arthur Brown at Lucky Friday, William Anderson at Star-Morning, Wallace Crandall and others in Idaho. Miner deliberately did not take part in Lakeshore. Instead, he held Hecla's Idaho operations in a jealous, protective, albeit frugal embrace while the company was preoccupied in Arizona.

Hecla had missed the first and second payments on its bank loans. Love negotiated extensions—that cost another $2.7 million—and the directors agreed to pay the banks partially with an issue of preferred stock, but the shareholders failed to ratify the new stock.

Hecla could not afford to keep Lakeshore on the shelf at $6 million a year. The property had to be sold. Bill Grismer mailed invitations to more than 500 possible buyers and advertised in foreign business journals, but with a stricken copper market, only a few bargain hunters sniffed at Lakeshore. One director, Horton Herman, told Love baldly that he "had nothing to sell"— a low-grade copper mine millions in debt amounted to a distress sale and every buyer knew it. Looking at their balance sheets, the pragmatic directors concluded that they might have to sell Hecla itself. If so, they meant to make the best deal they could for their shareholders.

Kuhn Loeb & Company, as financial advisors, recommended that "efforts to dispose of Hecla's 50 percent interest in the Lakeshore copper mine should be vigorously pursued as the first alternative." The next possibility might be "sale or merger of Hecla to or with a considerably larger corporate entity" which could sustain future losses at Lakeshore. On the other hand, Hecla was no longer a good buy, Kuhn Loeb pointed out, because the company had "lost its heretofore undiluted image as a precious metal/silver producer," and the "substantial operating losses and resultant shift in capitalization dramatically increased the financial risk implicit in an investment in Hecla." The losses at Lakeshore created a ratio of debt to capitalization "totally out of line" with other mining companies, many of them debt-free.

In the decade that Hecla had devoted to Lakeshore, the Coeur d'Alene district had changed. It had run out of elbow room. A 1967–68 boom in silver set off a rush that staked dozens of new claims pressing against old and new properties. A geologist who mapped the mines in 1980 found "great differences in property conditions" since 1965 and "many boundary conflicts." Surface lines notwithstanding, deep shafts—trunks with tunnels reaching like roots into nearby claims—commanded the district. Impecunious companies dealt perforce with those that owned the deep shafts: Sunshine, Asarco, or Hecla. And without a deep shaft, rising costs precluded all but the most modest development.

Directors of large companies often sat on the boards of beholden smaller ones, and on the boards of those that shared joint ventures or unitized areas. "Incest," they chuckled—everyone in everyone else's business. Inevitably, crowding and suspicion set one against another—rumors of takeover or fears of tunnels pushed stealthily into a neighbor's ore. It was an atmosphere of each his brother's keeper, a climate in which Bill Love judged that Hecla was losing money as a result of inept management of the Sunshine. During Hecla's critical need for cash flow in 1972–73, Love remembered, Sunshine had been closed by its calamitous fire and then by a yearlong strike. The fire was accidental; the strike, needless. Rather than profiting from its 33.25 percent of the unit area, Hecla had to chip in for rehabilitation and maintenance.

Sunshine had disconcerted the district, as a matter of fact, since New York investors ousted its Yakima directors in 1965 and named a Brooklyn linotype salesman, Thomas F. McManus, as manager. McManus fired geologists and engineers, cut staff, and gobbled surrounding claims—showing little understanding of their promise—with contracts that would reduce the unit area's share of profits. Investment bankers shooed clients away from Sunshine. Hecla, on the other hand, bought $2.5 million worth of depressed Sunshine stock.

A New York attorney, Irwin P. Underweiser, executor for one of the 1965 raiders, seized Sunshine's presidency in 1970. A series of lawsuits by the State of New York and the Securities and Exchange Commission alleged that Underweiser and associates used Sunshine money to buy two banks and a race track, exacted excessive legal fees, scuttled an insurance company, squeezed personal loans from banks handling Sunshine's deposits, altered minute books, and issued proxy statements with "material misstatements." Stockholders revolted. At its 1974 annual meeting, to blunt a proxy fight against "ineffective management," Sunshine put the leader of the dissidents on its board and bumped Underweiser upstairs to chairman.

One of Harry Magnuson's companies, Silver Dollar (9.6 percent of the unit area), also disparaged Sunshine's management. Magnuson and Bill Love discussed operations several times with Underweiser, a short, rotund, affable attorney who knew little about mining—Love found him "difficult"—but nothing changed. Sunshine needs expert management; it is a complex mine, more than a mile deep with an intricate tunnel network at numerous levels reaching into areas of joint ventures. Satisfying jealous partners is nettlesome, at best. Turnover is high. Sunshine has never been efficient or cohesive.

Under threat of the 1974 proxy fight, however, Underweiser hired a retired Asarco vice president of mining operations, C. E. Nelson, as chief operating officer. But Nelson was ill. Neither income nor efficiency improved. Battling like cats in a gunnysack, various partners sued Sunshine during the next eighteen months. In turn, Sunshine sued them, including Hecla, from which it demanded prorated costs of sinking its new number 12 shaft. Hecla and Silver Dollar together sued Sunshine for an accounting of antimony sales, and Hecla sued again, alleging improper payments to Nelson. In March 1976 the Sunshine miners walked out and, as the strike dragged into its ninth month, with Hecla losing $100,000 a month from the idle unit area, Love and Magnuson called in Joe Flom for advice on ridding Sunshine of its managers and directors.

In his practical way, Flom saw that Hecla and Silver Dollar, as small stockholders, were too weak to force changes at Sunshine. He advised Love and Magnuson to "look for someone who could bail us out"—that is, provide large sums for stock purchases—and to solicit proxies from Sunshine's 19,000 stockholders. Love and Magnuson settled on Charles E. Schwab, former president of Bunker Hill and now president of Golden Cycle Corporation, to head a stockholders' proxy committee. And as affluent allies interested in silver, they chose N. Bunker Hunt and W. Herbert Hunt, wealthy sons by his first wife of the late Dallas oil multibillionaire, H. L. Hunt, and heirs to one of the two or three largest family fortunes in history. Bunker was once quoted: "A billion dollars doesn't go as far as it used to"; and, another time: "People who know how much they're worth probably aren't worth very much."

Love telephoned the Hunts for a meeting. "Really, all we wanted to do was pressure Underweiser to make management changes," he has since insisted. He and Magnuson both deny an intention to take over Sunshine.

Magnuson, Love, and Schwab met the Hunts at their Dallas headquarters. As Magnuson remembers, they had barely settled in an unadorned conference room when Bunker Hunt exclaimed, "This room is bugged!" and bolted to another. There, Love lit a cigar. Bunker snapped, "Put that out!" (Love does not recall either incident.) Despite a disconcerting start, the portly

Hunts were cordial and interested. Within a week, their man visited Wallace, and shortly after, on March 21, 1977, their Great Western United Corporation, a diversifying sugar refiner, bought Hecla's and Silver Dollar's 334,070 shares of Sunshine. Three days later, Great Western United made a public tender offer of $15.75 a share for 2,000,000 of Sunshine's 5,600,000 shares outstanding.

Underweiser and his associates tried to stop the Hunt tender by lawsuits and were answered with lawsuits; one reached the U.S. Supreme Court as the first challenge to the constitutionality of an Idaho law requiring tenders to be filed with the state department of finance. (Idaho lost.) Within months, Hunt International Resources Corporation (HIRCO) had acquired 28 percent of Sunshine's stock, including that of Great Western United, and the Hunts were effectively in command. At Sunshine's annual meeting in Dallas, Sunshine elected a three-man board, all former executives of Great Western United.

The Hunt brothers transferred G. Michael Boswell, the brisk, ambitious executive vice president of Great Western United, to Sunshine as president. Full head of hair, square face, cleft jaw, fashionably dressed in suit with vest and Western boots, Boswell looks the new-breed executive.

Early in 1979, Sunshine, Silver Dollar, and Hecla dropped their legal actions against one another. In the middle of the year, Boswell and his board, to forestall domination by HIRCO, obtained a loan to buy out the Hunts and subsequently resold the stock to the Arab Investors Group SA, based in Luxembourg—an internal power play which the Hunts did not contest publicly and which gave control of Sunshine to the Boswell faction. Once in silver, however, the Hunts seemed enchanted by its possibilities. They bought extensively on low margins and by 1979 would own perhaps one-half of the world's production of refined silver, about 220,000,000 ounces—not merely paper, but metal, much of it stored in rented warehouses in the Dallas area.

Profits from the Sunshine Unit Area did not quickly improve with new management. Low-grade ores, damage to tunnels from rock bursts, and union work stoppages continued to impede Sunshine. Boswell's board sold off subsidiaries not directly related to silver mining or marketing for roughly $31 million. Thus well-financed, they began to buy mining stocks in the open market. In a reversal of their earlier positions, Sunshine acquired 5.3 percent of Hecla's stock within two years—and would begin to advise Hecla on how to manage its business.

The Hunts had captured Sunshine while Hecla was preoccupied with extricating itself from Lakeshore. In addition to widely circulated form letters and prospectuses, Bill Love wrote personal letters to mining company officers promoting this "uncommon opportunity" to buy a major copper mine, expressing confidence that the copper market, inert as an old dog by a warm fire, would revive by 1979 or 1980. He and Grismer journeyed to Toronto, New York, Houston, and other cities to sell Lakeshore—to no avail. When the directors met in the fall 1978, they had no offers for Lakeshore, even at salvage value. One prospective buyer, Alusuisse, a venerable Swiss aluminum company, had looked greedily over Lakeshore three times, but could not convince a pool of European investors to buy it.

For a time, Love thought he had sold Lakeshore to Superior Oil Company, brought to Hecla by Robert B. Fulton. As a Newmont vice president, Fulton had been "Malozemoff's man" on the Hecla board from 1968 to 1973 and was now chief executive of McIntyre Porcupine Mines, a Superior subsidiary. Love had dickered transcontinentally with Howard B. Keck, president of Superior, the beefy, imperious son of the company's founder. With Fulton playing matchmaker, Love and Keck talked in Toronto, discussed in Dallas, and in Los Angeles one weekend Keck signed a letter of intent: Superior would take Hecla's half interest in Lakeshore, paying royalties and an annual rental of $3 million, while Hecla continued to operate the mine; Superior would also buy 4,900,000 shares of Hecla at bargain prices from unissued stock and from an El Paso subsidiary. Love left Los Angeles with mixed feelings: he had shifted the burden of Lakeshore, but Superior, with roughly 45 percent of Hecla's outstanding shares, would dominate Hecla. Nevertheless, the deal seemed to be the best he could do, waiting only the formality of shareholders' approval at annual meetings.

Then two months later, at noon on a day near the end of May, Love's telephone rang and the voice at the other end barked, "This is Keck—Howard Keck. We've decided not to go ahead." Love asked why, and Keck responded, "That's not important. We're not going ahead. I have no further comment." And that was that. Superior would not take Lakeshore.

Archibald Witherspoon, the Hecla director and Spokane attorney who served as interim president of the company in 1951. Witherspoon commuted to Wallace weekly. (*Photograph courtesy of Neal Fosseen*)

Lester J. Randall, the Wallace CPA who, as president of Hecla 1951–66, acquired Lucky Friday to extend the life of the company. Randall was generally credited with reviving a moribund Hecla.

The Leduc portal camp at the foot of a glacier near the Granduc mine in northern British Columbia. Shortly after this photo was taken in February 1965, an avalanche wiped out the camp, killing twenty-six men.

A private pilot, Hecla President William H. Love flew in to inspect the avalanche disaster at Granduc. He conferred with Nick Gritzuk, manager at Granduc (*left, wearing hard hat*), shortly after arrival. In this plane, Love flew around the world after leaving Hecla. (*Photograph courtesy of W. H. Love*)

Hecla's presidents regularly prescribed underground tours for members of the board of directors. Bill Anderson, manager of the Star-Morning (*left*), answers questions. *Left to right:* Edward McL. Tittmann (*gesturing*), John R. Williams, L. J. Randall, and William T. Pettijohn.

In recognition of his service to the company, Hecla's directors gave L. J. Randall a table inset with silver dollars at the annual meeting, May 28, 1964. *Left to right:* Marcus D. Banghart, W. H. Love, Richard N. Hunt, Randall, Ross D. Leisk, John E. D. Grunow, and Harry F. Magnuson.

At Hecla's initial listing on the Pacific Coast Exchange in September 1967. *Left to right:* L. J. Randall, W. H. Love, Gordon Miner, H. E. Harper, P. J. Lindstrom, and W. J. Grismer. (*Photograph courtesy of H. E. Harper*)

Miners working underground in the Lucky Friday, 1979. *Foreground*: Lanie Keller, Jr., operates an Eimco mucker, and Bob Cossey, a Mancha battery motor and Granby dump oar at the 3650 level.

A Lakeshore drift showing the fault in the face. Note the steel "timbering" and the size of tunnels to allow mining by huge machines. (*Photograph courtesy of W. H. Love*)

The remoteness of the Lakeshore mine, in the Sonoran desert on the Papago Indian Reservation in Arizona, emerges from this aerial photo of early surface structures. Most workers commuted thirty-two miles daily to Casa Grande.

William H. Love, who made a reputation for distinguished mine operation at Atlas and Radon, was Hecla's president from 1966 to 1979. Love practiced personal management, going underground to see operations for himself. (*Photograph courtesy of W. H. Love*)

Electricians boarding a skip at the portal of Lakeshore's north decline. *Left to right:* Robert Peterson, Richard McQuillan, and Calvin Lorts. (*Photograph by Manley, Tucson*)

A silver medallion, face and obverse, struck to commemorate the merger of Hecla with Day Mines, Inc. The merger date marks stockholders' approval of the combination.

Lucky Friday surface buildings and mill (*bottom, center*) constructed by Hecla. The Silver Shaft, a third shaft from the surface, would begin in the area in the lower left-hand corner of this picture.

Miners in the Star mine boarding the lift to descend to working stations.
(*Photograph by Ted Johnson*)

Arthur Brown (*left*) and William A. Griffith. Brown became Hecla's tenth president in May 1986, succeeding Griffith, who continued as CEO and chairman until his retirement. Under Griffith, Hecla was judged by the *Wall Street Transcript* to be the best managed company in the silver industry.

A miner operates a jackleg drill in the Knob Hill mine near Republic, Washington, acquired with Day Mines properties. The Knob Hill has shown new life as a gold producer. (*Photograph by Photography Unlimited, Spokane*)

The new headframe for Lucky Friday at Mullan, Idaho, has been adopted as the model for Hecla's company logo. Lucky Friday sustained Hecla when the original Hecla mine had been exhausted. (*Photograph by Photography Unlimited, Spokane*)

An LHD (load-haul-dump) vehicle underground at the Lucky Friday mine. Mechanization and innovation continue to be hallmarks of Hecla mining operations. (*Photograph by Photography Unlimited, Spokane*)

When Knob Hill produced its two-millionth ounce of gold, Hecla displayed a five-foot cube showing the volume of that much gold. *Left to right:* Vice President–Metal Mining Ralph Noyes, Republic Unit Manager Josef Suveg, U.S. Senator Slade Gorton, and Hecla Chairman and CEO Arthur Brown.

Dave McCarroll, a crusher foreman at Hecla's Colorado Aggregate Company, scoops a handful of volcanic scoria from the conveyor belt. (*Photograph by Photography Unlimited, Spokane*)

In May 1986 Hecla dedicated this new corporate headquarters about two miles north of Coeur d'Alene, Idaho. The sculpted figure of a mining engineer (*left foreground*) carries surveying equipment.

(Later it developed that Keck had acted on advice of an old-time consulting metallurgist.)

Love sat numbly for a few minutes while the brief conversation sank in. He reflected that Hecla had devoted months to negotiations, and now that time was lost, with no other prospect in sight. That call he would remember as "a low blow—the bitterest blow of my career." Hecla contemplated suing Superior but concluded it was in no position to do so.

For several weeks after Keck's call, Love shut his office door while he restructured Hecla on paper. "I felt I had to go to the board of directors with a plan," he remembered. "The only way was to pare down the company to the bone and devote the next year or two or three, or whatever it took, to getting the debt down to manageable size and getting the company on a really sound financial footing again." He drew financial projections and organizational charts, revising and reordering, pretty much alone at his task. "A lot of people thought that Hecla was going down the tube bankrupt," he recalled. "We weren't going down the tube—we were really never close to that."

While Love worked on his plan, El Paso announced that it would dispose of its half of Lakeshore. Without El Paso's participation, Lakeshore would be even harder to sell. "Boy, that sure dried up prospects fast," Love said bitterly.

Love's financial plan assumed that Lakeshore would be sold or salvaged; that Liard would be sold for $3 million (it brought $94,811 more than that); and that layoffs and early retirements would save as much as $700,000 a year. As he worked, he was haunted by the possibility that the copper market would revive as Hecla dealt away Lakeshore. "If no unforeseen circumstances" upset his forecast, Hecla would survive: It would continue Lucky Friday, its Star-Morning, its Lisbon Valley uranium project (a joint venture with Union Carbide near Moab, Utah), and the Sunshine Unit Area—"a bare bones operation," he told the directors. He traded his three-year forecast for one from Callahan Mining with some preliminary discussion of merger.

As he drew and discarded organizational charts, Love erased every executive between himself and the mine superintendents. "It took me a long time," he would muse, "to realize that I had to take one guy—me—out of the company, so that we could promote somebody, so that Hecla would have a kinetic, moving organization, and the people who were left would have a future there." And so in December he went to the board meeting with a new organizational plan in which there was no place for Bill Love, and said simply, "This is what I think is best."

Love proposed to stay long enough to renegotiate Hecla's bank loans. He would retire after the annual meeting in May 1979. He recommended one of the senior vice presidents, Bill Griffith, the metallurgist who had designed the Lakeshore process, for executive vice president, gradually to take over operations and succeed him as president. Love apparently settled on Griffith believing that Griffith's skills in planning and budgeting offered Hecla a better chance of survival than the hands-on mine operating skills of Gordon Miner. When various directors had hinted that a flying accident might deprive Hecla of its chief executive, Love had replied that he had an envelope in his desk with the names and his personal appraisals of potential successors.

Now, however, he kept his decision to retire to himself, telling no one before the meeting. He surprised the directors, who had not seriously considered removing him. Some directors thought that Love took on himself too much blame for the Lakeshore failure. Others felt that a housecleaning might be in order. At least two directors, Horton Herman and Edward Tittmann, would have preferred to conduct a search for a new president, yet—confronted with Love's recommendation—Tittmann moved and Herman seconded Love's proposals for reorganization and his nomination of Griffith. (Edward McL. Tittmann, then president of Asarco, had come on Hecla's board after Leisk's death in June 1964.)

At the end of October 1978, Hecla and El Paso Natural Gas both terminated their Lakeshore leases with the Papagos, granting the tribe an option to buy the plant at salvage value. There remained some carryover contracts for electrical service which expired in 1985. At Casa Grande, said the *Arizona Daily Star*, "They are counting on agriculture—the town's traditional economic base—and a good tourist season to hold things together until the copper industry rebounds." Half of the town's payroll was gone.

As he intended, Love worked out a new credit pact with the banks: a three-and-one-half-year declining-balance agreement at 9 percent interest, with a pledge that Hecla would repay or refinance any principal remaining by the end of 1981. Love was "pretty proud" of the 9 percent interest—"a little under the prevailing rate and a fixed rate."

Hecla's 1978 annual report more or less summed up Lakeshore: "The basic problem," it read, "was the prevailing price of copper. . . . If the venture had been a success, the Company would have taken a quantum leap in increased revenue and earnings."

While Love was closing up Lakeshore and tying off his thirty years with Hecla, the price of silver started to rise. By the end of 1978 it had climbed 16.8 percent in twelve months, one of the greatest price swings since the beginning of the century. With rising prices, the Coeur d'Alenes produced the highest value of ores in any year to that time—$137.6 million worth. Only two mines lost money—one, the Star-Morning, where costs outran income by $105,939. The fourth quarter was good indeed to Hecla: a net income of $3.2 million, the company's first fiscal period in the black since the first quarter of 1976. The bank debt was reduced from $57.7 million to $51 million in that quarter alone. If silver continued to rise, Love was going to leave Griffith a very healthy company. For that, he could thank the irrepressible Hunt brothers and other speculators; their buying binge was driving the price steadily upward.

Hecla convened two shareholders' meetings in 1979, the first in January, where they approved an increase in capital stock to 20,000,000 shares but turned down a management proposal to issue preferred stock to pay off part of the bank debts. Although this was the first shareholders' meeting since the $96 million write-off of Lakeshore, newspaper reporters thought the shareholders "more resigned than angry." No rumored attack on Hecla's management materialized.

At the second meeting on May 4, Phil Lindstrom reviewed the metals markets, referring obliquely to "forces at work" which drove up the price of silver $4 an ounce in six weeks, advising his listeners to "take a position and wait." When shareholders again rejected preferred stock, the meeting was adjourned to May 25, when additional proxies authorized 1,000,000 preferred. Hecla issued 25,532 to the banks with a stated value of $100 a share, redeemable by 1988.

Love's customary report to shareholders was matter-of-fact and brief; he declared that earnings for the first quarter of 1979 were "the highest in the history of the company," noted that the debt had been further reduced, and formally announced his retirement. Love planned to fly around the world in his private airplane with his wife Carolyn, also a pilot, inspecting mines before starting a new career as a consultant.

Although Love had tutored him for more than six months, William A. Griffith would set his own course as president of Hecla. He could not emulate Love, who preferred hands-on mine operation, going underground and talking to the men. In twenty-nine years of mining, Griffith had achieved distinction as a research metallurgist in laboratory and mill. He had also watched mining change, from a business of selling metal for more than it cost to mine it, to a business that demanded forecasting, planning, budgeting, and advanced executive techniques. Griffith proposed to drag Hecla into the age of management by objectives.

A native of Sioux Falls, South Dakota, Griffith had earned his bachelor's degree in metallurgical engineering from the South Dakota School of Mines and Technology and his master's in metallurgy from the Massachusetts Institute of Technology. The American Institute of Mining, Metallurgical and Petroleum Engineers honored him in 1976 with its A. M. Gaudin Award for achievement in process metallurgy, and would vote him the prestigious Robert H. Richards Award in 1981. Love had hired Griffith for his skills in solving metallurgical problems. Griffith's design had made Lakeshore possible for Hecla, and perfidious Lakeshore had swept everyone else aside to give Griffith his opportunity to be president of Hecla.

A trim, didactic man, little given to chatting with miners, Griffith instituted staff retreats for executives. He told them in his flat voice, "I have some strong ideas on how things should be done, and only this one opportunity to try them out, so I am going to do this my way." Feeling that he had a relatively untried staff, Griffith's way would be to keep his finger on every aspect, even to approving press statements before release. His restrained manner—the *Wall Street Journal* called him "preacherly"—ruffled the booster clique among Wallace business and professional men and Griffith, in turn, disdained them. Astute, hard-working, with an exceptional memory, Griffith could be unyielding when his mind was set, and he could erupt in temper.

The new president felt that many of Hecla's brightest young men had left the company. "I took over a decimated staff," he would say. "There had been a mass firing which Bill Love did, bless his heart, because it had to be done." With Hecla riding buoyantly on the boom in silver, Griffith set out to rebuild, with different people, an executive corps for Hecla.

Arthur Brown, a native of South Africa who had been manager of Lucky Friday, moved up to manager of mines. Within a year, Brown would be one of three vice presidents, then senior vice president, and in May 1986, president.

Griffith believed that Hecla must diversify and grow aggressively. He saw the mining industry as a crowded arena ruled by primordial mentality—swallow or be swallowed—prowled by corporate predators using legal and fiscal stratagems that "our kind of people" shunned. And he saw domestic mines losing ground in a changing competitive balance between developed and undeveloped nations.

In Griffith's first months as president, he turned aside "serious offers" from Amax, Rosario, and Sunshine to buy Hecla. The directors, he told them, had "taken down the 'for sale' sign." Hecla would pay yesterday's debts with tomorrow's devalued dollars.

Boswell of Sunshine appeared one day carrying a salesman's case filled with printed prospectuses for the Silver Valley Company, a proposed merger of Hecla and Sunshine by exchanging stock share for share. One novel idea was that the Silver Valley Company would issue preferred stock redeemable in silver. Griffith dutifully took the proposition to his board, which thought it "unorthodox" and declined to pursue it. But perhaps this was the genesis of their later suggestion that Hecla pay a dividend in silver.

On the other hand, Hecla's largest shareholder, El Paso Natural Gas, sold its Hecla stock to Rosario Resources Corporation, as Rosario was about to be taken over by Amax, Inc., Griffith went directly to Amax's president, Pierre Gousseland, to ask his intentions toward Hecla, coming away somewhat awed. "A visit with Pierre is like reading the Bible," he marveled. "He speaks in parables." Griffith urged Gousseland to stop buying Hecla stock. The Amax president's meaning could not be mistaken later, when he reproached Griffith, claiming that Amax had forfeited a million dollars in stock appreciation by complying with the request.

To "monitor the actions of threatening parties" and hold off "creeping acquisition," Griffith employed three New York consultants experienced in mergers: Joe Flom's law firm; Merrill Lynch White Weld for financial guidance; and for a short time, Hill and Knowlton, financial public relations advisors, "to improve Hecla's communications with shareholders." Flom would persuade the Federal Trade Commission to sanction Amax's acquisition of Rosario only with the stipulation that Amax would not use Rosario to control Hecla. (That threat has been removed: Amax sold its Hecla stock, and Gousseland retired as president in 1986.)

Several directors deprecated Griffith's reliance on hired consultants. "We had people on the board who knew more than the consultants," one complained. Herman bristled when Griffith occasionally "passed along special knowledge to some members" of the board before meetings to cinch their votes. For his part, Griffith felt that Herman and Tittmann, both outspoken, tried to dominate meetings. He would work to convince the directors to select new members from diverse backgrounds—men who knew marketing, finance, industry, and other business fields.

Griffith took small personal credit for Hecla's remarkable resurgence after Lakeshore, but he meant to make the most of it. He meant to compel planning, budgeting, and reporting internally, and to diversify Hecla to ensure the company's future. Of Hecla's good fortune, he would observe candidly to shareholders that "when the Hunts ran silver up to $40, we could have gone to sleep and still made a fortune." On reflection, he amended this offhand remark: "Sure we were lucky, but luck comes to those prepared to take advantage of it." He kept Hecla's mines running. "I would not listen to excuses of a manpower shortage," he said. Silver rose even higher than $40 before the boom subsided—and Hecla in 1979 recorded a net income of $35.1 million, its topmost in eighty-nine years. One Hecla director, Jack Williams, drolly suggested that Hecla give a dinner in appreciation for the Hunt brothers.

Around Hecla's unadorned brick headquarters, a tacit consensus formed to forget Lakeshore, but even Lakeshore now contributed tax-loss carry-forwards that might save Hecla as much as $39 million in the next five years. Moreover, the Papagos in April leased Lakeshore to Noranda Exploration, Ltd., a Canadian company that bought the idle plant for roughly $9.4 million, and eventually with others assumed Hecla's obligation for electrical service from the tribal utility.

Griffith concluded that Hecla "had neglected its own backyard." He gave his geologists an exercise: to rank prospects that Hecla might consider in northern Idaho. Apparently on the geologists' advice, he told shareholders in his first report to them that Consolidated Silver was "the most promising project in the Coeur d'Alene mining district."

Consolidated Silver brought together Hecla, Silver Dollar (a Magnuson company), Sunshine, and Coeur d'Alene Mines in a new venture to deepen the Silver Summit shaft and explore adjoining properties. The delegates from the four participants, sitting as Con Silver's board, squabbled about shares and, as usual, Sunshine and Hecla could not agree, and, as usual, Magnuson's man, Norman M. Smith, sided with Hecla against Sunshine. Perturbed, Hecla and Silver Dollar gave up a little "to placate Coeur d'Alene Mines." The final division—"primarily to present a better image to the public shareholders"— gave Hecla 64 percent and the three others, virtually equal parts of 36 percent.

The vote for this agreement had been: four in favor, one against everyone else, one for a bigger slice for Sunshine, and two abstaining. Con Silver thus mirrored the mining industry: crowded competition. Griffith felt that animosities were exaggerated in news accounts. "We don't look on them as enemies," he said of Sunshine, "but simply as aggressive competitors."

Aggressive corporate growth should be Hecla's immediate target, Griffith recommended in his 1980 statement of goals, because as Hecla stood, it "was too small to be truly viable in the corporate world." Given the mood of the mining industry, aggressive growth could translate into abrasive growth. By and large, the directors agreed with their president's goals, although they inverted his ranking of ways to grow; acquisition (with emphasis on the Coeur d'Alenes) would be first, joint ventures next, and last, exploration. On the other hand, they understood the necessity for exploration and approved an exploration budget of $4 million, about ten times that of 1979. And the directors, who generally conceded that "if someone was going to take us over, we couldn't stop it," advised Griffith to "stop worrying about a takeover."

In August 1979, the board had authorized $26 million to sink a third and deeper shaft for the Lucky Friday, starting on the surface in Hunter Ranch ground leased from Day Mines—

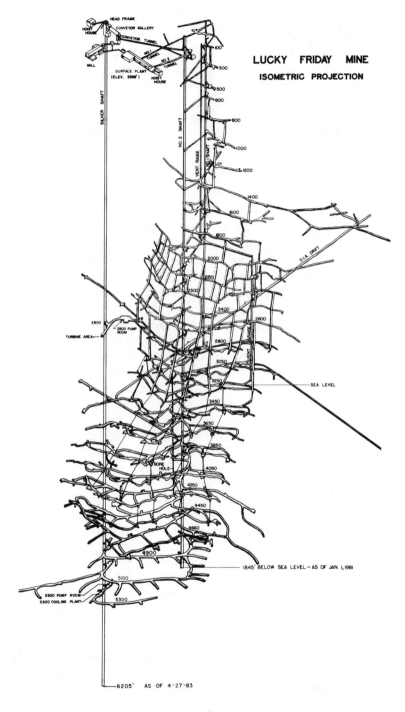

LUCKY FRIDAY MINE
ISOMETRIC PROJECTION

number 3 shaft, which Art Brown dubbed "the Silver Shaft." The name, Griffith laughed, was "more glamorous." The third shaft was necessary because the second could go no deeper. "We either sank deeper or went out of business," Griffith observed. Moreover, Hecla could maintain production from the second while sinking its third shaft.

The new shaft was, in a sense, a victory for new management, for the earlier plan had been to sink from a level inside the mine, and Brown and Bill Anderson had both opposed that. But Miner was penurious; he spent as little as possible on development and he considered an internal shaft to be cheaper. So one was begun, set aside, begun again, abandoned a second time. Griffith eventually acted on Brown's advice to build the new shaft from the surface. On the day ground was broken, Art Brown went up to the Lucky Friday to christen the shaft with bottles of champagne, happily popping corks into the hole. Hecla had known for nearly twenty years that Lucky Friday's so-called south split dipped toward Atlas and had tried sporadically to negotiate with Atlas to avoid litigation. The state supreme court had ruled in 1968 that Lucky Friday was entitled to pursue its vein into Atlas ground but questions remained: Was there also an Atlas orebody? And could Hecla crosscut through Atlas to its vein, rather than drift on the mineral?

In his time, Bill Love had tried for an accord with Frank J. Frankovich, Atlas's president. Handsome, with an eye patch, undoubtedly competent as a geologist, Frankovich mixed personal affairs with company and was consequently often at odds with Atlas's board. Love found Frankovich erratic, but he reached an agreement allowing Hecla to pass through Atlas ground in return for exploring it, with a 60–40 split if mineral were found. Atlas's directors turned down the compact. Frustrated, Love let Atlas lie while his ire cooled.

Now Hecla's board found a new opportunity to settle with Atlas, when the brokers, Bache Halsey Stuart, sued Frankovich, Atlas, and a Frankovich concern, Banner-Idaho Mining Company, for $9.6 million in connection with silver-futures losses. Frankovich's attorney called Griffith to suggest that Hecla buy Atlas for enough to bail out Frankovich, and Frankovich mailed Atlas shareholders a letter outlining a supposed Hecla purchase. But Atlas's board would not condone the deal. It removed Frankovich as president.

Griffith, hospitalized briefly in Spokane, discovered that Lavon Fausett, vice president and a director of Atlas, was also a patient. The two, perched on their beds in hospital gowns, bargained in a friendly way, inclining toward Love's 60–40 proposal. In court testimony, Griffith would recall that neither Fausett nor anyone else from Atlas questioned Lucky Friday's ownership of the vein, and that Atlas—idle, beleaguered by Bache, and short of funds—seemed eager to deal. Fausett did not let on that Atlas was also negotiating with Day Mines.

Consequently, Griffith was shocked—betrayed, he believed—when he learned on November 19, 1980, from Day that Atlas had contracted with Day on what seemed less favorable terms. Day had no shaft in the area—"no way to mine Atlas property," Griffith fumed. "There had to be something going on . . . and I didn't think it was quite on the level." He concluded that Day Mines meant to break its agreement that allowed Hecla to sink its shaft from Hunter Ranch ground, and that Day's president, William M. Calhoun, had aborted a Hecla-Atlas deal for a "rake-off." Calhoun had admittedly been resentful because Hecla did not invite him to groundbreaking for the Silver Shaft, and Calhoun and his staff concluded that Lucky Friday had run out of ore, that Hecla would seek to mine Atlas and Hunter. Griffith's suspicions may not have been far from the mark, for when Henry Day, retired chairman of Day Mines, heard about the Silver Shaft on Hunter Ranch property, he observed that the shaft "is unauthorized. . . . Let them [Hecla] sink it and we'll fight it out later."

Some Hecla directors surmised that Griffith had botched the Atlas assignment. They felt they had been duped. Griffith naturally resolved that neither Atlas nor Day would burn him a second time. Hecla retaliated by withdrawing its business from Osburn Drilling, Fausett's company, while the board informally approved Griffith's request to Merrill Lynch White Weld to buy up to 5 percent of Day Mines' stock on the American exchange (later raising the limit to 9.5 percent), explaining that Hecla wanted to expand its investment in the Coeur d'Alenes. Hecla disavowed an intent to control Day—although Henry Day himself apparently expected Hecla to demand a seat on Day's board. When the seat was offered, Hecla declined. Within six months, Hecla would be Day Mines' largest shareholder with approximately 7.5 percent of the outstanding stock. Even though he thought "Day took the Atlas deal to buy a lawsuit against Hecla," Griffith meant, by stock purchases, "to dispel some suspicion" in the Day camp, and hoped that Day Mines might not "be disagreeable to a major shareholder."

Rather than dispelling suspicion, Hecla's buys sharpened it. Both Calhoun and Henry Day suspected that Hecla was "onto something," reasoning that Hecla would not spend $26 million for a new shaft unless it knew something it would not reveal. Calhoun handed Day a memo asserting that his review of agreements "brings to light Hecla's primary intent to control all of Day Mines' property near the Lucky Friday." Through intermediaries, Calhoun approached Hecla to stop buying Day stock. Hecla did not stop.

And since secrets are the daily grist of conversations in the constricted community of Wallace, the mounting exasperation between Hecla and Day overflowed into the town. People started taking sides—an uncomfortable situation for Griffith and Calhoun, who had been friends, whose wives owned a small business together.

Shortly before Christmas 1980, Atlas filed suit against Hecla to define the Lucky Friday's extralateral rights to pursue the vein outside Lucky Friday boundaries. Early in March, Day Mines, Inc., joined Atlas as a plaintiff in the suit. Dismayed by Day's fighting stance, Hecla's directors, in a special meeting at Spokane's Sheraton Hotel, instructed Griffith to seek a compromise—even possibly a merger with Day Mines—to forestall a flurry of suits over mineral rights around the Lucky Friday. (Griffith would remember Herman's brusque counsel: "Take 'em over!") By this time, Calhoun and Griffith were wary and indignant, each man feeling that his reputation as a manager was at stake—a personal contest each meant to win. When Griffith proposed merger, Calhoun interpreted the offer as throwing down the gauntlet. He turned down the proposal, and Griffith went over Calhoun's head to the Day Mines board.

Griffith offered 1.65 shares of Hecla stock for each one of Day as a basis for merger, "purposely a very generous price" to stimulate a friendly consolidation. In a letter to Calhoun, Griffith pointed out that the offer represented a 38 percent premium over market value for Day shareholders and that a merger would create "the premier silver mining company in the United States."

Hecla had only recently split its stock, three shares for two. Even so, Gousseland of Amax, concerned about dilution of Amax's share of Hecla, objected that "Hecla was paying through the nose for Day." Now began a ritual thrust and parry: Day Mines asked for more information about mineral prospects in the Atlas, to evaluate Hecla's offer, but called Hecla's response a "tightly controlled, well-rehearsed, sham." Calhoun and Griffith traded snarling letters and telephone calls; each gave the other deadlines.

To the people of Wallace—indeed, to Hecla's people—a dismaying aspect of a contest between Hecla and Day was the unavoidable buffeting of Henry Lawrence Day, patriarch of the Coeur d'Alenes. Son of the discoverer of the singular Hercules mine, Day had come into the old Hercules partnership as a young engineer in 1925. For half a century, he had preserved and strengthened his father's company; without stinting, he has worked to advance Idaho and to raise funds for its enterprises and monuments. Conservative, honored by industry and state, Henry Day might not move fast enough for Harry Magnuson's younger boosters, but he was the heartbeat of Wallace, proud of his family's pioneering place in it.

If many of Wallace's interested citizens supported Day, another large faction backed Hecla, for Hecla's was also an illustrious past, and Wallace had also been nurtured by John Finch, Amasa Campbell, James McCarthy, Lew Hanley, Les Randall, Bill Love, and hundreds of Hecla employees. Hecla's office manager, David W. Morehouse, for one, won recognition from civic clubs, and the high school yearbook had been dedicated to him for his "unselfish interest in the young."

Hecla had filed a required statement, form S-1, with the Securities and Exchange Commission outlining its proposal to merge with Day Mines through a tax-free exchange of stock. But Day Mines had sued in federal court (bringing twenty-six cartons of documents for their case), petitioning the court to define Hecla's extralateral rights and to halt Hecla's alleged trespasses into Atlas ground. Day also asked the court to enjoin Hecla from pursuing a merger, charging that Hecla had "secretly devised a plan and course of action fraudulently to acquire common stock of Day Mines, Inc.," and that Hecla's alleged refusal to tell what it knew about ores in the Atlas "masked the true value" of Day stock. On the day Hecla filed form S-1, Day shares sold at $25.50 on the American, and Hecla, at $14.75 on the New York Stock Exchange.

Day Mines' petitions were denied by the federal district court, whereupon Day Mines appealed to the U.S. Court of Appeals for the Ninth Circuit, which declined to stay Hecla but set a hearing for the coming September. With the court's intervention likely, investment bankers for Day and Hecla gathered in Wallace to negotiate. On their bankers' advice, Hecla's directors, also meeting there, agreed to raise the ratio of Hecla to Day stock, on condition that the Day board accept the higher offer, drop its lawsuits, and stop seeking other potential buyers. Griffith carried the new offer and conditions to Day Mines, and Day's board and officers huddled in the Day building, where they "went to the blankets"—brought in blankets and pillows, and sent out for sandwiches—while they deliberated well past midnight. Barely two blocks away, Hecla's people waited restively in their building. Day Mines accepted the offer at 3:00 A.M., as approaching dawn greyed the mountain skies.

On the morning of July 8, 1981, consequently, Hecla and Day Mines signed an agreement to merge by an exchange of 1.8 shares of Hecla for each one of Day. Fifteen days later, Hecla's tender had brought it 61.5 percent of the stock of Day Mines, Inc. The merger was completed on October 20 with the favorable vote of Day's stockholders.

With Day Mines, Hecla acquired the Knob Hill gold mine near Republic, Washington; 5 percent of the Coeur and 12.5 percent of the Galena units operated by Asarco, the lowest cost silver producers in the Coeur d'Alenes; 18.5 percent of the Caladay unit, southeast of Galena; and Day Mines leases in Nevada and Colorado. And with Day's Hunter Ranch, Hecla finally owned 100 percent of Lucky Friday.

With the merger, Atlas agreed to settle its suit out of court. Hecla paid $200,000 for subsurface rights in Atlas's north property and pledged to spend $1.3 million exploring Atlas south of the Osburn fault.

The merger had cost Hecla 7,200,000 shares. It consolidated two pioneer companies into one less vulnerable to takeover— "A bigger fish is harder to swallow," Griffith remarked. Out of respect for Day, Hecla's directors toyed with calling the merged company Hecla-Day, but Hecla's employees balked because, as one pointed out, "Hecla is an old company with a reputation now known over the world."

Although it was a shotgun merger, begun in frustration and suspicion and propelled by umbrage, the merger was a good one for Hecla. "In a good merger," declared Bill Griffith, "two plus two equals five. That reflects the facts of percentage in a good merger." Indeed, in months to come, the acquisition of Day Mines (and subsequently, that of Ranchers) would seem as significant to Hecla's progress as purchase of Lucky Friday had been in its time.

The 1981 annual report crowed about "the new Hecla . . . the premier silver mining company in the United States." Although operating results had been "disappointing"—largely because silver and lead prices fell, a nine-week strike cut off income from Lucky Friday, and the company spent $7.1 million to complete the Day merger—Hecla was now larger and stronger. The years 1979 and 1980 had been the richest of Hecla's life, allowing it to sell 1,000,000 shares for $22.4 million to pay off its entire remaining debt, redeem preferred stock issued to banks, and restructure its line of credit. For the first time in decades, Hecla could resolve that, in any future consolidation, it would be the surviving entity.

When the depressed market and rising costs of environmental compliance persuaded Gulf Resources to close the Bunker Hill, the old giant of the district, Hecla, Callahan, and Coeur d'Alene Mines formed a partnership to buy the Crescent mine from Bunker Hill. They had gone so far as to draft an agreement that Hecla would be managing partner with 40 percent of the profits before discovering that Jack W. Kendrick, Bunker Hill's president, was "dealing under the table for himself," hoping that he and his associates could take over Bunker Hill. Hecla allowed its offer for Crescent to expire. Bunker Hill eventually went to the Bunker Limited Partnership formed in 1982 by Kendrick, Duane B. Hagadone, the Coeur d'Alene newspaper chain magnate, Magnuson, and J. R. Simplot Company.

With Hecla's resurgence, Griffith was invited to address the New York Society of Security Analysts, the first Hecla president to appear there in thirteen years. In 1983, Griffith would be elected chairman of the board of the Silver Institute, the industry's international trade association.

Griffith set new corporate goals—the consensus from staff retreats—aiming to increase Hecla's annual average productivity 20 percent within five years, and to diversify so that minerals other than silver and gold would generate 25 percent of the company's income.

Diversifying into minerals that would hold their markets as gold and silver lost theirs would be the challenge. Growth of this kind meant setting the company's sights beyond Idaho once again, for opportunities for mining combinations were limited in Idaho. And maneuvering in the corporate arena required freeing Hecla from the impediments of Washington state law. Consequently, the directors voted in February 1983 to reorganize Hecla in Delaware. At a board meeting in Spokane, two advisors from the law firm of Wachtell, Lipton, Rosen & Katz explained that, with a Delaware charter, Hecla could specify "super-majority voting requirements" and staggered directors' terms that would make Hecla harder to take over. A new charter under the "comprehensive, flexible, and modern" laws of Delaware, where courts were familiar with corporate law, would require a favorable two-thirds vote from shareholders. With their approval, Washington Hecla would merge into a new Hecla Mining Company of Delaware. Wachtell, Lipton, Rosen & Katz also recommended that Hecla provide job security for "key" executives, a measure now regarded as essential by many companies to attract and hold able men.

The rules of the New York Stock Exchange required that votes of the actual (beneficial) owners of shares held by brokers and nominees must be counted. By Hecla's estimate a little over 45 percent, or 7,200,000 shares, were in such "street" accounts, necessitating a cumbersome canvass of brokers who, in turn, solicited their clients to vote. At a reconvened shareholders' meeting in June, 69.3 percent of the shares approved the merger with Delaware Hecla, and Hecla became a Delaware corporation on June 7, 1983. The company again asked the Spokane Stock Exchange to stop listing its shares. This time the exchange complied, although it has since resumed trading in Hecla.

The year 1983 was exceptionally profitable for Hecla. The price of silver had risen 44 percent and mine production, 30 percent. The net reached $26.7 million, compared with $5 million in 1982. Salary rollbacks, instituted to save operating funds in June 1982, were revoked in January 1983. Again, that recently familiar phrase, "the best year in our history," appeared in the annual report—a polished booklet conceived by Hecla's public affairs manager, Elmer L. Bierly, with a silvery cover and a catch-phrase page headed, "Hecla is . . .," opposite a colored photograph of Wallace surrounded by hills bright with autumn's orange hues.

"Hecla is . . . 18,000 shareholders from each of the fifty states," it read, responsible for 15 percent of the newly mined

domestic silver each year, an employee family of 700. "At Hecla we have no designated 'key' employees," it went on, "because every individual is considered 'key' in his or her partic-
ular function." (Hecla in 1981 would offer guarantees for three
years—later cut to two years—to five executives, assuring their
incomes temporarily if displaced by merger or takeover.) The
caption read, in part, "Hecla . . . is proud to have its headquarters in this historic city," Wallace—a line that soon rang
hollow.

Indeed, Hecla's favor in its hometown had begun to erode.
In the opinion of some, Hecla, with its Delaware charter and
national repute, had gotten uppity. Wallace sensed that Hecla
was growing away from its origins. The town had regretted
the demise of Day Mines. It was dismayed in mid-1982 when
Hecla shut down the ninety-two-year-old Star-Morning, after
eighteen months of deficits, "to eliminate unprofitable operations." The old mines had lived as long as they did only because Hecla imposed economies and efficient methods. Now
the equipment was being salvaged and the lower levels allowed to flood. Jobs had been lost. With evaporating hope for
revival of Bunker Hill, the families and merchants of the district faced awesome transition. In their discontent, it was con-
venient to blame someone—and some blamed Hecla and Bill
Griffith.

Even as Hecla reorganized in Delaware, the company was
negotiating to absorb the Ranchers Exploration and Development Corporation of New Mexico, formed thirty years earlier
by Carl Anderson and ranch owners who pooled the mineral
rights on their grazing land. Ranchers' first mineral property,
ironically, had been a low-grade Arizona copper mine. The
company leased its claims to experienced miners who discovered uranium in 1956 and paid the first royalties two years later.
Unlike conservative Hecla, Ranchers' panache was legendary:
its owners stood off claim jumpers with lawsuits and gunfire;
paid its dividends in gold and silver; and for two decades had
been guided by old Carl's unconventional son, Maxie L. Anderson, an international balloonist—in 1978, first to fly the Atlantic.

Anderson, a combative, innovative manager who had once
cracked the ribs of an Anaconda attorney in a scuffle over mineral rights, had been seated on Ranchers' board at age twenty-
three by his father. And although old Carl did not sit on the

board, he took a chair in a corner of the boardroom and pretty well told his directors how to run the company. As president, Maxie had steered Ranchers into operating rather than leasing its properties, and into copper, gold, silver, clay, and volcanic rock production. The *Wall Street Journal* characterized Ranchers as "a swashbuckling company unafraid to use debt, diversification and a bit of dabbling in the futures market to help maximize its profits." In 1981, Ranchers had opened the Escalante mine about thirty-five miles west of Cedar City, Utah, a low-cost silver producer. Anderson stockpiled silver when he considered the selling price too low or sold on the futures market as a hedge against further weakening.

Maxie Anderson and Griffith began contemplating merger seriously in May 1983 after an investment broker, looking for a buyer, inquired about Hecla's possible interest in Ranchers. The broker represented Kelly Williams, hard-driving president of First Mississippi Corporation, a fertilizer, oil, gas, potash, and industrial chemicals firm which held 19.5 percent of Ranchers' stock as an investment. Williams, critical of Anderson's management, determined to get out of Ranchers. Obviously, with ball clay and volcanic scoria (industrial minerals) among its products, Ranchers offered some of the diversity that Griffith wanted for Hecla, but he would neither take First Mississippi's minority interest nor pay cash, as Williams's broker suggested. Hecla would only consider acquiring Ranchers wholly by stock exchange. With Williams's assent, Griffith telephoned Anderson to ask if Ranchers might be for sale, and Anderson invited him to Albuquerque to talk.

Griffith found that Anderson had tired of mining. He had shifted his enthusiasm to politics and ballooning, and he drove Griffith—in an old station wagon while his wife drove a white Jaguar—to see his real estate development. Before they parted, he gave Griffith two bottles of private-label wine. As Anderson affixed the labels, Griffith saw that the balloonist's hands shook badly. He concluded that Anderson must be ill.

They met again in New York on Anderson's way to Europe for ballooning, and afterward, John Motica, the geologist who had helped Carl Anderson build Ranchers, came to Wallace to review Hecla's assets. He was sitting in Griffith's office when a message came that Anderson had died (on June 27, 1983) in a balloon-landing accident. Motica went home. He soon reported that Ranchers was no longer open to merger.

In the meantime, Hecla's board again considered moving the company's headquarters from Wallace, where it had been since the Hecla records were transferred from Finch and Campbell's offices in Spokane in 1904. Hecla's new goals for diversity and expansion meant that it would need larger administrative quarters. Moreover, as Griffith pointed out, professional executives and engineers routinely turned down job offers from Hecla rather than live in Wallace. Before Ranchers broke off negotiations, its staff insisted that any merger must involve relocation of Hecla, for its people had no intention of moving to the confining mountain towns of the Coeur d'Alene district. Perhaps Colorado Springs, Denver, or even San Francisco. Griffith advanced Coeur d'Alene as a possible site. That seemed to suit the Ranchers people.

Everyone involved in Hecla's decision to move understood that it would be a blow to Wallace. The town was observing its centennial with sentimental pride in its durability through labor wars, floods, fires, snow slides, mining and timber recessions, and other calamities. Its people were justifiably exalted by their community spirit. Nobody at Hecla wanted to deflate Wallace in the middle of a celebration. The company would delay announcing its departure until an auspicious day, if ever there might be one.

Then Leland O. Erdahl, who had succeeded Anderson at the helm of Ranchers, called Griffith to reopen negotiations for a friendly merger with Hecla. Michael Boswell of Sunshine got wind of the merger deliberations—they really were not secret—and in Griffith's opinion, Boswell "shook the tree to see what might fall out." Boswell bid 2.5 shares of Sunshine for each share of Ranchers, threatening a proxy fight in which he would offer Ranchers' shareholders 27 percent more than the current market value of their stock. On paper, Sunshine's was a better offer than Hecla's, but Ranchers officers felt that Sunshine stock was overvalued on the market. First Mississippi and Ranchers both turned down Sunshine's bid.

On March 1, 1984, nevertheless, Griffith and Boswell both presented proposals to the Ranchers board. Griffith remembered that he, Grismer, and their investment advisors had crowded into a small rental car at the Albuquerque airport. When they drove into Ranchers' parking lot, they found that Boswell had preceded them in a chauffered limousine. During their separate presentations, Boswell answered a director's question by assuring him that the Sunshine and Ranchers pension plans would mesh well. There was no Ranchers pension plan, he learned with embarrassment—and angrily accused the Ranchers board of trapping him.

Seven days later, Boswell announced that Sunshine held 437,900 shares, roughly 7.7 percent, of Ranchers' outstanding 5,700,000 shares. He renewed Sunshine's offer to buy the New Mexico company. Griffith met a second time with the Ranchers board. By now Hecla held approximately 413,000 shares bought on the open market, and the Anderson family's and First Mississippi shares traded for Hecla stock, raising Hecla's holding of Ranchers to 36 percent.

On March 9 the boards of Ranchers and Hecla agreed unanimously to merge by stock exchange on the basis of 1.55 shares of Hecla common for each one of Ranchers. Together they sought a federal injunction to block further Sunshine attempts to take over Ranchers. The merger would give Hecla 67.8 percent, and former Ranchers shareholders 32.2 percent, of the stock of a combined company.

The terms of the consolidation called for expanding the Hecla board from seven to nine members, with former Ranchers directors taking the two added seats, and for the absorption of Ranchers executives and employees into an enlarged Hecla Mining Company. (Although the agreement did not call for it, Hecla would soon contribute $100,000 to a Maxie L. Anderson International Balloon Museum.) Awaiting only the predictable assent of shareholders, the merger would, Griffith told the New York security analysts, "create a company which is the largest domestic miner of silver . . . [with] significant diversification in lead and industrial minerals to protect it during dips in precious metals prices." The combined assets, he pointed out, would "about double those of Hecla today."

Buying Ranchers increased Hecla's assets, in fact, about 68 percent. With Ranchers, Hecla acquired the Escalante silver mine; the Kentucky-Tennessee Clay Company, a provider of clays to ceramic manufacturers; and the Colorado Aggregate Company, which quarried volcanic rock—black for briquettes in gas barbecues and red for landscaping. In this one transaction, Hecla doubled in size, diversified, and captured a silver mine producing about 2.3 million ounces a year at the lowest production cost of any large-scale silver mine in the country. For Hecla, the merger represented "a quantum leap," in the view of Arthur Brown.

Even though the Ranchers merger seemed all but final, Sunshine did not back off. Griffith asked Boswell to arrange a meeting where they would be unlikely to meet anyone they knew. Boswell set them up in a sumptuous Dallas hotel—gold-plated bathroom fixtures. There, he and Griffith reached a preliminary accord. Shortly after, at the Spokane Sheraton, with attorneys and investment bankers, they worked out details of the deal in thirty-six hours. (Griffith learned later than Sunshine's people wanted to call off negotiations after the first session.) They kept the attorneys in the hotel until an agreement was written and signed.

Under its terms, Sunshine withdrew its opposition to the merger and agreed to turn in its 437,900 shares of Ranchers in exchange for Hecla stock. Hecla also acquired 2,250,000 shares of Sunshine common and Sunshine's 13 percent interest in Consolidated Silver. Sunshine took Hecla's 33.25 percent interest in the Sunshine Unit Area—and Hecla was at last free of the aggravating unit area, leaving Griffith to contemplate whether, in fact, that had not been Boswell's purpose all along.

Even though seven former Ranchers executives soon resigned from Hecla and the Albuquerque offices were closed, the prospective increase in staff with acquisition of Ranchers compelled Hecla to act on its decision to move out of Wallace. Perhaps no delay would have softened the dismay there. Hecla already occupied two buildings, the Hecla and the former Day Mines quarters, and to stay in Wallace, would need a third one. If the company did not actively look for more space, its secret would come out, anyway.

Griffith had evaded stockholders' queries about a rumored move at their meeting ("because we were heavily involved in property negotiations," he explained later), but he convened Hecla employees at the Elks Club to break the news to them and, on July 10, disclosed in a press release that Hecla had purchased land in Coeur d'Alene, would erect an office building there, and move within one or two years. Only six weeks earlier, Sunshine had revealed that its executive offices would leave Kellogg for Boise. And Coeur d'Alene Mines Corporation planned to abandon Wallace for Coeur d'Alene.

Wallace's public reaction to Hecla's intended departure was

vehement and vituperative, voiced by Harry Magnuson's *North Idaho Press*. (He has since sold the newspaper.) No doubt the *Press* conveyed Magnuson's own indignation, for he had earlier fired an editor and reporter who disagreed with his political views. The *Press* headlined one editorial "Griffith the Barbarian," declaring shrilly that "like a thief in the night" Hecla would "steal out of Wallace." With exquisite disdain for historical accuracy, the editorial went on: "Local citizens have stood by Hecla during fire, flood, and economic downturns. Hecla has responded by gobbling up Day Mines, prematurely flooding the Star Mine and playing the poor man when it is time to ante-up for community projects."

Coeur d'Alene realtors' advertising leaflets began to appear on Hecla desks. Sixteen days after the press release, Griffith introduced himself with a grim smile to shareholders meeting in Wallace: "I am Griffith the barbarian."

The Shoshone County commissioners passed a sharp resolution urging Hecla to remain in Wallace, to which Grismer replied for the directors: "We do not consider it wise nor prudent to jeopardize [the company's corporate] health simply to support the ailing businesses of others or to attempt to support the declining economy of Shoshone County, which is only one of 10 or more countries nationwide in which we now have significant business operations." Five Hecla shareholders, including Henry Day, sued to enjoin consummation of the Ranchers merger and move from Wallace, but their petition was denied.

Outside Wallace, the reaction was more favorable. Griffith had been the target in Wallace but, the *Wall Street Journal* observed, his "preacherly demeanor has always played better on Wall Street than it has in Wallace," and reminded readers that "Griffith's conservative management style helped put the company back on the track after the disastrous copper venture." For three years running, the *Wall Street Transcript* had singled out Hecla as the best managed silver company in the nation, and, for five consecutive years, had named Griffith the foremost chief executive officer in the silver industry. The *Transcript* said: "Despite severely depressed silver prices, this management has prepared Hecla to weather the current crisis while positioning it for future growth. . . . Hecla boasts one of the soundest balance sheets in the industry, an attractive portfolio of investment securities and an excellent cost structure."

With cutting of a bright blue ribbon, Hecla dedicated its new corporate headquarters on May 9, 1986. The two-story grey stucco building stands in pines just off Hanley Avenue, approximately two miles north of Coeur d'Alene. It is only thirty-five miles west of the canyons where the company began, but in spirit far removed from the intrigues of clannish Wallace. On the day the building was dedicated, the directors reelected Griffith chairman and chief executive officer, and named Arthur Brown president and chief operating officer.

Born in Germiston, South Africa, and educated in mining and metallurgy at Witwatersrand Technical College, Brown came to Canada in 1962 with a roving assignment as superintendent and project manager for Cementation Company, Ltd. He and his wife, looking for a company and place to settle down, chose Hecla. Six feet, four inches, with boyish features, Brown sprinkles the soft accents of his native South Africa with an occasional salty phrase. He is outgoing in manner, suited to the Hecla tradition of leading by friendly persuasion.

Brown joined Hecla in 1967 as an industrial engineer. Three years later, he had risen to manager of Lucky Friday, walled off from Lakeshore by Gordon Miner. A patriotic man, Miner badgered the Browns to become United States citizens, which they did in 1978. Brown was among the key young executives whom Love did not sweep out after Lakeshore. Early in his tenure, Griffith intimated that Brown would have his opportunity for the presidency.

Within six years, Brown was executive vice president with an apparently clear track ahead, although Griffith brought him up short from time to time: "You're not president yet; so don't act like you are." But Griffith dispatched Brown with Elmer Bierly to get acquainted with security analysts, and he took Brown with him to represent Hecla before the New York Society of Security Analysts in April 1986; it was Griffith's fourth appearance in seven years, and he observed that "of our seven profit centers last year, only one had been in the company when I made my first presentation" in 1979. Indeed, Knob Hill, which Hecla regarded as incidental in its acquisition of Day, had become the company's most profitable property for the time being; second and third were the industrial minerals companies, Kentucky-Tennessee Clay Company and Colorado Aggregate, acquired with Ranchers.

Hecla had not, Griffith told the analysts, abandoned silver

and gold as "our primary businesses" but had "been prudent enough to arrange significant diversification, within the business we know, to help us through [depressed] times." And it is true that Hecla's stock price no longer precisely tracks that of silver.

Three weeks after cutting the ribbon at the new building, Griffith retired on June 1, 1986, succeeded as president and chief executive officer by Brown. And while he continued to live in Coeur d'Alene and to serve on Hecla's board, Griffith did not look in at the company's offices—"a guy who, for years, devoted twenty-four hours a day to this company," remarked one, "and when he retired—he retired. He does not come around to visit." Obviously, for Bill Griffith, to use one of his expressions when a task was finished, "She's deep enough." At a farewell party, Hecla presented Griffith with a 21-inch silver sculpture of a tired miner coming off shift, inscribed: "She's deep enough."

Griffith left Hecla financially sound with diverse products, and bastioned against unfriendly takeover by a shareholders' rights plan. Hecla no longer relies solely on the treacherous market for precious metals. Griffith rebuilt the staff and taught them management by objectives; he faced the ire of Wallace to relocate Hecla without abandoning its Idaho heritage, in a headquarters building symbolic of the company's enlarging prospects. When Griffith came into the presidency, Hecla's market value stood at approximately $35 million; on the day he retired, it was near $600 million. In world-wide mining, Hecla remains a medium-sized company, albeit on the verge of bigness.

Art Brown does not want to fashion Hecla into a big company; he proposes that it be larger but not large and, barring catastrophe, he is likely to be its leader into the twenty-first century. In broad terms, he sees Hecla continuing and expanding its current product lines. Although the Escalante mine gave up its last silver in 1988, Hecla pursues new precious metal prospects in Canada and Alaska; it maintains a Canadian subsidiary and Toronto office for exploration. Lucky Friday has continued Hecla's tradition of innovation with increasing mechanization. And Brown has expanded the company's presence in industrial minerals and specialty metals with acquisition of kaolin mines and mills in Georgia and South Carolina, and a germanium-gallium mine in Utah. Kaolin is essential to production of ceramics; germanium, to fiber optics and light-emitting diodes.

In the turbulent arena of mining, with increasing care for the world's environment, nothing is sure. Yet even somnambulent Granduc stirs with its Sulphuret gold project, and Hecla has enlarged its interests in Canada. Knob Hill near Republic, Washington, which seemed to be playing out when Hecla scooped it in the Day Mines basket, shows new possibilities southward and great promise into the second century. When Hecla acquired Day, it could brag that it had become the "premier producer of domestic silver." As its first century ended, with operations in twelve states and four provinces, Hecla could claim rightly to be a leading U.S. producer of newly mined silver and gold and a major supplier of ball clay and volcanic scoria, with expanding prospects in industrial minerals and specialty metals.

Hecla remains innovative in mining technology and aggressive in pursuit of new opportunities. Under friendly Art Brown, paradoxically, its employees feel greater pressure to meet the goals of divisional five-year plans. Brown will tell you that Hecla had always attracted the best, and he demands superior achievement. On the threshold of its second century, diverse, computer-driven, international Hecla has come a long way from the hillside claim of 1885 that sold for $150, long past the comradely days of McCarthy and Hanley, and in spirit is long gone from the narrow canyons of northern Idaho. But Hecla is not yet deep enough.

Sources

THIS SECTION CITES SOURCES BY PAGE NUMBER. TO LINK THE TEXT with sources, however, I occasionally use a topical heading or a key word in parentheses.

Minutes of meetings, annual reports, and similar sources are Hecla's, unless otherwise noted. Hecla's files, of course, are the foundation of this study.

Legal and newspaper citations, complete in this section, are not repeated in the Bibliography.

Chapter 1. The Milwaukee Connection

3. Wallace *Free Press*, June 2, 1888.

4. Shoshone County: *Wallace Press*, Aug. 29, 1891, quoting *Idaho Free Press*, n.d.; see Fahey, *Ballyhoo Bonanza*, pp. 18–19. Letters: *Weekly Missoulian*, Sept. 28, March 30, 1883.

4. Tiger was claimed May 2 and Ore-or-no-go, May 16, 1884, both before framing of a local mining code on June 3, 1884, which incorporated the lode-claim provisions of an 1872 federal law. Hecla: see Idaho Mineral Survey No. 949 indicating the Hecla was patented Oct. 14, 1891, at Boise City, and Shoshone County deeds, book O, p. 357. Toner's name does not appear on other claims in 1885 in Canyon Creek. Of course, after discovery of the famed Calumet and Hecla in Michigan, every mining camp had a Hecla.

4–5. *Wallace Miner*, March 27, 1930, recalls the "famed" Hecla mine 16 miles west of Melrose, Mont., active 1877–1905, which yielded $18 million in silver-lead ores. Hauser: see Fahey, *Inland Empire: D. C. Corbin and Spokane*, pp. 20–50, and, for Reed, pp. 51–53.

5–6. J. G. Butler, *History of Youngstown and Mahoning County*, passim. An appreciation of Henry Wick in *Youngstown Telegram*, Dec. 24, 1915. Names of men in the Youngstown syndicate appear in Campbell letterbooks in the Eastern Washington State Historical Society. (EWSHS).

6. Finch and Campbell are mentioned in the Wallace *Free Press*, Dec. 10, 1887, as examining properties. Finch obituary, *Spokesman-Review*,

June 21, 1915. Youngstown city directories, 1886–89. Personal communication from Mahoning Valley Historical Society. Biog., N. W. Durham, *History of the City of Spokane* 3:277. Campbell: obituary, *Spokesman-Review*, Feb. 17, 1912. A Campbell genealogy by the Salem (Ohio) Historical Society, June 1892. Clippings from "Builders of Youngstown" file, Reuben McMillan Free Library Association, Youngstown. Walter's obituary, *Youngstown Daily Vindicator*, Jan. 25, 1905. J. Edwards, *Illustrated History of Spokane County*, p. 639.

7–8. Quotation: Campbell to J. C. Wick, Sept. 17, 1900. Wages: *Coeur d'Alene Miner*, July 25, Oct. 24, 1891. Poorman: Wallace *Free Press*, July 30, Sept. 10, 1887. Union: Wallace *Free Press*, Sept. 24, 1887. See Shoshone County deeds, book N, p. 581; book O, pp. 14, 16, 18 for sales by various Poorman owners to Clark. Clark: *Spokesman-Review*, June 8, 1915; magazine, June 16, 1963; Wallace *Free Press*, May 18, 1888 (quotation).

8. Coeur d'Alene Mining & Concentrating Co., articles of incorporation at Spokane Falls, Nov. 22, 1887, filed in Shoshone County, Dec. 17, 1890. Sweeny: see Fahey, *Ballyhoo Bonanza*. Union: Wallace *Free Press*, Sept. 29, Oct. 13, 1888. "Eastern capitalists": Dec. 10, 1887. Durant: *Coeur d'Alene Miner*, Oct. 24, 1891; Campbell to H. Wick, July 25, 1903 (Sweeny). Gem: Wallace *Free Press*, July 13, 1889. The manager was J. J. Smith, not to be confused with J. R. "Hecla" Smith.

8–9. Dam: Wallace *Free Press*, July 16, 1887. Milwaukee Mining Co. articles of incorporation, Aug. 22, 1888, in Shoshone County Miscellaneous Records, book H, p. 590. Stock record in Finch papers, Eastern Washington State Historical Society. Gem: Wallace *Free Press*, Jan. 21, March 30, June 8, Oct. 12, 1889; March 22, 1890; *Coeur d'Alene Miner*, June 14, 1890 (quotation). Kipps: *Milwaukee Sentinel*, Jan. 11, 1884; Feb. 3, 1885; Dec. 30, 1887; Jan. 18, July 3, Dec. 12, 1888; Dec. 21, 1890; *Greater Milwaukee*, pp. 86–87; Gregory, *History of Milwaukee* 4:36–37, 39–40; Watrous, *Memoirs*, 2:994–96; Milwaukee city directories, 1889–1914 (some years missing).

9. Kipps: *Milwaukee Sentinel*, April 24, 1878; Feb. 3, 13, 1885; March 20, Dec. 30, 1887; Jan. 13, 18, July 3, 1888; Dec. 12, 1889; Dec. 12, 1890. Morning: Wallace *Free Press*, Aug. 10, 1889; *Mullan Mirror*, Dec. 29, 1899. Hussey: *Spokesman-Review*, Jan. 19, 1940. Toner's claim: Shoshone County deeds, book C, p. 61.

10. Hecla: *Coeur d'Alene Miner*, April 11, 1891; *Wallace Miner*, Aug. 19, 1915 ($150); Shoshone County deeds, book O, p. 357; book W, p. 602; book T, pp. 398, 571. *Coeur d'Alene Miner*, Dec. 29, 1890 [*sic*: correct date probably Dec. 28], says Hardesty and Healey bought the store of Harris & Rice, Burke. Quotation: *Wallace Press*, Jan. 2, 1891. Hecla Mining Co.: articles of incorporation, Shoshone County, filed March 24, 1891; certificates of stock record in Hecla files.

11. *Wallace Miner*, Nov. 23, 1911; Aug. 19, 1915. Humes: *Wallace Miner*,

Jan. 18, 29, 1917; Idaho First District Court, civil No. 4327. Humes had to wait out a lawsuit against her brother to collect.

11. Hecla Mining Co. stock register. Milwaukee Mining Co. stock register, Finch papers (EWSHS). Mammoth: *Coeur d'Alene Miner*, Sept. 17, 1890. Standard-Banner: *Coeur d'Alene Miner*, Dec. 20, 1890; May 30, Aug. 29, 1891.

11. Ransome and Calkins, *Geology and Ore Deposits*, p. 175 ($14,000). *Coeur d'Alene Miner*, April 11, 1891.

12. Republican Club: *Coeur d'Alene Miner*, July 19, 1890; Finch, Sept. 5, 1890; Campbell home, June 21, 1890. Banks: *Coeur d'Alene Miner*, Dec. 20, 1890. Morning: Dec. 26, 1891; Sept. 17, 1892; Dec. 30, 1893; Morning Mining Co., articles of incorporation, filed in Shoshone County Nov. 30, 1894, and Morning Mining & Concentrating Co., Feb. 6, 1894, filed Nov. 7, 1894. Clark, Finch, and Campbell with others organized a new bank in Wallace, soon taken over by Van B. DeLashmutt.

11–13. Gouging: A. W. Hoover interview, Aug. 31, 1962. Shiach, Henderson, and Averill, *Illustrated History of North Idaho*, pp. 1026–45, describes towns. Gem: *Wallace Miner*, July 11, 1929, quoting 1892 description. Railways: *Coeur d'Alene Miner*, Sept. 23, Nov. 29, Dec. 27, 1890. Burke: Bill Dunphy in *Wallace Miner*, June 30, 1977. Electric Co.: *Coeur d'Alene Miner*, July 18, 1891. Bender: Sept. 5, 1891. Coeur d'Alene Hardware: *Wallace Press*, Feb. 27, 1892.

13. Mines: Ingalls, *Lead and Zinc*, pp. 164–66; Ransome and Calkins, *Geology and Ore Deposits*, p. 82. MOA and unions: Fahey, *Ballyhoo Bonanza*, pp. 68–70; *Coeur d'Alene Miner*, July 25, Oct. 24, 1891; Fahey, "Coeur d'Alene Confederacy." Finch: *Wallace Press*, Jan. 1, 1892.

13–14. Labor wars are treated in detail in Fahey, *Ballyhoo Bonanza*, pp. 68–95; see also Fahey, "Coeur d'Alene Confederacy," and "Ed Boyce and the Western Federation of Miners." This abbreviated account also relies on the transcript, House Committee on U.S. Military Affairs, "Proceedings . . . ," 3 vols., 56th Congress, 1st sess., 1900. *Coeur d'Alene Miner*, July 16, 1892, reports the Gem battle and, April 22, 1893, an approach by Knights of Labor to Finch and Campbell as intermediaries "to adjust all labor troubles."

15–16. Finch: *Coeur d'Alene Miner*, Jan. 14, 1893. Clark home: *Spokane Chronicle*, Aug. 29, 1899. The house was placed on the National Register in 1975. Campbell to N. M. Smith, Dec. 28, 1899, indicates that Campbell bought Gross's stock in Hecla from his executor. Morning: *Spokesman-Review*, Aug. 6, 1897. Ore production: *Spokesman-Review*, Aug. 20, 1903; *Wallace Miner*, Dec. 3, 1914; June 23, 1977; Ingalls, *Lead and Zinc*, pp. 165–66; *Wallace Press*, Jan. 8, 1896; Shiach et al., *Illustrated History of North Idaho*, p. 1055.

16–17. McCarthy, "History of Hecla," *Mining & Metallurgy*, p. 276. Although McCarthy indicates assessments of one cent a share, in a

letter, Campbell to H. E. Allen, Oct. 17, 1898, assessments of eight
cents are noted. Hecla Mining Co., articles of incorporation, Shoshone County, July 12, 1898. Healey: *Coeur d'Alene Miner*, Aug. 27, 1892.
Hardesty: ibid., Dec. 2, 1893.

17. Campbell to H. Wick, Oct. 8, 1898. Prices: Campbell to H. Wick,
Oct. 19, 1898; *Wallace Miner*, March 7, 1907. Smith transferred the Mas-
cot to Hecla on Oct. 9, 1898, Shoshone County deeds, book Q, p. 469.
Frank had been associated with Van Dorn in the Denver and Leadville claims, Shoshone County deeds, book Q, p. 452; ibid., book M,
p. 474; ibid., book 11, p. 573.

17–18. Shoshone County deeds, book Q, p. 467; ibid., book M, p.
474; ibid., book N, p. 202; ibid., book 11, pp. 571, 573 (Van Dorn and
Frank); ibid., book 12, pp. 61–62 (Hecla Fraction); ibid., book B, p.
163; ibid., book 30, p. 108 (Ore-or-no-go); Campbell to H. Wick, Oct.
8, 1898 (purchase), Oct. 29, 1898 (driving). Campbell to B. A. Kipp,
March 17, 1899.

Chapter 2. Getting Started: McCarthy in Charge

19. Campbell to H. Wick, Oct. 29, 1898; to F. Kipp, Nov. 16, 1898;
to H. Wick, Oct. 19, 1898; to F. Kipp, Oct. 29, 1898.

19–20. Tunnel: Campbell to H. Wick, Dec. 27, 1899. Stock: Campbell to M. M. Smith, Dec. 28, 1899. Taxes: *Spokane Chronicle*, Aug. 13,
1909.

20. Moffitt: *Mining Truth* 6:2 (March 1, 1921), 11. Tunnel: Campbell
to H. Wick, Jan. 23, 1900. "Bulwark": *Wallace Miner*, Jan. 6, 1927. Hecla: Fahey, *Ballyhoo Bonanza*, pp. 171–73; *Spokesman-Review*, June 15,
1901; Ingalls, *Lead and Zinc*, p. 746; Hecla directors' minutes, April
1901; Dec. 31, 1901. The acronym "Asarco" did not come into use until
forty years later, but is used here for convenience. In the early years
of this century, most referred to the trust as "A. S. &. R."

21. Campbell to J. C. Wick, July 18, 1900. Directors' minutes, Jan.
1, 1901. Smith shares: minutes, annual meeting, Oct. 7, 1901. Smith
obituary, *Chicago Daily News*, Sept. 28, 1908. Clark: Campbell to D.
Hyman, Aug. 30, 1900.

21. Hecla directors' minutes, April 1901; Dec. 30, 1901.

21–22. Campbell to H. Wick, March 16, 1899; to Hyman, March 16,
1899. Minutes, annual meeting, Oct. 6, 1902.

23. Sweeny: Fahey, *Ballyhoo Bonanza*, pp. 170–84. Campbell to H.
Wick, July 25, 1903. Hecla bid: Campbell to Tod Ford, Aug. 31, 1903.

23–24. Campbell to Moffitt, Sept. 4, 1903. Directors' minutes, Nov.
11, 1903. Letters from McCarthy to Clagett, Dec. 1 and 21, 1902, place
McCarthy in the Hecla office nearly a year before the directors' meeting of November 1903. McCarthy: Hoban interview; Beal, *History of*

Idaho, 3:466; *Spokesman-Review,* biographical sketch no. 187, March 1, 1928.

24. Memo, "mules in service," Jan. 1, 1913. *Engineering & Mining Journal,* June 15, 1918, pp. 1071–72. *Wallace Miner,* April 27, 1916.

25. Asarco: *Engineering & Mining Journal,* Jan. 6, 1906, pp. 9–10. News release, "To Control Ore Smelting and Refining," New York News Bureau, May 10, 1905. Fahey, *Ballyhoo Bonanza,* p. 191. Fell, "Rockefeller's Right Hand Man," p. 559. Day quotation: H. L. Day to Bunker Hill & Sullivan, Federal, Hecla et al., Oct. 25, 1905. Bradley affidavit, *American Smelting & Refining (Asarco)* v. *Bunker Hill,* U.S. District Court, Oregon, No. 7555 (1917).

25. Sternfeld, letter and telegram to H. L. Day, May 5, 10, 1905. Salida contract: directors' minutes, November 1903. Pennsylvania: Manager's report, 1906. Salida smelter: *Engineering & Mining Journal,* Aug. 20, 1921, p. 307. International Smelter: ibid., Jan. 11, 1913, p. 65. *Wallace Miner,* Feb. 20, 1913. McCarthy to Clagett, March 5, 1904.

26. Railroads: Fahey, *Days of the Hercules,* pp. 73–76. McCarthy to Clagett, March 27, 1904; to Smith, March 27, 1904. Memo on proposed arbitration with O-WR&N, Northern Pacific Ry. Co. (NP), May 13, 1924. NP general freight agent to assistant general solicitor, March 26, 1924. J. M. Hannaford, 2d vice pres. of NP, to D. Miller, 1st vice pres. of Chicago Burlington & Quincy (CB&Q), April 15, 1905 (NP president's file 1064, Minnesota Historical Society).

27. McCarthy to Clagett, March 5, 1904; to Smith, March 20, 1904; June 8, 18, 1907; to J. Kelly, April 8, 1908. Fahey, *Days of the Hercules,* p. 37. Insurance: McCarthy to W. E. Guess, Dec. 18, 1910. Eight-hour day: *Idaho Press,* Feb. 4, 1905; July 21, 1906. Detectives: McCarthy to Finch and Campbell, Oct. 8, 1903.

27–28. Office: receipt for documents delivered Oct. 14, 1904. Mill: directors' special meeting, April 2, 1903. Dividends: L. J. Randall to directors, March 1, 1966, recapitulating earnings 1898–1965. Julia: notation on stock certificate.

28. Costs: manager's reports, Aug. 1, 1906; Aug. 1, 1907. Salary: directors' minutes, Oct. 6, 1906; at this meeting, McCarthy succeeded Moffitt as Hecla's attorney-in-fact in Idaho. Minutes, shareholders' meeting, Oct. 7, 1907. Landsee: Gregory, *History of Milwaukee,* pp. 168–69; *Milwaukee Sentinel,* Jan. 27, 1887; Aug. 25, 1889; March 3, 1890.

29. Smith: *Chicago Daily News,* Sept. 28, 1908 (quotation); Kipp to Campbell, Dec. 9, 1907; Smith to Swift & Co., Dec. 5, 1907; Smith to Armour, Dec. 6, 1907; McCarthy to Smith, April 8, 1908. Possibly Upman introduced Smith to the packing companies; he had invested in bonds of both.

29. Hussey to Campbell, Nov. 3, 1907. Finch to Campbell, Oct. 29, 1907. Easton to H. L. Day, June 3, 1908. McCarthy to Upman, Nov. 3, 1907. Upman to McCarthy, Campbell to McCarthy, Dec. 17, 1907. Directors' minutes, Dec. 16, 1907.

30. Johnson to Campbell, Dec. 16, 18, 1907.

31. McCarthy to Smith, June 20, July 7, 14, 1908. Profits: *Wallace Miner*, May 7, 1909. Campbell: McCarthy to Smith, July 7, 1908. Electricity: Fahey, *Days of the Hercules*, pp. 143–47. McCarthy to Smith, Aug. 18, 1908.

31–32. *Copper Handbook 1909*, p. 802. *Engineering & Mining Journal*, Feb. 23, 1905, p. 400; Feb. 1, 1908, p. 279; Feb. 15, 1908, pp. 379–80; Nov. 7, 1908, p. 923; March 27, 1909, pp. 673, 867; May 22, 1909, p. 1059; June 12, 1909, p. 1207; Aug. 5, 1922, p. 255. *Wallace Miner*, April 23, Dec. 31, 1908; March 18, May 6, Aug. 19, 1909; Jan. 20, 1910. *Idaho Daily Statesman*, March 19, 1909.

32. Costs: shareholders' minutes, Oct. 6, 1909. Tailings: 164 Fed. 927 (1908). Smith: marriage license, Cook County, Ill., Sept. 8, 1908; certificate of marriage, Sept. 25, 1908, by the Rev. Samuel Goodsell; death certificate, Department of Health, City of Chicago, Sept. 25, 1908, showing Smith's occupation as mine owner.

Chapter 3. The East Orebody

33. Minutes, annual meetings, Oct. 6, Nov. 10, 1908. Sarah: W. W. Hindley in *Spokesman-Review*, Jan. 23, 1927; Hoban interview.

34. Quotation: Wick to Campbell, Dec. 22, 1905. Directors' minutes, Nov. 10, 1908. Finch: *Spokesman-Review*, June 21, 1915.

34. Directors' minutes, Nov. 10, 1908. McCarthy letter in directors' minutes, Aug. 8, 1910. Directors' special meeting, Sept. 12, 1910. Letter, McCarthy to directors, July 6, 1915; McCarthy recalls Youngstown opposition to listing. McCarthy to Clagett, June 5, 1911. Vogelstein profile, upon acquisition by American Metals, in *Engineering & Mining Journal*, Jan. 10, 1920, p. 90.

35. Resolution, in directors' minutes, Oct. 6, 1911. McCarthy to Kipp, May 25, 1911. McCarthy to directors, Jan. 10, 1911; to traffic manager, Northern Pacific,—1911; to directors, Dec. 22, 1914.

35. Upman to McCarthy, May 22, 1911. Directors' minutes, Oct. 6, 1911. McCarthy to H. Wick, Oct. 18, 1911.

35–36. Directors' minutes, Oct. 6, 1911. McCarthy to directors, Dec. 29, 1911.

37. Special directors' meeting, Jan. 10, 1912, adjourned to Jan. 13, 1912. McCarthy to H. Wick, April 26, 1912. Landsee to McCarthy, Feb. 10. 1912, and response, Feb. 15 (?), 1912. Sarah Smith, testimony in *Day v. Hecla Mining Co.*, Washington Supreme Court, No. 17198, in which she calls Lonstorf "Longstroth." Campbell: *Spokesman-Review*, Feb. 17, 1912.

37. Directors' minutes, April 9, 1912. McCarthy to H. Wick, April 26, 1912. Fahey, *Days of the Hercules*, pp. 139–40.

38. McCarthy to Hecla foreman, Dec. 5, 1910. Quotation: directors' minutes, April 8, 1913. McCarthy to J. H. Frank, Sept. 23, 1912, describes the ore. Sorenson, "History of Hecla," pp. 2–3, says McCarthy "insisted" that crews continue their work. McCarthy, report to directors, April 14, 1914.

39. McCarthy and men: Tilford interview, confirmed by others.

39. Hecla: "Historical Record of Earnings"; *Wallace Miner*, May 9, 1912; May 1, 1913, gives net profits from mine reports to county assessor. *Engineering & Mining Journal*, Aug. 9, 1913, p. 280; Jan. 10, 1914, p. 65. McCarthy report, April 8, 1913. McCarthy to directors, Aug. 7, 1914 ("something due"); May 1, 1917 (retiring). Landsee to McCarthy, Nov. 14, 1914.

40. Directors' minutes, April 13, 1915; McCarthy report, same date. Finch: McCarthy to Finch, March 27, 1915; *Spokesman-Review*, June 21, 30, 1915; *Spokane Chronicle*, June 8, 1915; *Spokesman-Review*, June 16, 1963.

41. Special directors' meeting, July 28, 1915. Silver: *see* Jastram, *Silver: The Restless Metal*, esp. pp. 85–86. Kipp to McCarthy, June 9, 1915. McCarthy to Kipp, June 14, 1915 (McCarthy circulated this correspondence to other directors). McCarthy to directors, July 6, 1915. Special directors' meeting, July 28, 1915. L. E. Hanley to stockholders, July 31, 1915, assessment and dividend notice.

41–42. McCarthy to directors, Sept. 24, 1915. Lonstorf's action was approved by the directors, Oct. 11, 1915. McCarthy to directors, Dec. 24, 1917. For the curb: see Sobel, *Curbstone Brokers*, pp. 128, 141, 172.

42. *Engineering & Mining Journal*, Jan. 13, 1907, pp. 106–7; McCarthy to directors, Nov. 19, 1915; McCarthy report, April 11, 1916. Hecla annual reports, 1916, 1917 (Ore-or-no-go), n. p. Smelters: Fahey, *Days of the Hercules*, pp. 163–69; *Engineering & Mining Journal*, July 20, 1918, p. 91; *American Smelting & Refining* v. *Bunker Hill*, U.S. District Court, Oregon, No. 7555 (1917).

43–44. Shareholders' minutes, April 11, 1916. Smith: see W. W. Hindley in *Spokesman-Review* magazine, Jan. 23, 1917; M. Bean, ibid., Dec. 3, 1936. Dividends based on 92,000 shares at $1.55 per share in 1916.

44–45. Fahey, *Days of the Hercules*, pp. 178–79.

45. McCarthy to directors, Aug. 10, 1917 (quotation); to Kipp, Oct. 19, 1917. Fahey, *Days of the Hercules*, pp. 185–86. *Engineering & Mining Journal*, Jan. 19, 1918, pp. 145–46. Lovin, "Red Scare in Idaho," pp. 2–13.

46. *Wallace Miner*, May 2, 1918. Directors' minutes, April 10, 1917. McCarthy to directors, Oct. 17, 1917 ("booster").

46. Clagett retired in 1947, then Hecla's oldest living employee. He died in December 1950, according to *Wallace Miner*, Dec. 28, 1950. McCarthy to directors, Dec. 24, 1917; Feb. 14, 1918. Directors' minutes, April 9, 1918. *Wallace Miner*, Jan. 24, 1918.

47. Fahey, *Days of the Hercules*, p. 193. McCarthy to directors, May 10, June 11, 1919.

47–48. The union is discussed in Fahey, *Days of the Hercules*, pp. 177–202. McCarthy's statement from McWade's transcript of meeting June 25, 1919, pp. 31–33 (federal conciliation service).

48. McCarthy to directors, July 7, 1919 ("back down"); Oct. 7, 1919; Feb. 20, 1920.

49. Special directors' meeting, July 28, 1915. McCarthy to directors, Oct. 7, 1919.

50. Directors' minutes, April 9, 1918. McCarthy to Smith and Kipp, Dec. 4, 1920. *Spokesman-Review*, April 18, 1920. *Northwest Mining Truth*, Nov. 4, 1919, p. 1; Nov. 18, 1919, p. 1; Dec. 3, 1919, p. 1. McCarthy's suspicions about the Days appear in the transcript, *Day v. Hecla*, Washington Supreme Court, No. 17198. Eugene Day: shareholders' minutes, April 8, 1919; directors' minutes, April 13, 1920; April 12, 1921 ("beanery").

50. Special directors' meeting, Oct. 9, 1920. McCarthy to Smith and Kipp, Dec. 4, 1920. Shoshone County deeds, book 55, p. 1, a conveyance on Nov. 4, 1920, for properties by Federal to Hecla. Marsh lease, Shoshone County leases, book C, p. 103; July 20, 1916 (the lease expired in 1926). Hecla annual report, 1920. Directors' special meeting, April 12, 1921. Upman had moved to California in 1913. According to Los Angeles County Probate No. 44290, Upman held 40,000 shares of Hecla at his death. His estate, appraised for $548,725, was divided between his widow and adult son Walter. Neither widow nor son was considered as a potential successor on the Hecla board. Attorney E. J. Nolan, apparently at the widow's request, began acting before probate as the estate's representative to Hecla.

Chapter 4. Hitched to a Star

51. Based on tallies at annual meetings, esp. April 10, 1917.

52. Smith to McCarthy, Nov. 17, 1920.

52. *Spokesman-Review*, Nov. 24, 1921. Kipp to McCarthy, Nov. 30, 1920. McCarthy to Smith and Kipp, Dec. 4, 1920.

52–53. Nolan: McCarthy testimony, *Day v. Hecla*, 126 Wash. 50, 217 Pac. 1 (1923); Spokane County Superior Court, civil No. 65210, Wash. Supreme Court, No. 17198. Transcripts cited are from the supreme court files supplied by Geoffrey Crooks, commissioner. In appellants' (Day and Smith) abstract of the record for the supreme court, p. 107, Nolan is described as an attorney for a Los Angeles bank, apparently his exclusive occupation. Bradley: McCarthy to directors, May 12, 1921; Anderson, "Star Mine." Federal won in the lower court; Star in the Ninth Circuit Court of Appeals, which refused to rehear the case. The

U.S. Supreme Court refused Federal a writ of certiorari, at which time the parties settled. *Wallace Miner,* Nov. 24, 1921, on Star ore.

54. 23rd *Mining Industry of Idaho* (1921), p. 6. *Engineering & Mining Journal,* April 9, 1921, p. 638. Directors' minutes, April 11, 1921. At this time, the Hercules resumed its contribution to maintain the mines' employment office, according to letter, Jerome Day to W. H. Hoover, Dec. 31, 1921 (Day files).

54. Copies of scurrilous letters are in Hecla files. Shareholders' minutes, April 12, 1921. *Engineering & Mining Journal-Press,* April 30, 1921, p. 760. Transcript, *Day* v. *Hecla,* passim. At this meeting, shareholders ratified a settlement with Marsh. According to the *Wallace Miner,* April 14, 1921, Day had only 47,000 votes beyond his and Sarah's. The *Miner's* editor, Alfred Dunn, was unfriendly to the Days. He was also correspondent for *Engineering & Mining Journal.* Star: McCarthy to directors, May 12, 1921.

54–55. Wallace *Press-Times,* May 24, 1921. Testimony of Smith, Nolan, Lambach, and McCarthy (quotation) in *Day* v. *Hecla.* Dunn's allegations appear, for example, in the *Wallace Miner,* April 14, 1921; Feb. 9, 1922. *Engineering & Mining Journal-Press,* April 30, 1921, p. 760. *Spokesman-Review,* Nov. 24, 1921.

56. Sarah's feelings are mentioned in Searls to Hoban, Feb. 7, 1929. Special directors' meeting, May 25, 1921. If Searls was not available, Albert Burch was second choice. Contract: Smith and McCarthy testimony, *Day* v. *Hecla.* The contract was dated Aug. 11, 1921.

56–57. Complaint, *Day* v. *Hecla,* Spokane County Superior Court, civil No. 65210. Searls' report is part of the supreme court file. Shareholders' minutes, Aug. 18, 1921. Wallace *Press-Times,* Oct. 15, 1921.

57. Searls: *New York Times,* Oct. 23, 1968. Tilford, Love interviews. See also Ramsey, *Men and Mines of Newmont,* passim.

58. Letters, dated Oct. 21, 28, 1921, copies in Hecla files.

58–59. Judgment by Judge William A. Huneke, Feb. 2, 1922, Spokane County, civil No. 65210. Vote: Stockholders' special meeting, Feb. 4, 1922. Eugene Day: Fahey, *Days of the Hercules,* p. 233. Quotations: *Wallace Miner,* Feb. 2, 9, 1922.

59. Directors' minutes, April 11, 1922. Mayer: Milwaukee city directories, 1921, 1922; Watrous, *Memoirs,* pp. 61–62; *Wallace Miner,* April 13, 1922. Ingalls to Bradley, June 30, 1922, appended to Hoban, "History of Sullivan." Bunker Hill and Washington Water Power retained Ingalls to study the plant and projected electrical requirements.

59–60. Directors' minutes, April 10, 1923; Sept. 19, 1925 (quotation). Interview with C. Y. Garber, July 17, 1972. Garber was employed at the north mill on Woolf's crew. Ingalls's report to Bradley, June 30, 1922. Tainton, "Sullivan Electrolytic Zinc Plant," in *Mining Industry of Idaho* (1927), pp. 33–38. Woolf and Miller, "Electrolytic Zinc Plant," *Mining Congress Journal* 17:11 (1931), pp. 624–66. St. Louis: *Wallace Miner,* Jan. 7, 1932.

60. Sullivan Mining Co., incorporated May 22, 1917, with 500,000 shares at $3 par, acquired the Star on April 1, 1921, and the mill in 1926. Hoban, "History of Sullivan," appendix A is the contract between Hecla and Sullivan. St. Joseph: Woolf, "Idaho Zinc," *Mining Industry of Idaho* (1936), pp. 67–69; Ingalls to McCarthy, May 31, 1933 ("brilliantly"); Ellsworth, "Resumé of Zinc Practice," *Engineering & Mining Journal*, Sept. 2, 1922, pp. 406–8.

61. Directors' minutes, Dec. 15, 1921. Hecla annual report, 1922 (water). Hoban, "History of Sullivan." "Star—A Big Mine in the Making," *Mining Truth* 9:20 (Dec. 1, 1924), 9 (quotations). Anderson, "Deep Mining in the Coeur d'Alene District," talks of ground pressure.

62. *Engineering & Mining Journal-Press*, June 6, 1925, p. 936. McCarthy to directors, July 14, 1928. Costs: Hoban, "History of Sullivan"; Easton to McCarthy, July 14, 1928; Ingalls to McCarthy, May 31, 1933.

62. Hecla annual report, 1927. *Wallace Miner*, April 26, 1928 (test). McCarthy to directors, Feb. 28, 1928.

63. Hoban, "History of Sullivan." In addition to expenses, the Star in 1925 began paying royalties based on tonnage. Hecla annual report, 1930. Ingalls to McCarthy, May 31, 1933.

64–65. *Spokesman-Review*, Jan. 23, 1927; Sept. 10, 1930; Feb. 2, July 28, 1934; Oct. 22, 23, 1936; biographical sketch by M. Bean, Dec. 6, 1936; letter, C. F. Dement to editor, Jan. 15, 1947.

Chapter 5. Searching

66. "Historical record of earnings and dividends," manuscript summary by Hecla accounting department. McCarthy to directors, March 13, 1924. *Wallace Miner*, June 24, 1926; Aug. 18, 1927. McCarthy to directors, Sept. 4, 1924 (shareholders).

67. "Milling in the Coeur d'Alenes," 27th *Mining Industry of Idaho* (1925), pp. 16–24 (pages 21–24 describe Hecla practices). One of the early contributions of the Idaho Bureau of Mines and Geology, created by the legislature in 1919, was flotation experimentation. The Morning installed a flotation unit with daily capacity of 480 tons as early as 1914. Minerals Separation: directors' minutes, April 8, 1919; McCarthy to directors, June 11, 1919. See Montague, "Minerals Separation's Position."

68. Wallace *Press-Times*, July 15, 1923. *Wallace Miner*, July 19, 1923. McCarthy to directors, July 24, 1923. Directors' minutes, July 18, 1923. 25th *Mining Industry of Idaho* (1923), pp. 14–17.

68. Directors' minutes, April 10, 1917; April 11, 1922. McCarthy to directors, July 24, 1923. *Engineering & Mining Journal-Press*, Aug. 18, 1923, p. 265. *Wallace Miner*, May 29, 1924.

68. McCarthy to directors, Aug. 3, 1923; Jan. 31, 1924. Manager's annual report, 1923.

68–69. *Engineering & Mining Journal-Press*, Sept. 1, 1923, p. 384. Stevenson, "Reconstruction Methods." Wood, "Summary of Hecla Reconstruction."

70. J. P. O'Brien, gen. mgr. of O-WR&N, to B. O. Johnson, asst. to pres. of NP, Sept. 14, 1927 (NP pres. file 1064, Minnesota Historical Society). Zeigler, in 27th *Mining Industry of Idaho* (1925), pp. 21–24.

71. Based on talk by Henry L. Day, in *Wallace Miner*, Dec. 16, 29, 1926. Voynick, *Making of a Hardrock Miner*, passim. *Wallace Miner*, Jan. 8, 1920. Bitco: *Wallace Miner*, Dec. 14, 1939, and Tilford interview. Hirschberg, "Development of the Rock Drill in America."

72. *Wallace Miner*, July 27, 1922; Dec. 20, 1923; Jan. 10, 1924.

73. *Mining Truth* 10:2 (March 2, 1925), 4. *Wallace Miner*, May 26, 1921; July 27, Sept. 14, 1922; Dec. 15, 1932; March 30, Aug. 31, 1933. McCarthy to directors, April 30, 1927.

73–74. *Wallace Miner*, Oct. 19, 1922; Sept. 6, Dec. 20, 1923. McCarthy to directors, Dec. 9, 1924. Hanley: *Wallace Miner*, Aug. 31, 1922; Bean, "Mining Man—Hecla's Hanley," *Spokesman-Review* magazine, July 25, 1948.

74. *Wallace Miner*, April 20, 1922. Directors' minutes, April 11, 1922. Annual report, Federal Mining & Smelting Co., 1924, passim. See also Umpleby and Jones, *Geology and Ore Deposits*, passim. McCarthy to directors, May 9, 1922.

74. *Wallace Miner*, May 22, 1924. McCarthy to directors, April 16, June 16, 1924.

75. Olson and Wall Street: McCarthy to directors, Aug. 12, 1926. Red Bird: *Wallace Miner*, Nov. 27, 1924. South Butte: McCarthy to directors, Aug. 28, Dec. 24, 1926.

76–77. NP: McCarthy to directors, Nov. 23, 1926; Oct. 22, 1927. Mountain King: McCarthy to directors, Aug. 28, Dec. 24, 1926; July 29, 1927. Hasbrouck: McCarthy to directors, July 29, 1927. Minnie Moore: *Mining Truth* 10:1 (Feb. 16, 1925), 9. *Wallace Miner*, May 12, 1927. McCarthy to directors, Aug. 28 (quotation), Oct. 19, 1926; Oct. 12, 1927. Newmont: see Ramsey, *Men and Mines of Newmont*, passim.

77. Searls to McCarthy, June 30, 1926. McCarthy to directors, Aug. 12, 1926. Directors' minutes, Aug. 5, 1926. Red Ledge: McCarthy to directors, July 29, 1927; Feb. 28, 1928. McCarthy to Searls, April 27, 1928. *Wallace Miner*, Oct. 17, Nov. 7, 1929.

78. McCarthy to directors, Aug. 28, Oct. 19, 1926; Oct. 22, Dec. 22, 1927; Feb. 2, 1928. Profits: *Mining Truth* 12:19 (Nov. 26, 1927), 21. Hecla annual reports, 1931, 1932. Grand Forks (B.C.) *Gazette*, April 13, 1928. *Wallace Miner*, May 10, 1928; Nov. 26, 1931 (carload); July 20, 1933 (quotation).

79. Hecla manager's report, 1923. *Wallace Miner*, Feb. 23, 1928. He-

cla annual report, 1928. Directors' minutes, Aug. 12, 1930; July 8, 1936 (Pilot). Tailings: *Wallace Miner*, March 11, 1926; Aug. 18, 1927. Hecla annual reports, 1925, 1926. *Mining Truth* 11:3 (March 16, 1926), 19. *North Idaho Press*, Dec. 20, 1971 (Zeigler obit.). McCarthy to directors, April 11, 1933 (15 cents). Sunshine: Schultze, "Brief History of Sunshine"; 28th *Mining Industry of Idaho* (1926), p. 171; ibid., 34th (1930), p. 202; ibid., 42d (1940), p. 181; *Mining Truth* 12:7 (May 16, 1927), 3. *Wallace Miner*, Sept. 23, 1944; Feb. 1, 1945 (Tousley obit.). Shenon and McConnel, *Silver Belt*, p. 2.

81. Stocks: *Mining Truth* 12:24 (Feb. 1, 1928), 5–6. Polaris: *Wallace Miner*, May 24, 1928. Directors' minutes, April 8, 1930. Heyburn: *Wallace Miner*, Nov. 23, 1933; March 16, 1944.

81. Loan: directors' minutes, April 12, 1932; Nov. 8, 1933; Hecla annual report, 1933. *Wallace Miner*, Jan. 30, 1930.

82. Deepening: Hecla annual reports, 1924, 1925. Star: McCarthy to directors, Dec. 26, 1925; McCarthy to directors, Oct. 12, 1927.

83. *Wallace Miner*, July 26, Sept. 27, 1928; Oct. 24, 1929; 31st *Mining Industry of Idaho* (1929), p. 19.

Chapter 6. The Thirties

84. Charles Tilford, who was delivering newspapers then, often saw McCarthy walking to work as described. Kipp: *Wallace Miner*, Dec. 24, 1925. McCarthy to directors, Dec. 26, 1925.

84–85. C. Kipp: *Wallace Miner*, Sept. 10, 1925; *Mining Truth* 10:16 (Oct. 1, 1925), 19. Lambach: McCarthy to Landsee, Dec. 24, 1926. Landsee: *Wallace Miner*, April 16, 1931; June 21, 1934.

85. *Spokesman-Review*, July 6, 1931. *Wallace Miner*, Oct. 23, May 15, 1930 (trip). Tilford interview.

86. Prices: Hecla annual report, 1931. Star: *Wallace Miner*, March 20, 1930; Hecla annual report, 1931. Value: *Wallace Miner*, March 20, 1930. Net: May 4, 1933. Work weeks: Feb. 20, 1930; Hecla annual reports, 1930, 1931.

86–87. Pellette: directors' minutes, July 26, Dec. 12, 1932; Feb. 24, 1933. Reserve: directors' minutes, Dec. 31, 1931; Dec. 31, 1932. Losses: Feb. 10, Dec. 12, 1932. Ingalls: Dec. 12, 1932; and his report, 1933.

87. Meeting: *Wallace Miner*, Oct. 26, 1932.

88. Directors' minutes, April 14, 1931. Special directors' meeting, Nov. 8, 1933.

89. Directors' minutes, Nov. 8, 1933; April 14, 1936. *Mining Truth* 18:19 (Nov. 16, 1933), 8. *Wallace Miner*, Nov. 9, 1933; March 29, 1934. See Shenon and McConnel, *Silver Belt*, esp. pp. 1, 2, 6, 7.

89. Newmont: directors' minutes, Aug. 8, 1934; Hecla annual meeting, April 1, 1935.

90. 39th *Mining Industry of Idaho* (1937), pp. 32–33. "Polaris Mill,"

in *Coeur d'Alene Mining District in 1963*, pp. 19–20. Directors' minutes, Nov. 12, 1936 (loans); April 13, 1937. *Wallace Miner*, Dec. 31, 1936. Prospectus, Stratton's Consolidated Mines, 1927. Report to Silver Summit Mining Co. by Julius P. Hall, March 8, 1927.

90. McCarthy's address is reported in *Wallace Miner*, Nov. 28, 1935.

91. Jastram, *Silver: The Restless Metal*, pp. 51–53. *Wallace Miner*, Aug. 15, 1935; Dec. 31, 1936. NRA: *Wallace Miner*, Dec. 21, 1933. The zinc producers' code was administered by the American Zinc Institute, a national trade association.

92. *Wallace Miner*, Aug. 24, 1933; April 12, 1934; May 23, 1935. Taxes: based on county auditor's chart, 1903–25, in *Wallace Miner*, May 13, 1926.

92. Using a transcript of the regional panel's hearing in the Mine-Mill archives at the University of Colorado, S. S. Phipps, in his dissertation, "From Bullpen to Bargaining Table," pp. 213–30, 268–69, elaborates on union allegations of company intimidation against Hecla. His is a harsher view of the company than mine. Phipps, for example, quotes hiring agent George T. Edmiston as observing, "Mr. Hanley . . . control[s] the N.R.A. in Burke" (p. 216 of dissertation; p. 40 of transcript).

92. McCarthy to directors, Jan. 11, 1923. The discussion is based in part on the typescript of a paper by L. J. Randall, "Percentage Depletion."

93. McCarthy to directors, Sept. 12, Dec. 22, 1927. Directors' minutes, April 9, 1918. Shareholders' minutes, Aug. 18, 1921.

94–95. *Hecla v. Commissioner of Internal Revenue*, 35 Tax Board Reports 454, p. 460. Directors' minutes, April 13, 1926. Hoban: interviews with Hoban, Tilford, and Richard Magnuson; *Wallace Miner*, Sept. 16, 1948.

95. *Hecla v. Commissioner of Internal Revenue*; McCarthy to directors, April 8, 1913; April 14, 1914.

96. "Historical Record of Earnings and Dividends." *Wallace Miner*, May 27, 1937.

96. *Wallace Miner*, Aug. 18, 1932; May 18, 1933. Directors' minutes, July 26, 1932 (bonds); Nov. 9, 1934.

97. City: *Spokesman-Review*, June 17–22, 1930; *Wallace Miner*, June 26, 1930. Hanley: *Wallace Miner*, May 9, 1935. Mines: Hecla annual reports, 1935, p. 2; 1936, p. 3.

97–98. Hecla annual report, 1936, pp. 2, 5. *Wallace Miner*, Nov. 7, 1935. Craig, "Star and Polaris Mills," *Coeur d'Alene Mining District in 1963*, p. 17. Directors' minutes, Nov. 12, 1936. Fahey, *Days of the Hercules*, p. 254.

98. Sullivan: Hecla annual report, 1936, pp. 5–6, 8. Directors' minutes, Nov. 12, 1936; April 13, 1937. *Wallace Miner*, Oct. 17, 1929. Star: Craig, "Star and Polaris Mills," p. 18. Hecla annual report, 1937, pp. 2–3. Stocks: *Wallace Miner*, Oct. 31, 1937.

99. *Wallace Miner*, May 5, Nov. 24, 1938. Hecla annual report, 1938, passim. Hoban to stockholders, quoted in *Wallace Miner*, June 2, 1938.

100. Sorenson, "History of Hecla," p. 3. Directors' minutes, Nov. 27, 1939; May 14, Aug. 6, 1940; Feb. 7, 1942; Nov. 1, 1943. *Wallace Miner*, March 26, 1946. Hecla annual reports, 1939–53, passim.

100. Quotation: Lavendar, "Back to the Hills Again," *Travel* 63:2 (June 1934), 20. Special directors' meeting, Feb. 5, 1940.

101–2. McCarthy obit., *Spokesman-Review*, March 7, 1940. Interviews with Henry L. Day, James Hoban, and Richard Magnuson. *Wallace Miner*, June 10, 1926; April 2, 1936 (Anastasia obit.). Schoenberg, *Gonzaga*, pp. 397–98. Special directors' meeting, March 18, 1940.

Chapter 7. Hanley

103. Randall interview. *Spokesman-Review*, Nov. 17, 1952 (obit.). *Wallace Miner*, May 31, 1951. Directors' minutes, Oct. 6, 1911.

103. Randall, Richard Magnuson interviews. Biographical sketch by M. Bean in *Spokesman-Review*, July 25, 1948 (with portrait).

104. Signatures: directors' minutes, May 14, 1940.

105–6. Wages: 43d *Mining Industry of Idaho* (1941), p. 9; Hecla annual reports, 1942, 1943; *Wallace Miner*, Sept. 10, 1942. Women: interview with Ruby Sinrud Hill. Although Mrs. Hill believed herself the first woman employee at Hecla, and others confirmed this, a 1919 photograph of the Hecla office shows a woman at a desk.

107. Superannuated: directors' minutes, Jan. 31, 1944.

107–8. Special directors' meeting, Nov. 7, 1942. *Wallace Miner* (quoting *Engineering & Mining Journal*), June 8, 1944; Feb. 27, 1947; Dec. 30, 1948. Hecla annual reports, 1944–48. Hanley to directors, Dec. 31, 1948 (ribbing). The mill was insured for $221,900.

108. Directors' minutes, Aug. 6, 1940. H. W. Schultze, in *Coeur d'Alenes in 1963*, p. 67, dates the Sunshine-Polaris agreement to share costs and returns as early as 1934.

109. Sunshine: *Spokesman-Review*, May 5, 1948. Special directors' meeting, Nov. 7, 1942. *Wallace Miner*, June 12, 1943; March 16, 1944; July 19, 1945. Hecla annual reports, 1940–49.

109. Special directors' meeting, Nov. 1, 1943.

110. *Spokesman-Review*, May 7, 1948. *Wallace Miner*, July 19, Sept. 20, 1945; Dec. 26, 1946; April 10, 29, 1948. Hanley to Mayer, June 20, 1947.

111. Spirit: Ben Harrison interview.

111–12. Harry Magnuson interview, confirmed by others. *Wallace Miner*, Sept. 16, 1948 (Hanley's remarks on Hoban). *Spokesman-Review*, June 18, 1948. Hanley to directors, June 16, 1948. Neyman: interviews with Bill Love, Richard Magnuson; *Engineering & Mining Journal*, Aug. 1950, p. 109; *Wallace Miner*, April 28, 1977 (obit.). Magnuson resignation: Harry Magnuson interview.

112. Randall interview. Hecla annual report, 1947.

113. Special directors' meeting, Nov. 7, 1942; Nov. 8, 1946. *Wallace Miner*, Nov. 22, 1945. Under the Silver Purchase Act, amended July 31, 1946, the federal Treasury bought silver at 90.5 cents an ounce. "Big Five": Leon Starmont in *Spokesman-Review*, May 3, 1948; *Wallace Miner*, Jan. 17, May 9, 1946; June 27, 1948.

114. Special directors' meetings, Nov. 27, 1939; Feb. 5, 1940. Contract with Atlas, Jan. 25, 1940. *Wallace Miner*, Feb. 2, 1933; Feb. 1, 1940 (quotation); March 21, Aug. 22, 1940. Tilford interview. Hanley to Mayer, June 14, 1949. Hecla annual reports, 1951–53. *Spokesman-Review*, May 10, 1948.

115. Silver Cable: *Wallace Miner*, April 25, 1940; May 7, 1942; July 27, 1944. Directors' minutes, Feb. 7, Nov. 7, 1942; Nov. 1, 1943.

115. Blue Moon: directors' minutes, Nov. 1, 1943; Jan. 31, 1944; Feb. 4, 1946; Aug. 1, 1949. Hecla annual reports, 1943–46. *Wallace Miner*, March 11, 1943.

115–16. *Wallace Miner*, Feb. 6, 1947 (quotation). Hecla annual report, 1946. Directors' minutes, Nov. 8, 1946 (Hanley quotation). *Mining World*, March 1949, p. 38. Hecla annual report, 1948 (Hanley report).

116. Directors' minutes, May 26, 1949 (Searls quotation). Hanley to Mayer, June 14, 1949.

117. Hecla annual reports, 1950, 1952, 1953, 1955. *Mining Truth* 16:21 (Dec. 17, 1931), 5. *Newport Miner*, March 11, 1909. *Spokane Chronicle*, July 14, 1955 (obit.). Kinney, "Larsen." Stock: *Mining Truth* 13:2 (March 1, 1928), 6; ibid. 15:7 (May 19, 1930), 5–6. *Spokesman-Review*, Jan. 11, Feb. 2, 17, 19, 22, March 25, 1928. *Mining & Industrial Record*, May 1928, p. 88 ("hoodwinking").

118. *Spokane Chronicle*, Feb. 25, 1928 (house). *Spokesman-Review*, May 1, 1929; July 19, 1934; June 26, 1935; June 29, 1938. Hecla: Hanley to Mayer, April 15, 1948; Hanley to directors, April 15, 1948; contract May 4, 1948, with Hanley to directors, May 7, 1948. *Wallace Miner*, April 29, 1948. Hecla annual reports, 1951, 1954. Stock: special directors' meeting, Aug. 1, 1949. Hecla annual reports, 1951, 1952. *Spokane Chronicle*, May 24, 1951. *Wallace Miner*, May 31, 1951.

119. *Spokesman-Review*, Nov. 17, 1952 (obit.). Love, Randall, Neal Fosseen interviews.

120. Love, Randall interviews. Directors' minutes, Nov. 9, 1951. *Wallace Miner*, Nov. 29, 1951. There had been some sentiment among the board for Joseph McCarthy, who declined.

Chapter 8. Renewal

121. *North Idaho Press*, April 28, 1966. *Spokesman-Review*, April 29, 1966. "Historical Record of Earnings and Dividends," Hecla.

121–22. Randall to directors, Aug. 14, 1963 (physician). Shareholders' meeting, April 28, 1966. Randall to directors, April 12, 1966. J. Ralph Kirkpatrick to Hecla, Aug. 9, and Randall to Kirkpatrick, Aug. 15, 1949 (shareholder). Voltolini interview.

122. Randall to directors, Jan. 8, 1960. Randall interview. Retirement program, Jan. 1, 1947.

123. Randall to directors, Jan. 11, Feb. 18, 1952; March 6, 1964 (dissenters).

123–24. Herman interview. *Wallace Miner*, Jan. 11, 1962. Sullivan: proxy statement for special meeting of Hecla shareholders, Oct. 26, 1955, to consider exchange of Sullivan and sale of Pend Oreille stock, esp. p. 13. Randall to directors, Oct. 31, 1952. Report to Hecla shareholders, May 28, 1953.

124. John Matthews's notes of directors' meeting, Oct. 23, 1953. Randall to directors, May 2, May 4, 1955. Randall, personal communication. Directors' minutes, Feb. 18, 1952. Randall to Pollard, Feb. 25, 1952. Randall to directors, Oct. 31, 1952; March 24, 1953. Zeigler's work for Pend Oreille is documented in the Lewis P. Larsen collection (MS 42) at the Eastern Washington State Historical Society. Dozens of letters concerning Hecla's involvement are in the collection.

124–25. Notes from directors' meeting, Oct. 29, 1953. Randall to Hunt, Aug. 27, 1954. Proxy statement . . . Oct. 26, 1955. Shareholders' meeting, Oct. 26, 1955. *Wallace Miner*, Jan. 4, 1962, citing a Randall letter to stockholders.

125. Notes from policy meeting, Jan. 12, 1955. Randall to directors, Jan. 19, 1956. Balance sheet, Dec. 31, 1954.

126. Randall to directors, Oct. 31, 1952 (quotation); to directors, Jan. 15, 1958 ("prospect"). Directors' minutes, Jan. 25, 1962 ("interpretation"). *Wallace Miner*, Jan. 4, 1962; Aug. 22, 1963. Judge James Towles, Idaho First District Court, memorandum decision, Aug. 14, 1948. Matthews to directors, Aug. 22, 1963. Searls: R. J. Searls to me, Aug. 23, 1984.

127. Harper interview. Proxy statement for special meetings of Hecla and Polaris stockholders, Oct. 10, 1958, esp. pp. 6, 12, 25.

127. Randall to directors, April 12, 1957. Randall to directors, June 29, 1960, enclosing Matthews and Leisk memos. Directors' minutes, April 26, 1963.

128. Randall, draft letter to stockholders, in his letter to Jo Hall, April 28, 1960. *Forbes*, Jan. 8, 1958. Randall to directors, Jan. 9, 1958.

128–29. Polaris annual report, 1956. Randall to directors, June 25, July 11, 1956. Undated press release: dinner at Shoshone Club on Neyman's retirement. Hecla annual report, 1956. Neyman to directors,—1956. *Wallace Miner*, Aug. 2, 1956.

129. Undated press release. Sorenson: *Wallace Miner*, Oct. 30, 1969. Neyman: *Wallace Miner*, Sept. 14, 1961; April 28, 1977. Ace: Randall to

directors, July 15, Sept. 4, 1959. Harper to Randall (report on Ace), July 14, 1959. Hunter once remarked that after Hecla bought it, neither Randall nor Love visited Ace. Hecla annual report, 1976. Love interview. *Wallace Miner*, Sept. 16, 1976.

130–31. For accounts of Neyman's accomplishments, see articles in the *Wallace Miner* (quoting mining journals and a Bureau of Mines circular) Sept. 17, Nov. 24, 1949; Feb. 7, 1957; based also on Love interview. Directors' minutes, Feb. 18, 1952. Notes from directors' informal meeting, Oct. 23, 1953. Randall to Pollard, June 29, 1954. Hecla annual report, 1954.

131. Rock Creek: U.S. Bureau of Mines, *Information Circular* 7525 (1949). Wages: Randall to Pollard, June 29, 1954.

132. Harper's report, April 20, 1954.

132–33. See *New York Times*, June 1, 1974, July 11, 1948, for general reviews of Colorado plateau uranium exploration. Randall to directors, Aug. 12, Sept. 10, 1954; Jan. 19, Feb. 10, 1956. Randall to Joseph McCarthy, Sept. 8, 1954 ("criticism").

133. Randall to directors, Sept. 10, Dec. 3, Dec. 7, 1954. Hunt to Randall, Dec. 14, 1954. Hecla annual report, 1956. *Mining World*, April 1956. *Wallace Miner*, April 12, 1956. Gus Voltolini interview. According to the *Miner*, June 7, 1956, San Francisco stockholders were prevalent in six companies making up U&I: Caledonia Silver-Lead, Coeur d'Alene Silver Giant, Nancy Lee Mines, New Era Mines, Silver Bowl, and Signal companies. Matthews to A. R. Atkinson, Murphey-Favre Co., Spokane, April 18, 1955.

133. Love, Randall interviews. *Mining World*, April 1956.

134. Sorenson, "History of Hecla," p. 9. Hunt to Randall, Sept. 8, 1955. Love and Lindstrom, "Longwall Stoping." Lindstrom, "History of Hecla." Love interview. Hecla annual report, 1964, p. 12. *Salt Lake Tribune*, May 30, 1964. After recovering development costs, Hecla received 21.25 percent of net smelter returns from Radon and 50 percent from Hot Rock. U&I merged into Federal Uranium, Inc. (later Federal Resources Corp.), which did not alter terms of the contract.

135. Love interview. Love learned later that Charles Tilford had suggested him as Randall's successor.

136–38. Wafford Conrad in *Spokane Chronicle*, Jan. 15, 1958—a version of Lucky Friday's history reprinted by the *Wallace Miner*, and followed by Folwell, "Lucky Friday Mine:" Potts: Magnuson, *Coeur d'Alene Diary*, p. 35. 132 U.S. Tax Court Reports 139 (1972). Report to shareholders of Lucky Friday Silver-Lead, 1948. Wray Featherstone, "History of Lucky Friday (Hecla files)." *Wallace Miner*, Feb. 10, 1944. Proxy statement: To consider a statutory merger of Lucky Friday and Hecla, March 5, 1964. Also based in part on interview with Gus Voltolini.

138. Randall to directors, Dec. 24, 1958. Judge A. H. Featherstone

died in December 1956 (*Wallace Miner*, Dec. 20, 1956). *Wallace Miner*, Sept. 11, 1969. Love, Randall interviews, and Randall, personal communication. Harper's recollection.

139. Hecla annual report, 1958. Randall, personal communication. Special directors' meeting, Dec. 12, 1958. *Wallace Miner*, Oct. 16, Dec. 12, Dec. 18, 1958; Feb. 2, 1959. Strasser, Spiegelberg, Fried & Frank (for Hirshhorn) to Amex, Jan. 20, 1959.

Chapter 9. Investing

141. Love interview. Proxy statement . . . March 5, 1964.

141. Randall, personal communication. Hecla annual report, 1959. *Mining Industry of Idaho* (1960), p. 71. Randall to directors, July 7, 1958.

142. Investment: Randall memo to Lindstrom, Aug. 25, 1965.

142. Randall to Searls and Hunt, April 18, 1957. Randall to directors, April 15, 1957. New Park: Randall to directors, July 14, Nov. 6, 1961. Hecla annual report, 1962, p. 5.

143. Hecla annual report, 1972, p. 8. Reports on Mayflower appear in annual reports, 1961–72. *Wall Street Journal*, Jan. 12, May 4, 1965. Dunphy interview (gold streak). According to Hecla annual report, 1973, p. 13, Mayflower was the fifth largest domestic gold producer in 1971. Ruby Hill: Randall to Jo Hall, April 28, 1960, enclosing undated draft letter to stockholders; "Report on Ruby Hill," in Hecla files. *Eureka v. Richmond*, 103 U.S. 839.

143–44. Randall, personal communication. Hecla annual reports, 1962–66, 1966, p. 10 (quotation). *Salt Lake Tribune*, May 30, 1964. *Wallace Miner*, March 30, 1967. *Spokesman-Review*, May 29, 1964. Hecla's operating agreement took effect April 1, 1963. See also Love, "Ruby Hill Project, Eureka, Nevada." Eureka-Richmond had been sued for alleged failure to complete certain work and compromised by bringing Newmont and Cyprus into the project.

145. *Wallace Miner*, June 4, 1964. *Spokesman-Review*, May 29, 1964 (flattering). Directors' minutes, April 27, 1962. Randall to directors, July 11, 1962.

145. Leisk to Randall, July 3, 1962. Directors' minutes, July 19, 1963. Directors' special meeting, Sept. 9, 1963. Proxy statement . . . March 5, 1964. Randall to directors, March 6, 1964. Hecla annual report, 1964, "consolidated balance sheets," pp. 15–17.

146–47. Proxy statement . . . March 5, 1964, pp. 18–19. Directors' minutes, Jan. 17, 1963. Union: Hanley to directors, April 7, 1949; to Mayer, June 14, 1949; Hull to Sixteen Operators, Feb. 12, 1956, reassessing remaining members for his compensation; Hanley to Mayer and Pollard, Dec. 14, 1949 ("full crews"); *Wallace Miner*, Sept. 27, Oct. 25, 1951; *Spokesman-Review*, July 27, 1952; author's files of notes and dispatches to *Time* magazine. Fee, "1960 strike in the Coeur d'Alenes," pp. 44–49, 52–64, traces Kellogg high school students' opposition to Communist influence; her discussion is based largely on newspaper accounts.

147–48. *Wallace Miner*, Feb. 2, 1956; July 7, Sept. 8, 15, 29, Dec. 15, 22, 1960; Jan. 4, 1962. Randall to directors, Dec. 7, 1954. Hunt to Randall, Sept. 8, 1955 (Bunker Hill). Gus Voltolini interview.

148. SEC v. *Golconda Mining Co. and Magnuson*, 291 Fed. Supp. 126 (1968). *Wall Street Journal*, Nov. 3, 1969. Randall interview. The case was heard in U.S. District Court, southern district, New York. Harry Magnuson interview. Randall to directors, May 26, 1965.

149. SEC v. *Golconda*, 291 Fed. Supp. 126 (1968). *Wall Street Journal*, Nov. 3, 1969. Securities and Exchange Commission, vol. 34, bull. 4, p. 239, Litt. Rel. 4461, Oct. 31, 1969. The payments amounted to alleged profits plus interest. For tax savings, see 58 U.S. Tax Court Reports 139. NYSE: Randall to directors, Nov. 18, 25, 1964. *Spokane Chronicle*, Dec. 21, 1964. Hecla's listing application to NYSE, A-22053, Nov. 4, 1964.

150. *Spokesman-Review*, Dec. 27, 1964.

150–51. Hyams, *Hirshhorn*, esp. pp. 4, 25, 67–84, 183. *Fortune*, Feb. 11, 1980, pp. 152–59. *New York Times*, Sept. 2, 1981. *Wallace Miner*, July 9, 1936.

151. *Wallace Miner*, March 20, 1958. Randall memo to Matthews, July 29, 1958.

152. *Wallace Miner*, March 20, 1958; March 9, 1961. Hecla annual report, 1959. Newmont: *Fortune*, October 1965, pp. 132–37, 241–46. Hall: Randall to Hall, Nov. 28, 1958. Malozemoff took his degree from Montana Tech.

153. Randall to directors, March 12, 1959. *Spokane Chronicle*, March 25, 1959. Harrison, Herman interviews. *Wallace Miner*, Dec. 3, 1959 (Bradley). Hecla press release, May 2, 1960. Undated draft letter to Hecla stockholders, May—, 1960. Stockholders' minutes, May 6, 1960.

154. Randall to Banghart, Dec. 31, 1963. *Fortune*, October 1965, pp. 241–46. Directors' minutes, March 27, 1963. Ramsey, *Men and Mines of Newmont*, pp. 207–9.

154–55. Directors' minutes, March 27, 1964. Malozemoff to Hecla, April 16, 1964. Randall to directors, April 20, 1964. Love report, May 15, 1964. Randall to directors, May 21, 1964.

155. Ramsey, *Men and Mines*, p. 210. Love interview. *Wallace Miner*, May 23, 1968. Hecla conversion: Ramsey, *Men and Mines*, pp. 211–13. Hecla annual reports, 1974, 1976. *Wall Street Journal*, Oct. 15, 1965; Nov. 12, 1970. Granduc's first shipment of concentrates left Stewart for Japan on Jan. 24, 1971.

156. Hecla annual reports, 1974, p. 11; 1976, p. 27; 1977, p. 9; 1978, p. 8. *Wall Street Journal*, Jan. 23, April 12, June 29, 1978. Randall, personal communication. Before salvage had been completed, Esso took the Granduc lease, but after spending approximately $160 million, also

abandoned it. Plant and equipment have been removed. Day: Dunphy interview.

157. Harry Magnuson interview. Randall to directors, Jan. 5, 1966.

158. Hecla annual report, 1968, p. 12. *Spokesman-Review*, April 29, 1966. *North Idaho Press*, April 29, 1966. *Kellogg-Wardner News*, April 29, 1966. Randall to directors, Jan. 5, 1966.

158–59. Hecla annual reports, 1967, p. 8; 1961, pp. 5–6; 1965; p. 8. Hecla's listing application to NYSE, A-23088, Feb. 12, 1966, for 25,230 additional shares of capital stock, contains details of the 1961 royalty contract, dated May 1, 1961. James B. Robison, Callahan Mining Corp., in *Coeur d'Alene Mining District—Deep Mining*, observes that any shaft over 3,000 feet in length is considered deep, noting that several South African shafts have a continuous length of 10,000 feet.

159. Love interview. Randall to directors, Jan. 5, 1966. *Wallace Miner*, May 23, 1957 (mill); Oct. 8, 1953. *Star v. Federal*, U.S. District Court for Idaho, No. 678 (1921). Dunphy interview (Moffitt). Fahey, *Days of the Hercules*, p. 140. Leep, "Geological Features."

159–61. Hecla's listing application to NYSE, A-23088, Feb. 12, 1966. Directors' minutes, Jan. 27, 1966. *Wallace Miner*, March 23, 1967; Aug. 12, 1971. Hecla annual report, 1966, p. 5.

Chapter 10. Lakeshore

162. Barry Goldwater, in National Congress of American Indians *Washington Bulletin*, August 1949. Dobyns, *Papago People*, pp. 94–95.

163. H. E. Harper, in *Wallace Miner*, Oct. 23, 1969.

163. Hecla annual report, 1949, p. 9. *Forbes*, Dec. 1, 1969. Harper, "History of Exploration," p. 3. Randall to directors, Jan. 23, 1968. Harper interview.

163–64. Undated clipping from *Northern Miner*, 1968, in Hecla files, and March 20, 1969. Hecla Mining Co. and Wholly Owned Subsidiaries, Draft Prospectus. Hecla annual report, 1969, p. 6. Love interview. *Wallace Miner*, July 13, 1972. Liard is treated regularly in annual reports. British Columbia imposed a mining royalties tax on provincial-granted leases amounting to 2.5 percent of income after certain processing and transportation charges, which rose to 5 percent in 1975, and a mineral land tax on mineral extracted from private land beginning in 1975. See *Wall Street Journal*, Nov. 21, Dec. 24, 1974.

164. Hecla annual report, 1967, pp. 7, 10–11. *Wallace Miner*, March 7, 1968; April 20, 1972 (DIA).

165. Hecla annual report, 1968, p. 10; 1970, pp. 6, 10; 1971, p. 5 (suspends); 1979, p. 10; 1982, p. 5. Love to stockholders, Nine Corp., Feb. 21, 1969. In addition to Hecla and Day Mines, the Success, Nine Mile, and Inspiration Lead companies participated in the Nine Corp. project, 19 patented and 206 unpatented claims on 3,457 acres. Hecla

owned 56 percent. Con Silver: *Wallace Miner*, Feb. 8, 1968; Feb. 3, 1972. Silver Summit: Harper interview.

165–66. Hoist: *Wallace Miner*, Dec. 15, 1966. Silver: Hecla annual report, 1969, p. 15; Jastram, *Silver: The Restless Metal*, pp. 52–53; *Wallace Miner*, Sept. 21, 1967 (quotation); June 6, 20, 1968.

166. *Wallace Miner*, April 6, May 18, July 6, 1972; May 8, 1973. Love, Herman interviews. Hecla annual reports, 1968, p. 22; 1970, p. 4.

167. *Wallace Miner*, May 8, 1973 (appeal). Hecla annual reports, 1969, p. 17; 1967, p. 6 (quotation). Shareholders' minutes, April 25, 1967. "Crazy, wild stories": Griffith remarks.

167–68. *Wallace Miner*, June 20, 1968 (wages). Hecla annual reports, 1976, p. 7; 1977, p. 6. Goldberg to me, Dec. 14, 1984. The point should perhaps be emphasized that Bunker Hill's smelting rates affected primarily the profit margin of the Star-Morning. The arbitrator was Urban Roth.

168–69. Gulf Resources' takeover: account based on transcript of C. E. Schwab's statement to Bunker Hill employees, in *Wallace Miner*, Feb. 22, 1968. Hecla: Randall to Love, confidential memo, July 1, 1968; Harper interview; Love to directors, May 13, 1968; *Forbes*, Oct. 1, 1967, p. 69; *Wallace Miner*, Dec. 22, 1966; May 16, 1968.

169. *Forbes*, Oct. 1, 1967, p. 69. *Wallace Miner*, Aug. 1, 22, Dec. 9, 1968. *Wall Street Journal*, Dec. 12, 13, 26, 1968. The SEC alleged that Magnuson anticipated tax savings from transfer of his stock to Korholz. See 58 U.S. Tax Court Reports 139 (1972).

170. Harry Magnuson interview. *Wallace Miner*, May 16, Aug. 1, 1968. *Denver Post*, March 17, Sept. 25–26, 1968 (Collins). Meeting: Love interview. In a statement to Hecla stockholders, May 29, 1969, Magnuson listed merger possibilities.

170–71. Randall to directors, Aug. 30, 1968. *Spokesman-Review*, Sept. 8, 1968. Love interview. Love to stockholders, Sept. 3, 1968. *Wall Street Journal*, Sept. 4, 1968. *Wallace Miner*, Sept. 5, 1968. Called off: *Wall Street Journal*, Oct. 28, 1968.

172. Harper interview. Proxy statement, April 21, 1969. Hecla Mining Co., "Lakeshore Operations Review."

173. Harper interview. *Barron's*, April 21, 1969, pp. 8–9, 22. *Forbes*, Dec. 1, 1969, pp. 24–25 ($3.7 billion). El Paso had operated mines through a subsidiary, Rare Metals Corporation of America: mercury, uranium, copper, and coal.

173. Griffith resumé. Love interview.

173. A patent was issued May 13, 1975, to William Griffith, Nicholas Tschishow, and Theodore S. Jordan, and assigned to Hecla, covering a pollution-free sulfate-roasting, leaching, and electro-winning process for copper production. A second patent to Griffith, Howard E. Day, and Clarence A. Lefler, for acid recovery of copper, described a continuous method of producing cement copper by leaching. Love, Sandra Pope remarks on bid preparation.

175. Love, Harry Magnuson, and Randall interviews. Magnuson statement to stockholders, May 29, 1969. *Spokane Chronicle,* May 14, 1969 (Korholz).

176. Herman interview. Proxy statement, April 21, 1969, for annual meeting, May 29, 1969. *Spokane Chronicle,* April 17, 1969 (SEC letter). *Wall Street Journal,* May 5, 13, 1969. Judge's quotation from *SEC v Golconda Mining Co. and Magnuson,* 291 Fed. Supp. 126 (1968). Flom: *Fortune,* April 19, 1982, p. 91. Hecla retained D. F. King & Co., Inc., to aid in proxy solicitation.

176. *Golconda* v. *Hecla,* Spokane County Superior Court, civil No. 193262. See *Golconda* v. *Hecla,* 80 Wash. 2d 372 (1972). Hecla stockholders, at their annual meeting, April 27, 1967, had approved amended articles to specify the straight-vote as a consequence of changes in Washington corporation laws. Proxy: Randall to directors, April 18, 1969. E. Glenn Harmon, representing Magnuson, to Randall, April 16, 1969. Williams, memorandum opinion, May 23, 1969, entered June 23, 1969. Golconda appealed to the court of appeals, which affirmed Williams. See Court of Appeals, Div. III, Feb. 9, 1971. The Hecla annual meeting was postponed from April 24 to May 29, 1969, to clear proxy material through the SEC.

177. Stockholders' minutes, May 29 and 30, 1969. Typescript, statement of Harry Magnuson, May 29, 1969. Magnuson received 8,256 votes more than Golconda's 691,000 for director. All other directors received 3,522,520 each. (On April 11, 1969, Hecla had 4,957,575 shares outstanding.) Golconda sold its Hecla stock in 1973, according to *Wall Street Journal,* April 25, 1973.

178. Harry Magnuson interview. *Golconda* v. *Hecla,* 80 Wash. 2d 372 (1972). *Spokesman-Review,* April 29, 1972. *Forbes,* Dec. 1, 1969, pp. 24–25.

178–79. Love interview. Phillips, "View from Lakeshore," p. 1. Harper, file memo, April 2, 1969. R. W. Mullen, memo to W. Grismer, July 18, 1969. Segundo: Dobyns, *Papago People,* pp. 69–84. Berger: Mullen memo to Grismer, July 18, 1969. Grismer to Randall and Love, July 25, 1969. *Arizona Daily Star,* Dec. 16, 1981; Aug. 10, 1965; Nov. 6, 20, 1968; May 3, 5, 12, 18, 1973.

179. Love interview. Papago press release, Sept. 12, 1969. Leases H50C14200521 (mineral) and H50C1420911 (business), Sept. 12, 1969. Phillips, "View," p. 9. *Skillings Mining Review,* March 21, 1970, p. 12.

179. Dobyns, *Papago People,* p. 84 (Segundo died May 6, 1971). *Arizona Daily Star,* May 13, 1973. Phillips, "View," pp. 3–4. Hecla annual reports, 1970, p. 12; 1971, p. 9. Love interview.

180. Love, Herman interviews. Grismer to directors, Dec. 27, 1982. Phillips, "View," pp. 9–12, 23; Voynik, *Making of a Hardrock Miner,* pp. 96 ("irrational"), 161.

181. Hecla annual report, 1973, p. 9. Herman, Love interviews. Phillips, "View," pp. 26–28. Voynik, *Making of Miner,* p. 117.

182. Hecla annual reports, 1972, p. 2; 1973, p. 3. Voynik, *Making of Miner*, p. 142. Phillips, "View," pp. 17–19, 21.

182–83. Randall to Grismer, July 12, 1972. Love interview. Randall, "Remarks to Shareholders," typescript, April 30, 1970. *New York Times*, Jan. 9, 1974 (political weapon). *Wall Street Journal*, Sept. 20, 1974 (alloys); Jan. 2, 3, 1975 (68 cents). *Wallace Miner*, Oct. 18, 1973.

183–84. Love interview. Hecla Mining Co., "Lakeshore Operations Review," passim. Hecla annual reports, 1973, p. 7 (quotation); 1976, p. 3; 1977, pp. 8–9. Phillips, "View," p. 33. *Arizona Daily Star*, June 9, 1977.

184. Hecla annual report, 1976, p. 2. *Wallace Miner*, May 13, 1976 (quotation). Love interview. *Wall Street Journal*, Aug. 22, Oct. 18, 1977. Love to W. A. Robinson, Newconex, Toronto, Jan. 6, 1978.

Chapter 11. Two Plus Two Equals Five

185. Hecla annual report, 1978, pp. 3, 14. *Wallace Miner*, June 8, July 13, Aug. 17, 1978; Jan. 18, 1979.

185. Brown interview.

186. Hecla annual report, 1978, p. 3. Grismer and Mullen memo, Aug. 3, 1978. Herman interview. Kuhn Loeb & Co., "Preliminary Financial Analysis . . . Recommendations," Oct. 1977. Kuhn Loeb, at this time, merged as Lehman Brothers, Kuhn Loeb.

186. Map: Tibor Klobusicky deposition June 22, 1981, in *Day* v. *Hecla*, Eastern Washington District Court, No. C-81-342 (1981). Costs: annual report, 1978, p. 5.

187. *Wallace Miner*, March 9, April 27, 1967; March 7, Aug. 1, 1968. *Spokesman-Review*, April 22, 1967. McManus wrote contracts wih a 50–50 split rather than the customary 60–40. Underweiser: *Wallace Miner*, Jan. 6, 1969; May 6, 26, 28, 1970. *Wall Street Journal*, April 30, Oct. 24, 1974; Aug. 2, 1981; Sunshine's notice of meeting and proxy statement, Nov. 12, 1974, pp. 8–12. Pierson, Ball and Dowd, Washington, D.C., to SEC, May 1, 1970, on behalf of W. E. Schott, a Sunshine stockholder.

187–88. Hecla annual report, 1976, p. 8. Interviews with Love, H. Magnuson, and Harper. *Spokesman-Review*, Feb. 9, 1974. Suits: Hecla annual report, 1976, p. 8. *Wall Street Journal*, Oct. 24, 1974. *Wallace Miner*, July 31, Aug. 12, 1975; Nov. 22, 1979. Notes for meeting of Hecla's executive committee, Nov. 30, 1976.

188–89. Love, H. Magnuson interviews. *Great Western United* v. *Kidwell*, 577 Fed.2 1256 (1978). *Wallace Miner*, April 14, 1977. Schwab press release, Dec. 27, 1976. *Spokesman-Review*, Dec. 27, 1976. Skadden, Arps, Slate, Meagher & Flom to SEC, Dec. 27, 1976. Hecla, "Hecla Mining Co. and Wholly Owned Subsidiaries: Draft Prospectus."

189. Hecla annual report, 1979, pp. 7, 22–23. *Wallace Miner*, March

1, 1979. *Spokane Daily Chronicle,* July 12, 1979. *Wall Street Journal,* Dec. 12, 1979; Feb. 23, 1981. Love interview. *Great Western United* v. *Kidwell,* 577 Fed.2 1256 (1978).

189–90. Hecla annual report, 1979, p. 7. *Wall Street Journal,* Feb. 23, 1981. *Wallace Miner,* Sept. 20, 1979. Love to W. A. Robinson, president, Newconex, Toronto, Jan. 6, 1978. Love to directors, Oct. 18, 1978. Superior: joint press release, Mar. 14, 1978. Love to Hecla shareholders, March 15, 1978. *Wallace Miner,* March 16, 1978. Love interview. See *Wall Street Journal,* Oct. 21, 1983, for a report of Keck family disagreements over management of Superior.

190. Love interview.

191. Love interview. Love to directors, very confidential, Nov. 29, 1978. Lisbon Valley was placed on standby in 1982, fully developed and ready for production, due to a depressed market.

192. Grismer memo to files, March 15, 1979 (Love asked Hecla to pay his salary and benefits for one year). Herman interview. Conversation with W. Burney Warren, a Hecla director. Love to me, Sept. 19, 1986.

192. Hecla annual report, 1978, pp. 2–3. Love interview (quotation). *Arizona Daily Star,* Oct. 23, 1977. Silver: *Wallace Miner,* Jan. 18, Feb. 1, July 5, 1979. Hecla annual report, 1978, pp. 2, 24.

193. Love: "Remarks to Shareholders," typescript, May 4, 1979. Lindstrom, "Some Notes on Metals and Hecla," typescript, May 4, 1979. *Wallace Miner,* Jan. 18, May 10, Nov. 1, 1979; Jan. 25, 1979 (quotation).

194. Griffith, H. Magnuson interviews.

195. Griffith to directors, April 10, 1980. Griffith interview. Prospectus for Silver Valley Co. Griffith deposition. *Day* v. *Hecla* (Gousseland).

196. *Wall Street Journal,* Feb. 7, 1980 (Amax). Herman interview. Griffith interview, and remarks to shareholders, May 10, 1985. Hecla annual report, 1980, p. 20. Griffith to Herman, March 18, 1980. Williams to me, July 7, 1986.

196–97. *Wallace Miner,* Sept. 13, 1979, quoting the *Denver Mining Record.* Griffith deposition, *Day* v. *Hecla,* C-81-141, pp. 27, 49. Hecla annual report, 1980, p. 3. Con Silver: Griffith to directors, Dec. 11, 1979.

197. W. B. Warren and Griffith depositions, *Day* v. *Hecla,* C-81-141. Goals, Griffith to directors, April 10, 1980. Griffith, Brown interviews.

199. Brown interview.

199–200. Randall and Griffith depositions, *Day* v. *Hecla,* Love interview. Griffith, file memo, March 24, 1981. Love to Harper, Feb. 25, 1963, with Harper's note of March 6, 1963, that Hecla will negotiate with Day Mines before further drilling. *Hecla* v. *Atlas,* 92 Idaho 476 (1968); 445 Pac.2 225 (1968). See *Atlas* v. *Hecla,* Shoshone County Superior Court, civil No. 23000, Dec. 19, 1980, Fausett negotiations: Griffith, T. Sands, H. L. Day and Calhoun depositions, *Day* v. *Hecla*, C-81-141.

200–1. *Atlas* v. *Hecla*, Shoshone County civil No. 23000 (1980). Minutes of special directors' meeting, March 16, 1981. Griffith and Calhoun depositions, *Day* v. *Hecla*, C-81-141. R. Magnuson and Griffith interviews. Negotiations: Griffith and Calhoun depositions, *Day* v. *Hecla*, C-81-141. Griffith to Calhoun, March 20, 1981; Calhoun to Griffith, April 3, 1981; Hecla press release, May 21, 1981; Day Mines press release, April 5, 1981; *Wall Street Journal*, March 23, 1981.

202. See Fahey, *Days of the Hercules*. H. L. Day deposition, *Day* v. *Hecla*, C-81-141. H. Magnuson interview. *Wall Street Journal*, March 23, 1981. Complaint, *Day* v. *Hecla*, Nos. C-81-141 and C-81-342. *Spokesman-Review*, June 24, 1981.

203. Minutes of special directors' meeting, July 7, 1981. Calhoun to Griffith, July 8, 1981. Grismer to directors, July 17, 1981. Griffith, Brown interviews. *Spokesman-Review*, July 9, 1981. Directors' minutes, Aug. 5, 1981, say that Hecla owns 62.5 percent of Day Mines, that pending court actions have been dismissed, and that Day Mines has moved to withdraw from Atlas's suit against Hecla. Hecla annual report, 1981, p. 22.

204. Hecla annual report, 1981, p. 22. Griffith deposition, *Day* v. *Hecla*, C-81-141 (quotation). Directors' minutes, Feb. 12, Aug. 3, 1982.

204. Griffith interview. "Point sheet for terms of partnership agreement," typed document, May 12, 1982. *Wallace Miner*, July 26, 1979. Directors' minutes, Aug. 5, 1983 (goals).

205. Directors' minutes, Nov. 2, 1982; Feb. 11, 1983. Wachtell Lipton memo to Hecla, Feb. 4, 1983. Shares: Mike White file memo, Dec. 10, 1982, showing that at the 1982 annual meeting, 7.2 million shares were held by brokers; 8.6 million, by beneficial owners. For reorganization: NYSE to Grismer, Dec. 27, 1982 on rule 452, NYSE. Hecla shareholders' minutes, June 3, 1983. Directors' minutes, Aug. 5, 1983. *Spokane Daily Chronicle*, June 6, 1983. The merger was approved at a reconvened annual meeting after only 58 percent of the stockholders had voted in time for the regular May meeting.

206. Star: annual report, 1982, p. 5. Interviews with R. Magnuson and others requesting anonymity.

207. Griffith to shareholders, March 13, 1984. "Final report to shareholders and friends," Ranchers, July 26, 1984. Hecla directors' minutes, Feb. 10, 1984. *Wall Street Journal*, Oct. 19, 1984. Griffith interview.

207–8. Griffith interview. *Wall Street Journal*, Oct. 19, 1984.

209. Griffith interview. "Hecla: Two Years Later," typescript of Griffith address to NY securities analysts, April 6, 1984.

209. *Wall Street Journal*, Nov. 10, 1983. Griffith interview.

209. Directors' minutes, Feb. 10, March 10, April 26, 1984. *Wall Street Journal*, April 3, 9, 18, 26, 1984. Griffith to Hecla shareholders, March

13, 1984. Museum: directors' minutes, Aug. 10, 1984. Hecla's shareholders voted 63.3 percent in favor of Ranchers' acquisition on July 26, 1984. Ranchers' shareholders approved the merger on the same date in Albuquerque.

209–10. "Hecla: Two Years Later." *Wall Street Journal,* Oct. 19, 1984. Griffith's remarks to shareholders, May 10, 1985. Hecla annual report, 1984, pp. 3, 5–6, 23–33. Sunshine: directors' minutes, April 26, 1984. "Agreement in Principle" between Sunshine and Hecla, April 24, 1984, executed June 26. Directors' minutes, Aug. 10, 1984. Hecla annual report, 1984, p. 28, note 9 to financial statement.

210. Griffith, Bierly interviews. Hecla press release, July 10, 1984. Griffith, response to shareholder at annual meeting, May 10, 1985. *Spokane Daily Chronicle,* Nov. 1, 1984 (Ranchers resignations).

211. *North Idaho Press,* July 12, 1984. *Wallace Miner,* Aug. 17, 1978 (firing). H. Magnuson interview. Grismer to county commissioners, Aug. 13, 1984.

211. *Wall Street Journal,* Oct. 19, 1984. *Wall Street Transcript,* Dec. 9, 1985 (pp. 78, 787).

212–13. Brown interview.

Bibliography

T<small>HE MAJOR SOURCE FOR THIS STUDY WAS THE FILES OF THE</small> Hecla Mining Company, which were opened to me without restriction before the company moved from Wallace to Coeur d'Alene. These files, purged of documents regarded as no longer useful for business or history, have been deposited in the Eastern Washington State Historical Society archives in Spokane. The files, as I reviewed them, seemed reasonably complete—except, for predictable gaps due to shredding—and well arranged by Sandra Pope.

Most of the direction of the narrative emerged from interviews with persons inside and outside the company. Those who granted extended interviews, which I recorded and transcribed, are, in alphabetical order: Arthur Brown, William Dunphy, William A. Griffith, Herbert E. Harper, Ben Harrison, Horton Herman, Ruby (Sinrud) Hill, James F. M. Hoban, Harry F. Magnuson, Richard G. Magnuson, William H. Love, Lester J. Randall, Charles A. Tilford, and Gus Voltolini.

Several individuals wrote me useful letters about Hecla, including Love, Randall, and Jack Williams. A number of other persons answered my inquiries about specific points; they are credited in the notes. The rough-draft manuscript was revised after a number of individuals read it and suggested changes for historical or technical accuracy. Among these are: Elmer L. Bierly, Brown, Griffith, Harper, Richard Magnuson, Love, and George T. Krempasky. W. Burney Warren and Jack Williams read and commented on portions of the first draft. Once I had seen their suggestions, I talked with other persons to confirm the accuracy of their recollections.

Consequently, this study was written with a continuous balancing of documents and oral statements by persons who know Hecla, or aspects of its business and history, very well.

The following list includes unpublished and published documents. It omits legal and periodical citations that are complete in the section on sources. Most of the published materials are available in libraries. The University of Idaho holds incomplete runs of early Coeur d'Alene district newspapers and the *Wallace Miner* on microfilm. Bound copies of *Mining Truth* (sometimes *Northwest Mining Truth*) are in the collections of the Eastern Washington State Historical Society and the Spokane Public Library. The Campbell and Finch papers are held by the Eastern Washington State Historical Society.

Unpublished

Anderson, Robert L. "The Mining Engineer in Early Idaho." Typescript. Address to Idaho Society of Professional Engineers, Jan. 30, 1976.

Anderson, William. "Deep Mining in the Coeur d'Alene District of Idaho." Typescript. Paper presented at National Western Mining Conference and Exhibition, Denver, Feb. 5, 1972.

"Bunker Hill Company." Confidential memorandum. Prepared by First Boston Corp., October 1979, from data supplied by Gulf Resources & Chemical Corp.

Ettlinger, I. A. "Report on the Hecla Mining Company." Typescript. Prepared for General Development Co., New York, and Adolph Lewisohn & Sons, Jan. 31, 1935.

Fee, Elizabeth Tamplin. "The 1960 Strike in the Coeur d'Alenes: An Examination of Alleged Communist Influence." Master's thesis. University of Idaho, 1968.

Folwell, William T. "Lucky Friday Mine: History, Geology, and Development." Typescript (dated June 3, 1958). Paper presented at Pacific Northwest regional meeting of AIME, April 1958 (Subsequently published in part in *Mining Engineering*, Dec. 1958, pp. 1266–68).

Harper, Herbert E. "Hecla Mining Company: Exploration Department." Typescript. Aug. 5, 1976.

———. "Report on the Uranium Activity of the Colorado Plateau." Typescript. April 20, 1954.

———. "Some New and Current Developments in the Coeur d'Alene Mining District." Typescript. Address to the Idaho Mining Association, July 7, 1973.

Hecla Mining Co. "Hecla Mining Company and Wholly Owned Subsidiaries: Draft Prospectus." Typescript. July 1977.

———. "Lakeshore Copper Mine Operations Review." Typescript. July 1978.

Hoban, Leo J. "History of Sullivan." Duplicated. N.d.

"Joint Recommendations Relative to Making Common Use of the Facilities in Wallace-Burke, Idaho, Territory, by O-WRR&N and the Northern Pacific Companies." Typescript. Report of joint committee, 1924 (NP president's subject file 1064, Minnesota Historical Society).

Kuhn Loeb & Co. "Preliminary Financial Analysis and Recommendations Prepared for the Hecla Mining Company." Typescript. Oct. 1977.

"Lakeshore Project, Pinal County, Arizona: Vol. III, Process Operations and General Facilities." Parsons-Jurden Corp., New York, June 1972.

Leep, R. W. "Geological Features of the Star-Morning and Lucky Friday Mines in Idaho's Coeur d'Alene District." Paper presented to AIME sixteenth Intermountain Minerals Conference, July 18, 1980.

Lindstrom, Philip M. "History of the Hecla Mining Company: An Update." Typescript. Sept. 30, 1982.

Love, William H. "Ruby Hill Project, Eureka, Nevada." Typescript of article. May 5, 1965.

———. "Sinking the Atlas Shaft." Typescript of article. Dec. 2, 1953.

———. "Technological Change and the Supply of Mineral Resources." Paper presented at National Resources Public Policy Seminar, Graduate School of Public Affairs, University of Washington, March 6, 1969.

Love, W. H., and P. M. Lindstrom. "Longwall Stoping with Yieldable Steel Props at the Radon Mine." Typescript. N.d.

Matthews, John R. "Tax Effects of Elections to Aggregate Properties under IRC Section 614." Paper presented at Northwest Mining Association, Dec. 2, 1961.

Musgrove, Paul M. "Hecla Mining's Lakeshore Copper Complex." Paper presented at annual Arizona conference of AIME, Dec. 5, 1977.

Phillips, Tom W. "The View from Lakeshore." Typescript. Feb. 1981. One man's recollections from start to end of Lakeshore.

Phipps, Stanley S. "From Bullpen to Bargaining Table: The Tumultous Struggle of Coeur d'Alene Miners to Organize, 1887–1942." Doctoral dissertation, University of Idaho, 1983.

Randall, Lester J. "Effect of Present Federal Tax Laws on the Development of New Mines." Paper presented at Pacific Northwest Conference of Certified Public Accountants, June 3, 1950.

———. "Mining Industry of the Spokane Inland Empire." Paper presented at Inland Empire Industrial Exposition, Sept. 28, 1962.

———. "Percentage Depletion." Address to Northwest Mining Association, Dec. 3, 1954.

———. "Tax Problems of the Mining Industry." Address to Mountain States Accounting Conference, June 4–7, 1952.

———. "Tax Relief Needed by the Mining Industry." Address to American Mining Congress, Sept. 23, 1953.

———. "Excessive Federal Income and Excess Profits Taxes are Largely Responsible for the Plight of the Small Mine Operator." Statement to the House Small Business Committee, April 27, 1953.

———. "Statement on Behalf of the American Mining Congress." Statement to Mines and Mining Subcommittee of the House Interior and Insular Affairs Committee, June 8, 1965.

"Report on Ruby Hill." Typescript. 1961.

"Silver Valley Company." Typescript. Confidential prospectus for proposed merger of Sunshine and Hecla, Sept. 20, 1979.

Sorenson, Robert E. "History of Hecla Mining Company." Typescript, April 9, 1962.

Articles

Anderson, William. "Star Mine." In *Coeur d'Alenes in 1963*, pp. 15–16.

Aulbach, Adam. "Early History of the [Coeur d'Alene] District." *Idaho Mines and Metals* 2:9 (April 4, 1907), 19–43.

Bean, Margaret. "Mining Man—Hecla's Hanley." *Spokesman-Review* magazine, July 25, 1948, p. 2.

Broyles, Glen J. "Spokane Free Speech Fight, 1909–1910: A Study in IWW Tactics." *Labor History* 19:2 (Spring 1978), 238–52.

Craig, Gordon. "Star and Polaris Mills." *Coeur d'Alene District in 1963*, pp. 17–18.

Dayton, Stanley H. "Lucky Friday Now Has a Bright Future." *Mining World* (reprint), April 1958.

Ellsworth, John T. "Resumé of Electrolytic Zinc Practice." *Engineering & Mining Journal-Press*, Sept. 2, 1922, pp. 406–8.

Fahey, John. "Coeur d'Alene Confederacy," *Idaho Yesterdays* 12:1 (Spring 1968), 2–7.

———. "Ed Boyce and the Western Federation of Miners." *Idaho Yesterdays* 25:3 (Fall 1981), 18–30.

Fell, James E., Jr. "Rockefeller's Right-hand Man: Frederick T. Gates and the Northwestern Mining Investments." *Business History Review* 52:4 (Winter 1978), 537–61.

Folwell, William T. "Lucky Friday Mine: History, Geology, and Development." *Mining Engineering*, Dec. 1958, pp. 1266–68.

Gaboury, William J. "Stubborn Defense: Idaho's Losing Fight for Free Silver." *Idaho Yesterdays* 5:4 (Winter 1961–62), 2–10.

———. "From Statehouse to Bullpen: Idaho Populism and the Coeur d'Alene Troubles of the 1890s." *Pacific Northwest Quarterly* 58:1 (Jan. 1967), 14–22.

Hirschberg, Charles A. "Development of the Rock Drill in America." *Engineering and Mining Journal*, Oct. 25, 1919, pp. 677–81.

Howell, Don E. "Hecla Became Mining Giant." *Mining Record* (reprint), May 30, 1968.

Ingalls, H. W. "Saga of the Hecla Mining Company." *Compressed Air Magazine*, Nov. 1941, pp. 6591–95.

"Joe Flom's Marvelous Money Machine," *Fortune* 105 (April 19, 1982), 91.

Kinney, Lindsay M. "Lewis P. Larsen." *Big Smoke 1982*, pp. 43–47.

BIBLIOGRAPHY

Lavendar, David. "Back to the Hills Again." *Travel* 63:2 (June 1934), 20–23, 56. Reopening old mining camps.

Love, W. H., and P. M. Lindstrom. "Longwall Stoping at the Radon Mine." *Mining Congress Journal* (reprint), Aug. 1958.

Lovin, Hugh T. "Moses Alexander and the Lumber Strike of 1917: The Wartime Ordeal of a Progressive." *Pacific Northwest Quarterly* 66:3 (July 1975), 115–22.

———. "Red Scare in Idaho, 1916–18." *Idaho Yesterdays* 17:3 (Fall 1973), 2–13.

———. "World War Vigilantes in Idaho, 1917–1918." *Idaho Yesterdays* 18:3 (Fall 1974), 2–11.

———. "Idaho and the 'Reds,' 1916–1926." *Idaho Yesterdays* 69:3 (July 1978), 107–15.

McCarthy, James F. "History of the Hecla Mine, Burke, Idaho," *Mining and Metallurgy* 5:210 (June 1924), 276–77.

———. "History of the Hecla Mine, Part I." *Compressed Air Magazine* 33:6 (June 1928), 2447–49; E. L. Wood, "Part II," ibid., 33:7 (July 1928), 2473–75; A. C. Stevenson, "Part III," ibid., 33:8 (Aug. 1928), 2507–9.

Magnuson, Harry F. "The Idaho Mining Industry: What It Means to Idaho." *Mining Industry of Idaho 1965*, pp. 22–31.

Montague, Gilbert H. "Minerals Separation's Position under the Patent Laws and the Anti-Trust Laws." *Mining and Scientific Press*, Dec. 11, 1920, pp. 883–90.

"Papago People." *See* Sylvester.

Rice, Claude T. "Flotation in the Coeur d'Alenes." *Engineering and Mining Journal*, April 20, 1918, pp. 707–16.

Schultze, H. W. "Brief History of the Sunshine Mine Operations." In *Coeur d'Alenes in 1963*, pp. 65–67.

Sharp, Franklin H. "Silver—A General Review." *Mining Industry of Idaho 1962*, pp. 28–32.

Sims, Robert C. "Idaho's Criminal Syndicalism Act: One State's Response to Radical Labor." *Labor History* 15:4 (Fall 1974), 511–27.

Smalley, Eugene V. "The Coeur d'Alene Stampede." *The Century* 28:6 (Oct. 1884), 841–47.

Stevenson, A. C. "History of the Hecla Mine, Burke, Idaho, Part III." *Compressed Air Magazine* 33:8 (Aug. 1928), 2507–9. *See* McCarthy and Wood for parts I and II.

———. "Reconstruction Methods of the 'Hecla' Electrical-Mechanical Equipment." *Mining and Metallurgy* 5:210 (June 1924), 273–75.

Sylvester, Edward J., et al. "Papago People: At Home in the Desert." Tabloid supplement to *Arizona Daily Star*, April 24, 1977.

Tainton, U. C. "Sullivan Electrolytic Zinc Plant of the Sullivan Mining Company." *Mining Industry of Idaho 1927*, pp. 33–38.

Wells, Merle W. "Western Federation of Miners." *Journal of the West* 12:1 (Jan. 1973), 18–35.

Wood, E. L. "Summary of Hecla Reconstruction." *Mining and Metallurgy* 5:210 (June 1924), 270–72.

——. "History of the Hecla Mine, Burke, Idaho, Part II," *Compressed Air Magazine* 33:7 (July 1928), 2473–75. *See* McCarthy and Stevenson for Parts I and III.

Woolf, W. G. "Idaho Zinc." *Mining Industry of Idaho 1936*, pp. 67–69.

Woolf, W. G., and E. R. Crutcher. "Making Electrolytic Zinc at the Sullivan Plant." *Engineering & Mining Journal* 140:8 (Aug. 1939), 72–77.

Woolf, W. G., and R. M. Miller. "Electrolytic Zinc Plant of the Sullivan Mining Company." *Mining Congress Journal* 17:11 (Nov. 1931), 624–26.

Books and Reports

Beal, Merrill D., and Merle W. Wells. *History of Idaho.* 3 vols. New York: Lewis Historical Publishing Co., 1959.

Bruce, William. *History of Milwaukee City and County.* Chicago: Clarke, 1922.

Butler, Joseph G. *History of Youngstown and Mahoning County.* 3 vols. New York: American Historical Society, 1921.

Coeur d'Alene Mining District—Deep Mining. Pacific Northwest Metals and Minerals Conference, *Proceedings*, April 12–14, 1973, sponsored by AIMMPE, Coeur d'Alene, Idaho.

Coeur d'Alene Mining District in 1963. Moscow: Idaho Bureau of Mines and Geology, pamphlet 133 (Dec. 1963). A series of papers commemorating the 60th anniversary of the Idaho Mining Association.

Cook, E. F. *Silver Lining in Idaho Mining.* Moscow: Idaho Bureau of Mines and Geology, information circular 12 (Feb. 1962). A review of the industry in 1961.

Crosby, Garth M. *Guidebook to the Geology of the Coeur d'Alene Mining District.* Moscow: Idaho Bureau of Mines and Geology, bulletin 16 (April 1961).

Dobyns, Henry F. *The Papago People.* Phoenix: Indian Tribal Series, 1972.

Durham, Nelson W. *History of the City of Spokane and Spokane Country, Washington, from Its Earliest Settlement to the Present Time.* 3 vols. Spokane: Clarke, 1912.

Edwards, Jonathan. *Illustrated History of Spokane County, State of Washington.* Spokane: Lever, 1900.

Ellsworth, Lawrence E. *Community Perception in the Coeur d'Alene Mining District.* Moscow: Idaho Bureau of Mines and Geology, pamphlet 152 (March 1972).

Fahey, John. *Ballyhoo Bonanza: Charles Sweeny and the Idaho Mines.* Seattle: University of Washington Press, 1971.

————. *The Days of the Hercules.* Moscow: University Press of Idaho, 1978.

————. *Inland Empire: D. C. Corbin and Spokane.* Seattle: University of Washington Press, 1965.

Foreman, Charles H. *Mining Methods and Costs at the Hecla and Star Mines, Burke, Idaho.* Washington: U.S. Bureau of Mines, information circular 6232 (Feb. 1930). Mimeographed.

Fryklund, Verne C., Jr. *Ore Deposits in the Coeur d'Alene District, Shoshone County, Idaho.* Washington: U.S. Geological Survey, *Professional Paper 445* (1964).

Greater Milwaukee: Financial, Commercial and Biographical. Milwaukee: Milwaukee Journal Co., 1911.

Gregory, John. *History of Milwaukee, Wisconsin.* 4 vols. Chicago: Clarke, 1931.

Hobbs, S. Warren, Allan B. Griggs, Robert E. Wallace, and Arthur B. Campbell. *Geology of the Coeur d'Alene District, Shoshone County, Idaho.* Washington: U.S. Geological Survey, *Professional Paper 478* (1965).

Hurt, Harry, III. *Texas Rich.* New York: W. W. Norton, 1981. A biography of H. L. Hunt with references to his sons and silver.

Hyams, Barry. *Hirshhorn: Medici from Brooklyn.* New York: E. P. Dutton, 1979.

Ingalls, Walter Renton. *Lead and Zinc in the United States.* New York: Hill Publishing Co., 1908.

Jastram, Roy W. *Silver: The Restless Metal.* New York: John Wiley & Sons, 1981.

Magnuson, Richard G. *Coeur d'Alene Diary: The First Ten Years of Hardrock Mining in North Idaho.* Portland: Metropolitan Press, 1968.

Proceedings in Relation to the Coeur d'Alene Labor Troubles. 3 vols. Washington: House Committee on U.S. Military Affairs, 56th Congress, first session (1900).

Ramsey, Robert H. *Men and Mines of Newmont: A Fifty-Year History.* New York: Octagon Books, 1973.

Ransome, Frederick L., and Frank C. Calkins. "Geology and Ore Deposits of the Coeur d'Alene District, Idaho," U.S. Geological Survey, *Professional Paper 62,* Washington: GPO, 1908.

Reid, Rolland R., ed. *Guidebook to the Geology of the Coeur d'Alene Mining District.* Moscow: Idaho Bureau of Mines and Geology, bulletin 16 (April 1961).

Schoenberg, Rev. Wilfred P., S.J. *Gonzaga University: Seventy-five Years, 1887–1962.* Spokane: Gonzaga University, 1963.

Shenon, P. J., and R. H. McConnel. *Silver Belt of the Coeur d'Alene District, Idaho.* Moscow: Idaho Bureau of Mines and Geology, pamphlet 50 (2d ed., Oct. 1939). Mimeographed.

Shiach, William S., John M. Henderson, and Harry B. Averill. *Illustrated History of North Idaho.* Chicago: Western Historical Publishing Co., 1903.

Sobel, Robert. *Curbstone Brokers: Origins of the American Stock Exchange.* New York: Macmillan, 1970.

Umpleby, Joseph B., and E. L. Jones, Jr. *Geology and Ore Deposits of Shoshone County, Idaho.* Washington: U.S. Geological Survey, *Bulletin 732* (1923).

Voynick, Stephen M. *Making of a Hardrock Miner.* Berkeley: Howell-North Books, 1978.

Watrous, Jerome, ed. *Memoirs of Milwaukee County.* 2 vols. Madison: Western Historical Association, 1909.

Index

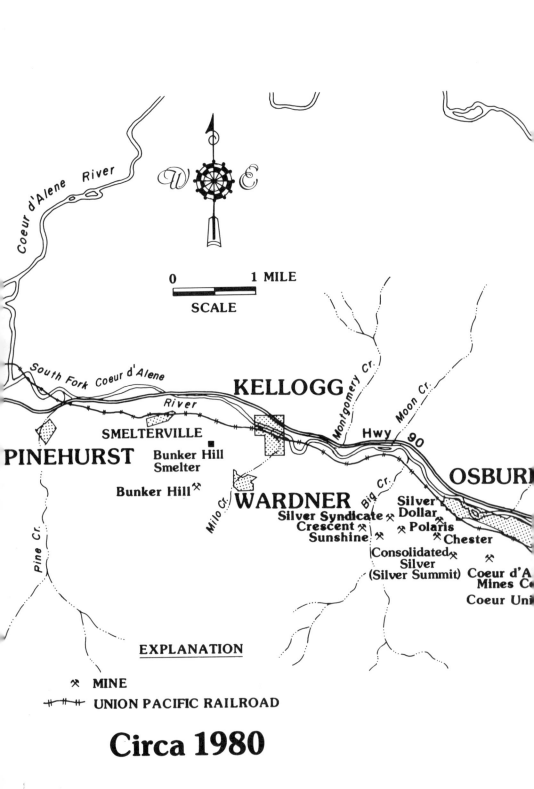

Coeur d'Alene River

W   E

0   1 MILE

SCALE

South Fork Coeur d'Alene

KELLOGG

River

Montgomery Cr.

Moon Cr.

SMELTERVILLE

Hwy   90

PINEHURST

Bunker Hill
Smelter

Big Cr.

OSBUR

Bunker Hill

Milo Cr.

WARDNER

Silver Syndicate
Crescent
Sunshine

Silver
Dollar

Polaris

Chester

Coeur d'A
Mines C

Coeur Uni

Pine Cr.

Consolidated
Silver
(Silver Summit)

EXPLANATION

MINE

UNION PACIFIC RAILROAD

Circa 1980